WEALTH
CODES

SACRED STRATEGIES FOR ABUNDANCE

JEN PICENO

FEATURING: KELLY CAMERON, HANNAH CHAPMAN,
THAIS CONTE, EIRIKAH DELAUNAY, LAURA DI FRANCO,
KIMBERLY COOPER, R. SCOTT HOLMES,
MORRIGHAN LYNNE, LAURA MAZZOTTA, KELLI MURBACH,
JAMIE LEE MURPHY, KELLY MYERSON, HOLLIE RENEA,
NATASHA SHARMA, MEREDITH SIMS, KRISTI H. SULLIVAN,
LULU TREVENA, WANDA TUCKER, DAMAYSI VAZQUEZ,
KRISTINA WHITE, ATLANTIS WOLF, JESSICA A. WOLFE,
AMBER WRIGHT, STEPHANIE ZITO

Wealth Codes
Sacred Strategies for Abundance

Jen Piceno

©Copyright 2022 Jen Piceno

Published by Brave Healer Productions

Paperback ISBN: 978-1-954047-67-9

eBook ISBN: 978-1-954047-66-2

WEALTH CODES

CODES

SACRED STRATEGIES FOR ABUNDANCE

JEN PICENO

FEATURING: KELLY CAMERON, HANNAH CHAPMAN, THAIS CONTE,
KIMBERLY COOPER, EIRIKAH DELAUNAY, LAURA DI FRANCO,
R. SCOTT HOLMES, MORRIGHAN LYNNE, LAURA MAZZOTTA,
KELLI MURBACH, JAMIE LEE MURPHY, KELLY MYERSON, HOLLIE RENEA,
NATASHA SHARMA, MEREDITH SIMS, KRISTI H. SULLIVAN, LULU TREVENA,
WANDA TUCKER, DAMAYSI VAZQUEZ, KRISTINA WHITE, ATLANTIS WOLF,
JESSICA A. WOLFE, AMBER WRIGHT, STEPHANIE ZITO

Inky Black Design, LTD was created with three core foundations: The Visual Story, Freedom, and Destiny.

Guy Graves and Dayna Fellows developed a fully integrated traveling art department with forty years of combined expertise. Offering all clients unique designs from graphics to fine arts.

It's an absolute honor to be a small part of this masterpiece. The vision and the work spoke right away. Freedom manifested in all forms of wealth.

You dream it. We design it.

Let's create something spectacular together.

inkyblack.design

DEDICATION

To the divine essence of money, thank you for teaching me how to give soul to every transaction that passes through my hands. With gratitude, I honor and respect these teachings and pass them forward with purpose.

Love and appreciation to the mentors, coaches, healers, teachers, shamans, and mystics who have impacted my life. Thank you for the tough love, warm embraces, honest feedback, and for seeing the real me. You ignited my journey and amplified the Wealth Codes mission. Thank you.

To my ancestors, thank you for working with me through stubborn generational patterns and beliefs so I could prepare my mind to fully embody the lessons to amplify wealth. With your guidance, I've dared to lead the mission of creating wealth in the lives of others.

Thank you to those who have purposely pushed me to my limits, challenged, hurt, or betrayed me. You unknowingly fanned my flames, ignited my power, and led me inward to align more deeply with the truth of who I am and what I'm here to do.

To my co-authors, thank you for pouring your wisdom and magic upon these pages. I know your power, see your integrity, trust your teachings, and am deeply honored to have you in my life.

To our readers, I honor you. No matter your history or current circumstances, know I believe in you. I know you're worthy of more, and I'm excited that you are here. This book found you because you, too, are ready for an abundance of wealth. It's your divine birthright. You have within you gems and treasures to illuminate your path forward. As you move through this book, remember that you are exquisite, you matter, and it's your turn to claim the life of your dreams.

If you want individual support, reach out to me directly. Schedule a complimentary Discovery Call here: www.jenpiceno.com/book_now

A GIFT FOR YOU

This book comes with a Wealth Codes meditation that's charmed with magical intentions to activate your wealth journey.

You have access to my abundance meditation to accelerate this experience too. It's a channeled light language transmission translated into English. This is a sample of the potent magic I share and offers a high-frequency activation and energetic balancing to enhance abundance. Get both meditations and more at: at www.jenpiceno.com/resources

Bringing wealth into all areas of life is woven into everything on The Ecstatic Living Podcast. To amplify the Wealth Codes and integrate them into your lifestyle, this is the show for you. Together we'll embrace magic and energetically align with the vibration of prosperity consciousness. Tune in here: www.jenpiceno.com/podcast

Women readers are invited into my complimentary Facebook Community, Mystic Circle at www.facebook.com/groups/jenpiceno

INTENTION STATEMENT

May we empower every life we touch with love, magic, wisdom, and sacred intentions to activate holistic wealth around the globe.

May we ignite change in our lives and the lives of others with each word written and shared.

May we honor and trust the impact of the wealth potentiality we hold as change-makers, healers, and conscious-minded business professionals.

May we share our hearts and sacred strategies wisely, passionately, fiercely, and with great purpose.

May we change lives with each turn of the page for all who read this book.

May you, our readers, expand beyond your wildest imagination and claim wealth as your divine birthright—then share this book with others.

DISCLAIMER

This book offers words of wisdom with regards to physical, mental, emotional and spiritual wellbeing and is designed for educational purposes only. You should not rely on this information as a substitute for, nor does it replace professional medical or business advice, diagnosis or treatment. If you have concerns or questions about your health, business or mental wellbeing, you should always consult with a physician, other healthcare professional or business professional. Do not disregard, avoid or delay obtaining medical or business related advice from your healthcare or business professional because of something you may have read here. The use of any information provided in this book is solely at your own risk.

Developments in research may impact the health, business and life advice that appears here. No assurances can be given that the information contained in this book will always include the most relevant findings or developments with respect to the particular material.

Having said all that, know that the authors here have shared their tools, practices and knowledge with you with a sincere and generous intent to assist you on your journey to being unstoppable in business and life. Please contact them with any questions you may have about the techniques or information they have provided. They will be happy to assist you further!

TESTIMONIALS

"I read Wealth Codes: Sacred Strategies for Abundance at the perfect time. As someone who grew up without money, and in a church that seemed to demonize money and people who had it, I had a lot of false beliefs around finances, earning, money management, and self-worth. Needless to say, those are not helpful beliefs to subscribe to if you're an entrepreneur.

What I loved most about Wealth Codes is that it covers many types of wealth (financial, spiritual, physical, relational, and emotional) and from all different angles. No matter what objection my logical brain could come up with as to why I shouldn't or couldn't have wealth, I would gravitate toward a specific chapter that explained in great detail not only why I was worthy of this desire, but easily laid out how to get there from where I was.

No matter your current beliefs on wealth and abundance, I know you'll learn several new techniques and enlightening perspectives that will shift you into the right mindset to receive and accept that good things are coming your way. I'm so excited to see what happens next!"

~ Alice Sullivan

"One thing that stood out to me about Jen's visionary outlook on the growth of wealth came into light during one of her group education spots. Jen tantalized us when she posed the following question.

Write down how much money you would like to make in one month to live the life you dream about?"
Her following profound statement uncovered our true worth. Add a zero at the end of your number."

Naturally, After grabbing our jaws off the floor, Jen started to explain the only difference between asking someone to pay you 10K vs. 100K is ultimately all in mindset.

At the time, I said to myself, "Well, Damn!" So you now understand what an honor it is to receive this opportunity to write this embodiment to wealth codes from Mystic Jen's wisdom.

Jen has a way of transforming you from a reader to a primal trance that starts to vibrate at a frequency that invigorates you to become part of the unlocking process of your wealth codes. In simple terms, you can say it's M.A.G.I.C

M= Money Magnetic Mindset

A= Abundance Amplified Arousal

G= Graciously Giving Gratitude

I= Imaginative Impactful Intentions

C= Consciously Creating Curiosity

Miracles are spiritual motivations held sacred to your true self. So I encourage you to embark on your odyssey and unlock your wealth codes today!"

~ S. A. Grant, Host of The Boss Uncaged Podcast

"We have such a distorted view of wealth. We tend to see it as it pertains just to money. There is the practical, real world side to wealth, but there is also the understanding that wealth is a feeling, an attitude, and a mindset that really has nothing to do with money.

Wealth is internally driven which can be a challenging concept for most people. There is a spiritual aspect to it that we seldom, if ever, have looked at. How can I see the wealth in my life if I don't have a healthy perspective of myself?

That is definitely the focus of Wealth Codes. Along with the practical, real world conversations, there are stories, and tools to help you grow as your idea of wealth shifts.

Lead author Jen Piceno and the authors of Wealth Codes have come together to present another perspective counter to wealth as it relates to our human experience. Each section was lovingly put together to invite you, the reader, to re-think your idea of what wealth means to you so you can let go of old stereotypes and integrate a healthier, more powerful relationship with wealth. If you come with an open mind you will learn something about yourself that may very well change your life."

~ James Kawainui, Native Hawaiian Healer and Spiritual Strategist

TABLE OF CONTENTS

SPECIAL NOTE TO THE READER

I'm so excited you're stepping into this sensational phase of expansion.

No matter where you are or what you've experienced along the way, you're here now. You've been led to receiving Wealth Codes.

Wealth Codes are offered to anyone ready to claim their divine birthright, limitless wealth, love, joy, vitality, and personal and financial freedom.

Our collaborative book shares innate wisdom and sacred strategies. We're wisdom keepers, change-makers, practitioners, and business professionals on a mission to create worldwide holistic wealth.

We've chosen a conscious-minded, soul-aligned, and expansive lifestyle of intentional living. We invite you to step into Wealth Codes to claim limitless wealth that transforms life on all levels. It's delicious, sensational, and full of pleasure.

Are you ready?

Cozy up and imagine our tribe of authors sitting with you, fully engaged and present for your initiation into the codes. You deserve this celebration, and we're thrilled you've been led here. It'll activate wealth and so much more.

Beautiful gifts and sacred strategies to guide you towards claiming authentic desires are being handed to you with each turn of the page. We're cheering for you with each life-altering shift that offers more joy and pleasure. We believe in you, your purpose, and the value you hold. Today, we're reminding you that you get to have the life you desire.

This book is an extension of our sacred space, and now, you've been invited here as we defy time, crush limitations, and do more than what others believe is possible.

Trust the journey. These pages are filled with purpose. Feel, sense, and know you are ready for more because you are.

Take a few deep, spacious breaths. Come into your body and remember that you are sacred, whole, and worthy. Breathe in love, peace, and abundance as you feel stress gently melting away. Imagine me there with you. I'm placing my hand on your shoulder. As your Prosperity Priestess, I lead you forward into expansion.

Boom-boom, boom-boom. The seductive sound of a drum flawlessly pulses with your heartbeat. Bring your attention into your heart space. Feel an inner fire build within the center of your chest, noticing the sensation of heat as your heart opens.

The wind blows and gently kisses your skin, and you know your spirit guides are with you. My tribe of healers anoint and bless you as I offer a sip of ceremonial cacao to inspire the opening of Wealth Codes. You're at peace, trusting that your mind, body, and soul are ready to claim the whole experience of wealth. Cacao is the food of the Gods. Sip it slowly to savor the medicine as it activates visions of soul-aligned desires.

Your body deeply relaxes, and you feel safe and protected. I'm guiding you into the codes for your highest human potential.

With your next deep, spacious breath, invite the essence of wealth to fill every fiber of your being. Feel it, know it, and remember that wealth is your divine inheritance. It's your birthright. It's now awakening within your cells, blood, and bones.

In celebration, we dance with wild abandon joyously in your honor. You have been initiated into the Wealth Codes.

As you journey through these pages, do so with an open heart and the willingness to receive. There is an expansive transformation waiting for you. It's already started!

Skip from chapter to chapter, reading whatever demands your attention. Trust the process; you're being led to exactly where you need to go. Enjoy the adventure.

With big love, I wish you all that you desire.

INTRODUCTION

Magic and miracles are always within our reach. I've experienced and witnessed unexplainable shifts and better than expected outcomes in my personal and professional practice. I've seen lives change over time and instantaneously.

If you want results, it's important to take note of what's not working and be grateful for what is. Then, be open minded enough to create space for receiving these teachings of change and transformation so they can work magic in your life.

I'm on a mission to create wealth in the lives of others, but it's the kind of wealth that's richer than money alone.

This book guides readers into achieving wealth in all areas of life by compiling what we know works when people are willing to step outside the box of confinement and into a world of limitless possibilities.

We're sharing sacred strategies, practices, and solutions that shifts energy, mindset, and unhealthy patterns that keep people stuck.

Money and financial freedom are definitely part of the Wealth Codes plan, but what I want you to experience more than anything is the ecstatic, expansive feeling of wealth in everything you see and do.

The teachings in this book and my courses at www.jenpiceno.com/ academy take you on a journey into creating holistic wealth: prosperity, abundance, wealth consciousness, and ecstatic living.

You're invited to savor life. It's not a quick fix. It's a lifestyle choice that makes ecstatic living a priority. As we increase wealth in all areas of life, money flows with ease, and we become magnets for abundance through prosperous living that embraces soul-aligned intentions.

Take time with these sacred strategies for living life fully so you can soak up its goodness. The pages are enchanted with prosperity, love, and truth to guide readers to achieve wealth in all forms. Each section holds the power of the sacred elements (earth, water, air, fire, and Spirit). If you're not familiar with that, no worries, it's weaved into the pages in this collection of stories.

You'll find everything interconnects, and you get to receive pleasure from it all, with sacred strategies, and delicious practices that enhance everything.

Join me in savoring life.

MONEY

Working with the elements (earth, water, air, fire, and Spirit) is part of the foundational practice in my online academy. It takes students deeper within themselves, activates spiritual gifts, enhances awareness, and deepens intuition. This work is profoundly helpful in all areas of life.

I've enchanted and blessed this section of the book with the element of earth.

As we journey within, we can see life through a different lens, and our spiritual gifts become more apparent, as does the purpose within lessons learned.

Earth symbolizes things we possess, safety, security, and material things, including money.

It offers wisdom from our ancestors and anchors us into this time and space. She invites us to heal anything limiting our sense of security or feelings of not-enough-ness. Then, she lovingly reminds us that prosperity and wealth are limitless.

She offers us roots and teaches us how to embody spiritual lessons.

Lovingly, she takes what no longer serves us into her fiery core. All wounds, fears, outdated beliefs, and limitations are composted with a sacred purpose to create a richer landscape for beauty to grow with overflowing abundance.

RITUAL: Sit quietly with soft lighting and tap into a deep appreciation for all you have and all that is coming to you. Have your journal, matches, and unlit candle nearby.

Light the candle. As the flame ignites, say, **"Everything I need comes to me."** Feel this truth in your physical body. Allow this nurturing earthy energy to move through you effortlessly as it heals misalignments so you can turn away from feelings of lack and step into prosperity consciousness.

Journal from a place of deep appreciation as you write a thank you letter to the Universe/God/Goddess/Highest vibration of light/or higher power of your choice. When you're complete, relax into the feeling of gratitude.

Receive a complimentary activation into the wealth codes
at www.jenpiceno.com/resources

Experience an initiation into practical and sacred wealth-building strategies, spiritual and business expansion, and enhanced intuition.

Visit my academy:

www.jenpiceno.com/academy

CHAPTER 1

MONEY MAGNET

CLEARING BARRIERS TO PROPERTY

Jen Piceno, Wealth Consciousness Coach

"If you want to give birth to your true self, you are going to have to dig deep down into that body of yours and let your soul howl. Sometimes, you have to take a leap of faith and trust that if you turn off your head, your feet will take you where you need to go."

~Gabrielle Roth

MY STORY

I'm living proof that this work takes people on a journey away from worry, fear, family beliefs, scarcity, and all the dangerous places the human mind goes when times are challenging. I've learned what ecstatic living tastes like.

Time stopped as I moved effortlessly to the trance-like rhythm. It was seductive and erotic and made my body feel alive and delicious. Each snake-like movement took me deeper into altered states of consciousness. It was ecstatic and sacred.

I became one with my goddess self at that moment. I felt powerful, sexy, primal, and holy. Each breath connected me profoundly with all that is and took me on a spiritual journey deeper within myself. The air was intoxicating as it blessed my skin with the scent of frankincense.

Connected to my higher self and rooted with the ground beneath my bare feet, my soles tingled with pleasure and full body rejuvenation. *Wealth is everywhere, and it's yours to claim.* My body felt wild, free, and sacred as I danced. The whisper spoke again as my eyes gently closed. *You are the wealth you seek.* All physical sensations turned on like a light switch. Complete body stimulation shot through me like a lightning bolt as I received divine wisdom. *Be quenched by pleasure and delight in the experience life offers you. Stop holding back.* Shakti flowed powerfully through my body. This intensity caused my legs to quiver. Energy gradually moved from my legs and through each chakra on the front and back of my body.

The word shakti represents feminine energy that accentuates all living things (gender doesn't matter). This energy poured into my human form with pure power and life force energy. It's sexy. It's holy, and it amplifies everything beyond measure. In Sanskrit, 'shakti' is power.

Powerful it is! When it arises within our physical bodies, life is forever changed. I've been on my spiritual journey for over three and half decades with a full spectrum of mind-blowing experiences with divine feminine and masculine energy. Because of its potency, I share this work with other women and guide them through spiritual awakenings and life transformations.

This time, shakti penetrated my flesh, blood, and bones. It commanded me to hold even higher energy frequencies, expanding and shifting everything instantaneously. Spiritually, this is what shakti does, she expands consciousness, and it was time for me to uplevel yet again. I'm obsessed with personal expansion. This power, strength, and sexual oomph had my full attention and willingness to explore whatever was next.

Mystery and magic surrounded my body. *Let go,* the voice whispered. I let out a moan of pleasure to release stagnant energy from my physical body. I felt held, safe, and divinely guided as I surrendered to the life force energy pumping through me. The music took me exactly where I needed to go, and shakti energy moved through my system with intensified sexual power. *All things birth through you,* she said. I twirled and danced with my arms to the heavens. Then, I sent fierce intentions to the cosmos, awaiting the answers to birth through me.

Spirit guides joined my space, dancing with me in celebration as the Greek goddess Aphrodite revealed herself. Her beauty filled the room, and her aura was vibrant with the scent of roses. She touched my heart, then my womb, enhancing my sexual power. She whispered in a strong, sultry voice, *are you listening?* Nodding my head with an expressive, full-body yes, I leaned into her with pure intentions of receiving her sacred teachings. *Sensual essence must integrate into your prosperity-filled life. Priestess, amplify what you send out into the Universe. Then, feel, receive, and be one with the luxurious wealth that lives within you.*

The trance-like-state guided each dance movement like a fluid moving prayer. My body spun, and my hips softened into a sensual figure-eight motion full of sacred wisdom. Then, with a shaky inner voice, my body shifted into raw, primal passion as I questioned what I had just heard with curiosity. A title wave rush of adrenaline flooded my physical body. Sensations of heat flushed my face with dewy sweat, and I felt aroused with vitality, enhanced with charms of pleasure.

Shaking my head back and forth took me deeper into a trance as my hair flew from side to side like a wild woman in the heat of ecstasy.

Yes, dear, amplify everything you send out into the world with your intentions, and don't hold back. Hear me from your divine higher-self, not your human mind. The secret, my dear, is to amplify everything—live life with pleasure. Submit to your desires. Invite the essence of love, joy, and pleasure into the human experience with every sensation it offers you. Rich rewards draped in wealth will return to you.

Everything you wish to receive must be infused with attention, adornment, energy, and willingness to amplify prosperity frequency laced with love and appreciation for all things. This law of the Universe will serve you well. There's no shame in lusciously living life to its fullest. It's a gift to your human experience. Everything is designed for giving and receiving. Life is filled with abundance. Pay attention and you'll taste how decadent and rich it is.

Energy exchange keeps abundance moving, flowing, and evolving. It's masculine and feminine and longing to be unified in sacred balance. There's an energetic wave, and you're invited to ride it.

Create a flow of abundance by igniting frequency at higher octaves by sending your unique energetic imprint into the world with love, beauty, kindness, and financial wealth distribution. Each sacred element supports your mission (earth, water, air, fire, and Spirit). These elemental powers reside within the codes and live within you. You hold the principles, sacred teachings, and codes, my dear.

Bring this through your physical being and out into the world. Trust that the Universe will respond to your actions with generosity beyond your wildest imagination. The bigger vision will soon reveal, my dear. Trust this calling. You are a carrier of the Wealth Codes. You're a Prosperity Priestess, an activator of wealth, change, and transformation. Teach the tantric ways of living life through sensation. Ignite passion. Anoint the masses with the principles of ecstatic living and continue to attract prosperity with great intention and purpose.

With a deep sigh and jaw-dropping self-realization, I thanked the goddess and felt the energetic alignment ripple through my physical body. Air gently entered with the sensation of breathing in wealth, freedom, and love with soul-aligned pleasure and prosperity. I swallowed the sweetness of my saliva and felt the purpose of this mission move through my body. It resonated—soul deep.

Amplify everything you send out! Her voice whispered again. I repeated the words until they anchored into my heart. My body coiled spirally like a serpent to honor the transformation happening. Energetic vibrations shot up my spine as kundalini energy sent me into an energetic orgasm. Seductively, my body melted with each sway of my moving hips. My breath slowed and deepened as I embodied the teachings. Clarity landed within me and ignited my Spirit.

I came back into my body slowly, fully present and centered. I slowly opened my eyes and knew I was no longer the same woman. This experience shouldn't have surprised me, yet its potency did. As a divine feminine leader, shamanic practitioner, Priestess, expert in energy medicine, and a master of the sacred healing arts, interactions with the divine are part of my everyday life.

This shook me to my core in the best possible way. Shivers of energy still traveling up and down my spine with orgasmic tingles while I processed the expanded consciousness I was embodying. The art of living an ecstatic life is essential in my core teachings. This upgraded everything for me and what I offer my clients.

I sat with the goddess's energy, words, and wisdom, cross-legged with red rose petals on the floor. I savored my oversized cup of coffee, which tasted more decadent than ever. I drank in the vibrations of wealth with understanding and appreciation. I remembered a quote from *The Secret*: "All the money I spend comes back to me multiplied." I started thinking about my relationship with money and how I'm a magnet that intentionally attracts it for the higher good through intentional spending, giving, and receiving.

Money is powerful, and we command the power it holds through our intentions. I choose to work with money consciously, intentionally, and purposefully. I choose to live my legacy now. *Wealth Codes* is part of that legacy.

Being on the goddess path, I've stepped into the art of activating change and transformation for worldwide impact. Mmm, just the sound of that gives me delicious full-body tingles.

Zap! Vivid images blasted through me with bright flashes of light. Deep-rooted knowing exploded like fireworks and lifetimes of lessons flooded in with the secret to prosperity.

My body tingled from head to toe. Nothing else mattered at that moment. Impacting millions of lives and businesses flashed in my mind's eye like a movie screen. The how didn't matter. There was peace in every cell of my being.

Words from my mentor Honorée Corder came to mind: "Everything is circulation or congestion. The truth is that there's always enough. All we need, all the time is always there. If someone is not abundant the solution is circulation." Light bulb moment! We create a conscious circulation of purpose-driven abundance and an energetic frequency that activates and attracts prosperity by consciously and generously keeping money in circulation by activating the law of giving and receiving. If you are not feeling abundant, ask where you can give instead of focusing on what you want to receive.

The experience I share here in my story happened at a financially, physically, and emotionally challenging time. My health was jeopardized, our marriage was rocky, and medical bills were stacked up. It seemed all the pillars of wealth were tumbling down, and I was in the rubble underneath it. I was exhausted, and my vitality was depleted from the overwhelm of trying to find a way out.

It's those things that cause blockages, congestion, and barriers. Congestion stops the flow of abundance. I've discovered ways to clear obstacles and ignite financial flow anchored in prosperity consciousness for myself and those I serve.

I've purposely aligned with prosperity in every area of life. It's a rich, delicious journey that breaks limitations. I invite you to join me on the path to personal and financial freedom laced with practices of fully savoring life.

My superpower is to simplify everything with divine feminine and masculine balance, mystical practices, sacred strategies, and practical action steps that save time, energy, and resources.

If you're ready to clear the barriers blocking prosperity and crave a life filled with passion, pleasure, purpose, and prosperity, continue reading.

The sacred strategy below invites you to clear barriers so you can ignite prosperity. Be open to receiving this work. It's designed to clear, activate, and align your energy centers with wealth consciousness for your highest potential.

To work privately or to accelerate your Wealth Codes journey, schedule a Wealth Codes Discovery Call here: www.jenpiceno.com/book_now

THE STRATEGY

Wealth consciousness offers an entirely sensational experience. It invites you to clear barriers blocking pleasure from every area of life. As you energetically align with wealth codes for prosperity, you come back into divine wholeness.

You'll find it appear in every area of life as you go deeper into this work with me.

This is simply the beginning where we clear the barriers blocking the path to holistic wealth. My intention is to awaken your senses so you can step into ecstatic living with the energetic frequency of wealth on all levels of your existence.

You decide where to go from here. I'm here for you when you're ready for more.

CLEARING BARRIERS TO PROSPERITY

Proceed only when you have time and space where you will not be interrupted.

Have an unlit candle and matches within arm's reach.

Center and ground yourself by taking a few deep, spacious breaths in through your nose and out through your mouth. Allow stress to evaporate with each exhale.

With divine powers, I now bless your space for a sacred ceremony to clear the barriers to prosperity.

I call upon the elements of earth, water, air, fire, and Spirit to transform blockages into opportunities for your fullest potential. I invite miracles guided by the highest vibration of light to embrace you throughout this clearing with ease and grace.

To earth, we call in our ancestors to release us from generational karma, wounds, and patterns that restrict, limit, or harm our soul's path to prosperity. We clear all chains, contracts, and agreements, keeping us in scarcity, oppression, or fear that has traveled through our lineage. We send healing to all involved through all lifetimes, time, and space.

To water, we release feelings of brokenness, trauma, anger, and grief from all relationships that still lay heavy on our hearts. We cleanse and purify every cell in our being with sacred water. Forgiveness is now being sent to all involved, including ourselves. May we be blessed with a juicy, abundant life.

To air, we release ourselves from the mental anguish that holds us back from moving forward into ecstatic living. We invite in the winds of change to release anxiety, fear, frustration and worry now so that we may be blessed with liberated personal and financial freedom.

To fire, we dance with the power and vitality of your sacred flames to burn away the past and charm us with the courage to rise from the ashes with lessons learned. May the heat of this activation clear limitations and ignite a life filled with prosperity, passion, and purpose.

To Spirit, we consciously release all heaviness, doubts, and unconscious barriers that keep us from living in prosperity consciousness. We invite you to cleanse, clear, and rejuvenate our mind, body, and Spirit through all time and space to reveal the truth of our sacred essence so that we can fully claim our divine inheritance now.

Take a moment to let this clearing work within you. Listen, sense, know or feel any personal messages that want to come through. Then, when you're ready, receive these words by Tzu Lao: **"When you realize there is nothing lacking, the whole world belongs to you."**

Let the words enter your body, receiving them at a cellular level. Say it a few more times and receive the words into your heart. Sit quietly for a moment to integrate with all we've done so far before moving on.

From today forward, be conscious of your words about money and life, having and not having. You create what you speak.

Now, take your candle and light it while speaking this mantra out loud.

"I'm aligning with prosperity and becoming more aware that the whole world belongs to me. I'm a money magnet attracting exactly what I need for my highest good."

This is a sacred truth if you choose to accept it. The sooner you align with these words, the faster prosperity will shift in your favor.

Repeat the mantra, but this time use your magical voice. My students laugh when they hear me say that for the first time. It means to speak with intention, heart, and soul. Mean what you say and say what you mean. When we tap into the source of divine power and speak with pure intentions, it activates our manifesting capabilities. From the belly up, harness your energy and place your faith in the words you speak. Draw personal power from the center of your being and bring it up and out of your mouth with purpose.

Your voice will sound deeper, purposeful, and filled with intention, heart, and soul. The Universe will respond accordingly.

Words hold power, and so do you. Go ahead, give it a try, **"I'm aligning with prosperity and becoming more aware that the whole world** belongs to me. I'm a money magnet attracting exactly what I need for my highest good."

Notice the vibration in your physical body when you use your magical voice. It feels so good. You may even feel the words activate and expand within your chest. I feel the vibration move through my body as it shifts and dissolves energy blocks. That's what we want. The shift! Prosperity is your divine birthright, and it's time for you to claim it.

If this is a stretch for you, take your time to get comfortable with the practice. Keep repeating it until it feels natural.

The more you integrate this work, the more things shift with ease and grace.

To work privately or to accelerate your Wealth Codes journey, schedule a Wealth Codes Discovery Call here: www.jenpiceno.com/book_now

Group programs and eclectic online experiences for personal and professional growth are available at my online academy. Visit: www.jenpiceno.com/academy

Complimentary resources, rituals, and activations are available at www.jenpiceno.com/resources

In the meantime, female readers may join Mystic Circle, my private Facebook community, for soulful conversations, holistic wealth, and accelerated business and spiritual growth.

https://www.facebook.com/groups/jenpiceno

Jen Piceno, Wealth Consciousness Coach, Prosperity Priestess, ORDM, RTM, LMT, THP.

Begin the transformation you crave and live your legacy now.

Jen is a coach, energy medicine practitioner, and modern mystic with 30+ years of experience in the healing arts. She'll help you bust through limitations to solidify your purpose and make sure you have fun doing it.

Align with everything you're meant to be in ways you've never experienced. Jen takes clients on an epic adventure that crushes time and limitations. Then, she welcomes you into an ecstatic life without sacrificing success, passion, or pleasure.

Jen is a bestselling author of Sacred Medicine, Mystical Practices for Ecstatic Living, and the host of The Ecstatic Living Podcast. She's a motivational speaker, ghostwriter, and sassy mompreneur. She savors life while teaching others to do the same.

Jen prevailed within corporate America, graced the stage as a professional salsa dancer, and trained as an amateur boxer, martial artist, and figure competitor. She approaches life as a lifetime student of human potential and mystical practices.

Jen's mission is to create worldwide wealth and happiness in homes, lives, and businesses. She believes in keeping what matters most at the forefront without sacrificing family, love, pleasure, or success. She works with women entering new phases of life, high achievers, athletes, and celebrities. She's sought after as an innovator who helps you clarify purpose and jumpstarts transformation.

To work with Jen, schedule a Discovery Call at:
www.jenpiceno.com/book_now
Visit her online academy at www.jenpiceno.com/academy or get
access to all quick links here: www.jenpiceno.com/links
Visit: https://www.JenPiceno.com

CHAPTER 2

MONEY STORIES

CREATING A WORLD
IN WHICH YOU (WE ALL) PROSPER

Meredith Sims, CSRIC®, Financial Advisor

MY STORY

A little girl sits on the warm concrete step, feet in running water, short blonde hair catching the sunlight as she bends over her task. She's holding a strange grey-purple and off-white striped rock, and beside her, one can see more of these beautiful stones.

Her mother has told her, "It is the flow of the water that makes the stone smooth." The young girl is polishing her stones.

I'm laughing now because, of course, the missing element here is time and perhaps friction. My mother could have told me, "Over time, you will be polished by the currents and tumbles of life," though I would have been too young to hear the deep truth of that.

Zebra rock is what held my attention as the water tickled my toes. Found only in the East Kimberley region of Western Australia, one of the Zebra rock's meanings that resonated for me is that this is a grounding stone that keeps you connected to the earth. *How appropriate,* I thought.

Another: Zebra rock balances the masculine and feminine aspects of self and helps balance the positive and negative, too. *Hmm, helpful!*

In my early childhood years, Dad got a job with the Public Works Department, and we moved from Perth to Kununurra, a remote new town founded as part of a project to use the Ord River for agricultural irrigation. Cotton was one of the crops trialed and a glitter-covered cotton boll, raptly held at the Cotton Queen festival, is an enduring memory for me.

As it turned out, those early cotton crops weren't sustainable. In my adult life, I was surprised to hear of the plague of insects being dealt with when visiting an old family friend who farmed in the area. The crops were heavily reliant on chemical pesticides.

The Americans assisting with the cotton trial may explain why our yard was complete with Pawpaw trees, as they're not native to Australia. Delicious, luscious, juicy Pawpaw! It's been way too long since I've eaten you. We had a good old-fashioned scarecrow to keep the birds away.

Nature was everywhere in our little town, from the nearby red rock bluff to the King Brown snake in our neighbor's yard. The bluff shone a beautiful deep orange in the closing light of day and provided a spectacular view of the surrounding area. Known to us then as Kelly's Knob, I discovered much later its true aboriginal name of Thegoowiyeng. The name Kununurra itself is derived from the English pronunciation of the word Goonoonoorrang which means river in the language of the Miriwoong people of this region.

Our small area of the Kimberley was a land of red earth, red rocks, and incredible natural beauty. With no television or other devices, my brother and I spent most of our time outdoors, amusing ourselves in the front or back garden or exploring the country around us.

Not surprisingly, my strongest memories are nature-based. My eyes widening at the sight of a huge green stick insect spreading its red-tipped wings; gazing at my first lily blossom as we clamber through the beautiful rock formations of Mirima National Park, known to us back then as Hidden Valley; picking our way carefully as we navigate the rocky track to reach the swimming hole at Black Rocks Falls. For me, there was a magic to these adventures.

It wasn't all happy times.

Our house was on stilts, and one day I went downstairs to find a joey (a baby kangaroo) jumping around. My brother and his friends found it abandoned and brought it home with them. It was upsetting for my mum because she tried to feed it, but sadly, a few days later the joey died.

Another time, seeing a cow on the distant flood plain, I asked, "What is it doing there?" "It's probably stuck in the mud," my dad replied. It still makes me sad today.

My brother and I built a sand cubby in the backyard. This was basically an underground fort. What could go wrong? Fortunately, we noticed the poisonous red-back spiders that took up residence before we used it again.

Mum and Dad loved the outdoors, and we had many a picnic on a riverbank where Mum would sketch and paint, and Dad would help my brother and me explore and search for interesting things like rocks or the freshwater crayfish I remember Dad proudly holding up for the camera.

There was a wonder to living in a part of the country filled with beauty and unexpected treasures. Discovery was and still is a delight for me.

As kids growing up, we had an old-fashioned bank book. I believe the teller even stamped it, which was exciting for me as a child. Those stamps seemed so important! And they were—each stamp a visual of our increase in savings.

I also recall standing in the one and only store, my attention on the sparsely filled shelves, hot coin in my hand. There wasn't a lot you could get for one small coin, but I found a tiny plastic bag that was in my budget and bought it. It's my earliest memory of money and possibly, of the constraints that can exist around it.

Other than that, and the bank book, I don't recall money being much of a point of discussion in our household. Mum made most of our clothes, our fancy dress for parties and fancy hats for festivals; we were well fed. And we never felt as though we went without.

There was a simplicity to this young life that resonates with me today. I still love rocks, nature, being in the water, exploration, and discovery and nothing delights me more than seeing a kangaroo bounding in the distance or a flock of pink and grey galahs when visiting home. Kununurra must have been idyllic for our parents too. Lots of social events and time to chill out. Not like life can be now.

Back in Perth, when my parents downsized, we bought them a fountain for their much smaller backyard. In their new shed, I found a big box of rocks. Oh, what lovely rocks of many colors—no doubt their collection from our time up north and perhaps from other trips. The fact that they kept a box of rocks after downsizing from their spacious suburban home makes me think that they also felt the connection to the earth and the relaxed times they represented. I admit to a pang of loss as those rocks were disbursed after Mum moved into care.

Fortunately, my sister-in-law kept some for me.

Zebra rock is a stone that brings compassion; I also read. How interesting that this story from my past came forward as I wrote for this book. I still have Zebra rocks today, bringing their energy of compassion into my home and, with these memories, into my life.

Compassion for myself.

Compassion for others.

Compassion for the planet.

I'm not sure if it's because of those early years in the North of Western Australia, but I've long had an affinity for the natural world and all things in it. As I write this story, there were certainly many lessons to learn from that time, unknown to my young self and only apparent now.

When I moved into finance, I never thought about where I might end up, but events over time led me to realize that focusing on sustainable investing is very much aligned with what I care about.

There's a lot of contention around climate and the environment, among other things. But politics and the media can't skew the basic fact that Mother Earth doesn't care—she is neutral.

Of course, sustainability can be applied to more than investing. It's about sustaining the life of a company, species, waterway, forest, or community. Oh, and what about your own quality of life? Building a financial foundation that sustains you is equally important.

THE STRATEGY

So, what does my story have to do with money, really?

I believe we have a divine connection to the things that inspire us if we're only awake enough to heed them. Often, we lose ourselves along the course of our journeys, but there may be times in our life that shine bright and illuminate them, as my story does for me. Nature. Beauty. Discovery. Adventure.

To be inspired is to be animated or imbued with the spirit to do something. What is the spirit of money for you? What is its purpose? Is your use and relationship with money fulfilling this purpose?

If we connect enough to our own desires and what's important to us, we can direct money for our own highest and best use. This is not a product of income or wealth. As I've written before, you can be broke on any income, and you can be unfulfilled with any amount of wealth.

In the steps to directing your money according to your values and building your own version of wealth, let's start with step number one, getting clear about what you value. This series of journaling exercises can be taken in one sitting or over a period of several days—one exercise a day. Allow yourself a quiet space to focus on the questions and your answers. Also, be okay with proceeding imperfectly.

If money is challenging for you, remember the Zebra stone essence in my story. Have some compassion for yourself and bring a playful sense of curiosity and discovery to the process. If you already have an empowering money story, yay you! Use these exercises as an opportunity to further elevate your money connection.

You can write out a detailed response to these questions, or when appropriate, you can also answer with a simple yes or no. Your wise self knows your truth.

JOURNALING EXERCISE # 1

Your values and money story.

1. Think back to those times when you were really happy or excited about something. What emotions were you experiencing? What values or desires did that event or person, or experience connect with?

   If you are struggling to define your values, I have a reference sheet for this on my resources page, listed at the end of this chapter.

2. What are the causes you are passionate about? This is another perspective you can take to look at what you value.

3. What is your money story? What do you tell yourself about money?

4. How does your money story, and what you tell yourself, relate to your own sense of value? What is the impact of that on your life?

   Don't judge yourself here, just notice what comes up. And, for the record, I've done some really dumb things in my life, all of which have been related to me undervaluing myself, judging myself as unworthy, or thinking that someone else's needs were more important. My most harmful money story was that I was undeserving, and the symptom of that was that I was passive and sloppy around my money exchanges.

As I wrote these questions, I spoke with a friend who told me that her story is that she always has no money. She's never destitute. When she has no money, she always survives, and when she has money, she always spends it. Another way of looking at this is her money temperature gauge is set to "Just Squeaking By."

Another friend has a different temperature gauge. Hers is set to "Always Finds a Bargain"—and I'm not talking about bargains as in junk; I'm talking about getting the things she wants at her preferred price.

I believe this is partly due to our ability to manifest our desire when there is no resistance and partly due to the embedded stories we have around money.

Your money story might vary in different parts of your life. When it comes to travel, my gauge is set to "Easy." Even when my resources were limited, somehow, it always worked out. For example, many years ago, out of the blue, a friend who didn't even live in the US sent me an airline ticket voucher. He'd received it due to canceled travel and had no idea when he would be able to use it.

But here's an example of where I put someone else's needs above my own. This is one of those dumb things I've done. I once loaned someone I worked with $2,000 to get their jewelry out of the pawnshop (I know, I know, really dumb!). When they gave me the jewelry as collateral, I didn't even blink when they kept the Rolex and diamond ring aside. I wasn't at the time a jewelry or watch expert (still not), but at least I now know the value of a Rolex, albeit an old one. I had to push and push to receive even monthly re-payments, which eventually sputtered out. Years later, a friend advised me to energetically reclaim that money. My house was broken into, and by some miracle, all they took was most of the collateral jewelry and an old laptop, not my sentimental and inherited jewelry pieces. The insurance claim repaid my money. Thank you very much, Universe!

Now, back to you.

JOURNALING EXERCISE # 2

How does your spending line up with your values?

1. When did you last exchange your money for something that felt really good? Did it feel good because it matched a value you distinguished in the first exercise? Or was there another reason?

2. When do you feel resistance to spending money? Why do you think that is?

   From my own experience, I've noticed that resistance around spending has nothing to do with how much money I have. It's usually either because I'm doing something based on someone else's idea or rules or based on another frequent culprit for wasting money—fear of missing out.

3. When did you receive something you wanted easily? It might have been with no money exchange or just felt effortless. What emotions, desires, or circumstances allowed this to happen?

With the awareness you have from the prior two exercises, let's move on to how you can better direct your money.

JOURNALING EXERCISE # 3

Writing a new money story.

1. What deep desires or dreams are you focused on? Is your money supporting those dreams? And if not, are there places where you are using your money that does not support you?

   This is an opportunity to redirect your money to its highest and best use for you.

2. What makes you happy? Is there enough of this in your life, and if not, what can you add in? If so, how can you add in more?

   This doesn't always have to be around money. Sometimes what brings us happiness is free.

3. Write a new and happy money story for yourself. You may want to include gratitude, appreciation, and partnership in your story. Above all, give yourself permission to have it all. You deserve it!

   Keep your new money story close and re-read it whenever you feel yourself slipping back into your old story.

Finally, I wanted to talk a little about money and prosperity in the world. I'm a firm believer that expanding prosperity for ourselves creates a ripple effect that can impact our communities and the planet. And I love that developing an awareness of what we value and how we direct our money can flow through to supporting organizations, companies, and movements that make a difference.

You all know the story below, I'm sure; here is my version:

A young girl walks along the beach, where many starfish, washed up by the high tide, have become stranded. As she walks, she picks up a starfish and gently returns it to the sea.

Her father admonishes, "Why are you wasting your time? There are too many. You can't possibly make a difference."

The young girl looks up at him, light shining from her eyes and her heart.

"It made a difference for that one," she replies.

Every day you vote with your dollars, and your time about the life you want to create for yourself and the world you want to live in.

Make it count.

For you.

For your families.

For the planet.

Meredith Sims is a chartered SRI counselor and independent financial advisor specializing in Financial Planning and Socially Responsible and Impact Investing.

She loves empowering women to step up and take charge of their money, helping them to build a solid financial foundation aligned with their values. Her love of nature and compassion for each living being drives her interest in spending and investing money in a meaningful and earth-friendly way.

As an advisor, Meredith has long been interested in the subject of money from the perspective of conscious connection, using money as a tool and platform to support living a fully expressed life, whatever that may look like for each individual—building wealth and building a wealthy life.

A spiritual seeker and artist at heart, Meredith came to Atlanta, Georgia, by way of Perth, Brisbane, London, and Sydney. She believes in the beauty of seeing the individual, the inherent goodness in humanity, and that living a fulfilled, joyful life is a birthright, while not necessarily an immediate destination. She loves getting on a plane and traveling somewhere, has been working on mastering the French language for many years, and no doubt will be for many more. She loves to garden, create, paint, and write, and her happy place is on the water. Meredith has previously written for The Art Section, an online journal of art and cultural commentary, and for the collaborative book *Wholehearted Wonder Women, Courage, Confidence and Creativity at Any Age.*

Meredith can be contacted at
www.heartstrongwealthplanning.com/contact
More money resources can be found at
www.heartstrongwealthplanning.com/resources
Connect with Meredith:
Website: www.heartstrongwealthplanning.com

CHAPTER 3

FINANCIAL ABUNDANCE
AFTER MAJOR HARDSHIPS

YOUR TRUTH SURPASSES
PAST CIRCUMSTANCES AND MONEY CHOICES

Kimberly Cooper, EA

MY STORY

After I'm dead, no one is gonna say, "Aww, it's a shame she ruined her credit score."

My past hardships and failures do not define my truth.

The downward slope began in 2006 when I was prescribed a medication that literally shut my ovaries down and put me into a post-menopausal state overnight, at 37. I couldn't work or do everyday functions. The only thing I could tolerate was a dark room, a washcloth over my forehead, and my momma rubbing my back and hair for comfort. Bills piled up, all specialty doctors were clueless, and my two girls couldn't depend on their momma. I was having a nervous breakdown.

Scared shitless that something was wrong with me, I told Doug, my husband, "I don't want to live to pay for this house. I want to sell and downsize. This nightmare has made me realize I don't want or need this house or its stuff. None of it matters."

Doug reassured, "Let's get you feeling better, then we will sell the house."

Several months later, my daddy set up a time for us to look at a house a friend of his, Ellen, was selling. It was a brick ranch on the street right behind my parents' home.

Ellen said, "Listen if you want the house, I'll be happy to wait until you sell yours. I have three years until I retire, so I'm not exactly in a hurry. This arrangement will help us both because I won't have to go to the trouble or expense of listing it with an agent." This house was about $100K less than the house we owned and would be such an answer to prayer! Relief and excitement washed over me.

Fast forward three years, slouching on the oversized leather chair, I took in my expansive open living room and all the unnecessary luxuries. Where gratitude once prevailed, guilt and desperation were front and center.

I don't want to live to pay for this house and all this stuff anymore! I feel so trapped! I need out! But how? I am an accountant, dammit! How the hell did I get in this damn predicament? Health issues, anxiety attacks, inability to work for months, returning to work part-time. I know how, but why has this happened to me? I have the perfect house waiting for me, but now my credit is shit! I spent so much energy on that damn credit score, too. Now, what does it matter? I cared too much about looking like I had my shit together. What a joke that is now. I'm so tired! How can I get out of this when I don't have what it takes to take it on mentally?

Not even a second later, I received my answer. So very unmistakable; a physical, emotional, and spiritual revelation came out of nowhere:

Quit being so damn prideful! What matters in this world has zero to do with your credit score, worldly standards, or others' opinions. Trust. File bankruptcy to get out from under this house and ask Ellen for owner financing. Just trust your intuition, and the abundance will follow.

It was received so simply, so matter-of-fact.

In an instant, I felt peace and clarity through every cell of my being. I completely trusted. I trusted the Divine, my intuition, and knew everything would align perfectly. This was the first time I consciously thought my intuition was more than a gut instinct—a gut feeling I always felt but never trusted to this magnitude.

It didn't take fear long to take control of my head talk. All the negative thoughts flooded my mind—*the audacity! You can't file for bankruptcy; what will people say? People will see me as weak. I know I can be bold, but damn, what sane person would ask someone to finance their house personally? Oh my God! Doug is gonna think I've lost it, and so are Momma and Daddy. Let's do a little searching because I don't want to look like an idiot.*

I opened my computer, hands sweaty and heart beating out of my chest.

I feel so naughty.

Kim, stop overthinking this!

I pulled up information on the types of bankruptcy and started reading through all the legal jargon. *I know I'm not stupid, but this is over my head.* I Googled a bankruptcy lawyer near me and made an appointment for the end of that same week. *Damn, this is happening fast!*

That evening I spelled out my day to Doug and told him about my scheduled appointment with the bankruptcy lawyer. Doug said, "See what the lawyer says, and I'll do whatever you think is best." Next, I called my momma and daddy, "Hey Daddy, get Momma on the other line, so I don't have to go through this twice." I retold my story.

A couple of days later, during the appointment, my lawyer explained that even though I was working part-time, I made $600 too much to file for bankruptcy. The calculation included all household wages earned through that period. Doug's wages were constant, so if I stopped working, then we could qualify the next month.

What? My answer appeared to me like magic, my husband is on board with my crazy, I get an appointment the same week with a lawyer, my parents are my biggest supporters, and my wages are only $600 over the threshold to be able to file? There is no way this timing is so perfect! Luck or coincidence? No way! This is what you call Divine intervention. Yes! Yes! Yes! Trust, I am trusting. Thank you!

My momentum is building now! Hope is something I hadn't felt in the last three years. Boy, did it feel amazing! It was just what I needed to take the next steps. I knew gratitude energetically raises your vibration, and that vibration attracts abundance. I started throwing gratitude at everything.

Thank you for the support of my parents. I am so grateful for my health bouncing back. Thank you for the unconditional love of my fur babies.

Abundance started flowing in all forms: love, money, freedom, and self-confidence. It was time to start acting upon that abundance of self-confidence.

I needed to talk to Ellen about the house for this grand plan to work. "Ellen, I want to be completely honest and let you know about our hardships over the last three years," I explained. I gave her the backstory and exactly how my heart yearned for a much simpler life focusing on what truly mattered. "You know we've been trying to sell, even before the recession, but we haven't had anyone look at the house since the recession. I want to ask you something that is really out of my comfort zone, but I am desperate."

You can do this.

I sighed heavily, then continued, "Would you be willing to owner-finance the house to us? And wait, before you even consider it, let me explain. I'm thinking about filing bankruptcy to cancel the debt of this house. To file, I have to stop working while the bankruptcy goes through. I won't be able to get a mortgage because the bankruptcy will ruin my credit," I told her matter-of-factly.

We talked for at least an hour, and even though it was a bold move on my part, it was raw and one of the most vulnerable things I'd ever done. I was nervous but trusted and felt safe sharing with her. The conversation ended with Ellen saying, "Let me talk to Howard, and I will get back to you in a couple of days. Recurring income might be nice since I'm retiring. But I need to talk to him."

Wow! I am a badass! Mental note for the future—don't think, just do! I feel so empowered. I don't know her answer, but my intuition already knows her answer!

Two days later, I answered my phone, "Hello?" Ellen greets me, "Hey Kim, do you have a minute to talk about the house?" "Absolutely!" I replied. Ellen continued, "We think this arrangement will benefit both of us, so let's move forward," Ellen's words were music to my ears.

Thank you, thank you, thank you! I'm grateful for the ease of everything falling into place.

Now it was time for the call I didn't want to make. The call to my employer was one of the hardest conversations I've ever had. These people are my family. I grew up with them, going to the same church, and worked for them for over 13 years. I respect and love them. No matter how difficult, I was trusting and moving forward.

I cried after that call. I told my mom, "I'm so sad and relieved at the same time. My career, my identity, not seeing my work family daily are lost, but I also have so much peace, hope, and gratitude."

Thirteen years later, I'm very grateful for all the lessons learned through my hardships. My circumstances brought me to my knees with a precious understanding to never take anything for granted. Because I was open to trusting something bigger than myself, I cut the chords of my pride.

Today, abundance overflows in every aspect of my life. It's an absolute privilege to use my experience and expertise to offer trusted accounting and advisory services with a unique twist of understanding that others in my industry don't manifest.

THE STRATEGY

Do you feel judged because of your past money choices?

Do you feel ashamed because of your past circumstances?

One purpose that came from my hardships is to offer a safe space for my clients. You'll never feel any judgment from me because I'm human and lived through my own shit.

Everyone has secrets, but they do not define you. Your truth surpasses your present or past circumstances and money choices. Trust your intuition and find your inner circle of those that lift you and cheer you on. There's no room for judgment or negativity within your inner circle. You should feel peaceful and safe.

Heart-centered people and businesses are changing the world. I'm proud that my firm is part of this movement. Our strength is eliminating your stress around bookkeeping and tax preparation for holistic and alternative entrepreneurs! Your peace of mind is invaluable.

If you ever think your financial failures or money choices are more important than the person you are, think to yourself: *After I'm dead, no one is going to say, "Aww, it's a shame they made that money choice."* Let's put things into perspective and change your current circumstance with financial abundance.

Any abundance, including financial, doesn't just happen. Start the flow.

Simple rules to live by:

1. Love and kindness are at the center of making this world a better place.

2. Listen to your intuition.

3. Raise your energetic vibration with gratitude practices every day.

4. Meditate.

5. Journal: Write down three to five things you are grateful for at that moment.

6. Visualization: Think of something you are grateful for. Visualize it in your mind and physically feel your vibration rise and your heart expand with love and appreciation.

7. Share with others why you're grateful for them.

8. Find a penny and thank the Creator for the abundance.

9. Let nature fill your soul—trees, birds, the seasons.

10. Give to those less fortunate.

11. Plan for your future.

There is limitless abundance all around you, waiting for you to claim it.

Let's have a virtual coffee to see how I can support you and create a plan for your financial abundance. http://intuitivebookkeeper.com/resources/

Learn more about The Intuitive Bookkeeper, LLC
http://intuitivebookkeeper.com/

Kimberly Cooper, EA, is the owner of The Intuitive Bookkeeper, LLC. She earned a bachelor's in Accounting from The University of Georgia and is currently an advanced ProAdvisor with QuickBooks Online and a Xero certified advisor.

Kimberly's experience includes 35+ years of bookkeeping, two years of public accounting, and 13 years of job cost accounting. She founded The Intuitive Bookkeeper, LLC in 2017.

After years of health issues and side effects from pharmaceuticals, Kimberly turned to a more holistic approach which became her passion. She practices many holistic modalities and understands the industry. Kimberly is an intuitive empath. Most accountants are left-side brain processors, but Kimberly is 50/50, an oddity in accounting. She uses the left-side brain for detail and analytics, like every other accountant, and uses the right-side brain to look into creative ways to decrease your tax liability and to explain things in easy-to-understand language.

She partners with entrepreneurs who want complete financials, trusted advisors, and strategic planning for success.

Kimberly is the mother to two daughters and Mimi to twin grandsons. Her free time is spent with family, traveling, reading, self-development, serving others, organization, a good movie, a Netflix binge, and tons of laughter!

Learn more about The Intuitive Bookkeeper, LLC, Kimberly, and The Intuitive Bookkeeper Team.

http://intuitivebookkeeper.com/

CHAPTER 4

SACRED SPACES FOR MONEY FLOW

FENG SHUI YOUR WAY TO THE BANK

Laura Di Franco, MPT, Publisher

MY STORY

"The back left corner of the room is your money corner."

My money corner? Now you tell me!?

"Take the Bagua map and line it up by standing at the entrance to your home or room. What's that back left corner look like?"

Cluttered. Bland. Uninspiring. I've got some work to do. I think it needs a plant.

I've learned a lot of things about money, but until I understood Feng Shui and how my internal and external spaces created a clog in my pipes, so to speak, I was only relying on what I was taught:

You'll have to rely on a man for money.

You'll have to be perfect to earn money.

You'll have to work your ass off to make money.

You'll never be smart enough to be rich.

This is hard and complicated, and you're not good enough.

Crap, you know what? I could keep typing, but this is embarrassing. These old, conditioned, outdated, unhelpful, unhealthy beliefs kept me stuck—for a long time. Let me flip the switch for you now that my dirty thought laundry is out on paper. Here's the good stuff, now that I know what I know about the law of attraction, Feng Shui, and the energy of money:

Money is energy, like everything else, and you attract what you are. So be amazing!

Money is easy to make.

Like love and other forms of energy, money flows freely when you keep it in circulation.

Money doesn't buy happiness. However, financial freedom is really nice and achievable.

The only thing stopping you from being rich is you and your beliefs and actions around money.

How you respect and treat money is part of the reason it's difficult to accumulate.

And I'll repeat for emphasis:

Money is energy, and like all forms of energy, you attract what you are. So be amazing!

Do you know what's truly awesome about this? I could keep typing this list, too. I've learned so much about keeping in the flow of money that it's a fun game now. Before I learned the tips and tricks about Feng Shui (from the amazing Dana Claudat) and removed my money blocks (with the help of several coaches, a course, and a lot of mindset practice), I was constantly worried about money. My divorce (the one I asked for) was the biggest trigger. I was terrified I wouldn't be able to continue to pay the mortgage and bills and take care of my kids, who were both headed for college.

"I'm not sure what I'm going to do. I will have to refinance the house. I don't know if I can afford the bills here by myself. I don't want the kids to have to move, though. I feel like I will wreck their lives."

I vented to my mom about everything, but mostly the money.

"Don't worry; everything will work out."

Mom has a way of reassuring me that "it will all work out" no matter what we're talking about. I remember doing some exercises in a money course and calling her up one night:

"Mom, can you tell me more about how we were raised around money? Were you and Dad worried about it?"

"We always had everything we needed. There was no real stress around money," she said.

I didn't believe her. There was some serious anxiety coming down the DNA line to me. I could feel it as chest pain.

"It's all ancestral," I heard my friend Amy say.

"Are you sure?" I questioned Mom again. "What do you remember?"

I grilled her for a while about how she was raised and how my sister and I were raised. I come from a pretty long line of entrepreneurs, including my mom, dad, and grandparents on my dad's side. I realized my money triggers might have come from my parents and grandparents, but I also realized I was feeling many things we never spoke about out loud. I had no context for the anxiety.

Why am I always so worried about money? Never in my life have I ever not had enough money! I always have enough to generously take care of myself and everyone I love.

That last line became a regular affirmation in my life. It was true. I didn't really even need to use it to help manifest it. It was just my truth.

Enter the inner Feng Shui. I journaled the shit out of my thoughts, beliefs, and past behaviors around money. I laid it all out so I could look at those pages. One time I finished writing and thought: *Whoa, do I believe that?*

The awareness was a huge key. The journaling, and resulting awareness, started to help me shift my mindset in a split second. I call that badassery my "ninja moves."

I worked the money blocks in multiple ways, with numerous people, in various journals, and during multiple ceremonies. I released, burned things, prayed to the full moon, shared my fears with healer friends, and questioned everything I knew about it. I wasn't afraid to talk about it anymore. I started busting through the taboo I learned from the silence I experienced at home and in my grandparent's homes, as well as the way-too-verbal way my ex constantly worried and expected me to worry about money.

Everything I think about money has been taught to me by others. I don't even know what is what anymore. I think I'll go wash my front door.

Cleaning and decluttering was the first step of the Feng Shui boot camp and the Cash Catalyst program by Feng Shui Dana; enter the external Feng Shui. I've always been super tidy. Ask my mom about how I organized the stuffed animals by size and color along the wall when I was five. But after a lifetime's worth of accumulating stuff, two kids and four dogs later, you have a whole other level of decluttering challenge. It took me a year after the divorce to fit my car into the garage. Happy to report I fit two cars in there now.

And my income is higher than it has ever been in my life. My little ol' divorced mom of two college kids self was able to pull in more income than in her last thirty years. Was it the cleaning? Who knows? I do work hard. But here's what I know (and want you to know) about the flow and what I now believe about money and how to attract more of that flow into your life:

When I declutter and clean my spaces, more money shows up.

More money shows up when I prioritize joy and make my day about that.

When I stop "working" and clean (my car, the junk drawer in the kitchen, the front door of the house, the stovetop, underneath my bed, the patio), money shows up.

When I Feng Shui my spaces and create rooms I can breathe better in, my income increases.

When I let go of any unhelpful beliefs about money and get more money in circulation, more shows up.

When I respect money, track it, and allocate it, more money shows up.

When I create from joy, my programs fill up.

When my mind is free of money worry and focused on flow, I'm so much happier.

There are real strategies to getting into a better flow (mental and physical) with money. It's about awareness. It's about how you think, believe, speak, and act. It's about the thoughts, beliefs, words, and actions you choose to make a daily, moment-to-moment part of your life. It's time to catch your bad habits in action, flip the switch, and retrain yourself.

Yes, you should wash your front door and organize your money corners.

THE STRATEGY

FENG SHUI YOUR SPACES FOR MONEY FLOW

THE INTERNAL SPACE

Step 1: This first part is a journaling and awareness exercise. Grab a notebook and pen, and find a quiet, sacred space where you can honor this exercise without being rushed.

Just like I did above, take a few moments to write down any past limiting thoughts, beliefs, or behaviors around money that you've practiced. The first step to shifting anything is to understand what you're dealing with. With awareness, you get a choice.

Louise Hay said, "If you want to clean house, you first have to see the dirt."

So, write out the dirty thought laundry about money in a list form. I'll wait until you're done. Imagine the Jeopardy theme music now while you write.

Step 2: Next, change every negative statement you wrote down into a positive "why" question. Thanks to Dr. Noah St. John for his book, *Millionaire Afformations* (yes, afformations, not affirmations). He teaches the power of turning statements into questions.

Example: One of my beliefs above was: "You'll have to work your ass off to make money."

The why question: Why is it so easy to make money? Or, why is it always so easy to increase my income?

Dr. Noah reminds us that the brain is wired to find solutions to problems. So when you ask a question, you move into that solution mode, which is way better than always trying to fake your way into a statement or affirmation that you can't quite believe fully.

Great job; you're already shifting your old money beliefs into new questions that will spark change and flow and attract more money!

THE EXTERNAL SPACE

Now for some of your external spaces. Start with decluttering. You're going to have to let go of the crap. Check for items in your home that are:

- Broken
- Stained
- Not sparking joy (yeah, I went there)
- Not functional
- Outdated
- Not being used
- Forgotten items that have been packed away for years
- Ripped, torn, or worn
- In disrepair
- Not enjoyable to use or look at

Ready?

Get rid of them.

Go get your garbage bags out, schedule a pick up from Salvation Army, list the stuff on Posh Mark; I don't care. But clear out your spaces. Make room for new things to move into your life.

Start small, like with a small drawer. Go medium, like with a closet. And then just go for it, like your whole garage. The attic was my last frontier of decluttering. I'm happy to report I no longer have anything up there, and I can't say I miss the trips up the tin pull-down stairs into the Hell-sauna in the middle of the summer to find shit.

Once you've cleared out, it's time to clean and organize.

"Make sure to clean your stovetop." One of my coaches told me that the stovetop, particularly, was aligned with abundance. Mine has stayed spotless ever since.

"Go wash your front door." Yeah, there it is again. Another coach talked about the door. I landed three deals adding up to $30,000 after washing mine. I can see you running for the bucket and soapy water now.

And after I completed a money corner organizing and beautifying day, I opened up my email to see that Bank of America ruled in my favor over a scam that I was fighting. That was a $2500 day. You better believe that the money corners of my home are looking pretty amazing.

Truth is, even when you finish with the whole apartment or house, you'll always be in maintenance mode. I make decluttering and cleaning a regular part of my week—of my abundance strategy. I especially love to wash my car. I do these activities as a kind of meditation, paying attention to the great feeling of clearing and cleaning the space. I enjoy a deep breath as I step back and look at those spaces I spend my life dwelling in. I feel great, grateful, wealthy, and abundant as I honor my home, the objects in it, and the spaces I live my life in.

THE MONEY SPACE:

Now think about everything I've had you work on, both the inner and outer spaces, as they relate to your actual money.

Begin to pay attention to:

- Your bank and bank accounts
- Your thoughts when a bill arrives in the mail
- Your wallet or purse (time for a new one?)
- Your computer and online apps that help you with your finances and accounts
- Your financial team (CPA, bookkeeper, CFO, or coach)
- Your thoughts when a check arrives in the mail
- Your reactions to money
- The words you speak when it's about money
- The way you track your money and expenses

- The way you allocate money
- How you feel when you have to look at your accounts or spreadsheets
- What you say to your friends, family, spouse, or co-workers about money
- What you hide
- What you feel good about

Grab your journal and pen and do some free writing on the above items, especially the ones that bring up the most resistance or passion. Take a deep breath and fill in the blank: I feel _____, when it comes to (the line item above). Write as fast as you can without censoring yourself. Write until you're surprised!

One of the best things a mentor said recently to me about how to reframe the money thoughts was, "Think of your money like someone you're in love with. How do you treat that person? What do you say to them? Do you respect them? How do you show it?"

Oh, whoa! I'm treating money like it's something I loathe. I remember so many times I'd walk to the mailbox, find a bill, and whisper, "Fuck!" out loud to nobody, with the feeling of true dread in the center of my chest.

Yeah, that was an Aha moment. I began to fall in love with money and started to think about all the ways I could think it, speak it, show it, and practice it.

Now, when I see a bill, I think: *I'm so grateful to be able to afford this and to be able to help someone else pay their bills and live a good life.*

It took a while to get to that ninja move in my awareness and mindset around money. Some days are still harder than others. But as I keep the flow going, things work out and keep working out even better than I ever could imagine.

Just like the flow of love energy I shower on the people I adore, I think about, believe in, and act about money in the ways that most resemble higher vibe frequencies: gratitude, joy, inspiration, excitement, expectation, etc. I catch myself in stuck, heavy moments and resistance and think: *Now, look here you sexy, badass, hippie, warrior of love, that's a waste of your precious time. Try something a little more healthy, aligned, and awesome.*

I remind myself that since I woke up to the moment, it's my choice to shift it as quickly as possible and manifest the life (and money) of my dreams.

And I do.

It's that easy.

I love money.

I love love.

I love the energy of gratitude and joy.

When you bake a cake with those ingredients, watch out world, cuz you're about to understand some of the most powerful, profound, and exciting secrets of the universe. And you'll have to be careful what you wish for.

Chocolate. For sure, chocolate.

Laura Di Franco, MPT, is the CEO of Brave Healer Productions, where they specialize in publishing and business strategy for healers. She spent 30 years in holistic physical therapy and 12 of those in private practice before making the pivot to publishing. With 14-years of training in the martial arts and 30 books and counting, including over two dozen Amazon bestsellers, she knows how to help you share your brave words in a way that build your business and your dream life.

Her daily mission is to help fellow wellness professionals do what they need to do to change the world in less time and with fewer mistakes and heartache on the journey. She shares her authentic journey, wisdom, and expertise with refreshing transparency and straightforward badassery. Hold on to your seat because riding alongside her means you'll be pushed into and beyond your comfort zone and have way more fun with your purpose-driven fears on a regular basis.

When Laura chills out, you'll find her with a mojito at a poetry event with friends, driving (or washing) her Mustang, bouncing to the beat at a rave, or on a beach in Mexico with something made of dark chocolate in her mouth.

Connect with Laura:
Website: https://www.LauraDiFranco.com or BraveHealer.com
LinkedIn: https://www.linkedin.com/in/laura-di-franco-mpt-1b037a5/
Facebook: https://www.Facebook.com/BraveHealerbyLaura
Instagram: https://www.Instagram.com/BraveHealerProductions/
Twitter: https://www.Twitter.com/Brave_Healer
YouTube: Brave Healer Productions and Positively Purposeful Poetry

CHAPTER 5

LIGHT UP YOUR DESIRES

EXPONENTIALLY GROW YOUR WEALTH AND BUILD A LIFE YOU LOVE

Hannah Chapman, CFP®, APMA®, CRPC®, Wealth Advisor

MY STORY

The more closely you can align your business and actions with your desires, the more money you will make.

I stared at my notebook after writing down what just came into my mind like a flash download.

"It can't be that simple, can it?" I asked my dog, Leif. He was the only one home, and he didn't know. But he was a good listener!

As I sat there and contemplated if it could truly be that simple, my hand kept on writing as if my higher self knew she had to prove the point.

- *A consultant leaned into her love of travel and connected with her partner on a business retreat cruise and is now working through hundreds of thousands of dollars worth of contracts doing creative consulting work.*

- *A coach leaned into her deep desire to help teens create mental resilience and is now working on a multi-six figure contract with a youth academy.*

- *A lawyer realized she desired to only work on estate planning in her law firm and leave family law behind, and now she's making more income and working fewer hours than she ever has before on the part of the law that lights her up.*

How had I not seen all of this before? It was right under my nose! I was taking my clients through the same process I went through to build my wealth advisory firm, and I hadn't even taken a minute to sit down and realize the connection!

Follow your desire. The money is a result, a side effect of following your deepest, truest "why" in your business.

I set my pen down and thanked my higher self for letting that pour out of me and onto the page. And then I thought about the journey I've taken doing the exact same thing: Following the sparks of desire over and over again until I created a bonfire that attracts the exact clients I love working with and allows me to make more money than I've ever made before!

Leif was waiting so patiently. "Do you want to go for a walk?" I asked him. He did know the answer to that question! He bounded to the door to get his leash, and I spent time walking and thinking back over my career and life.

My experience in the financial industry started in 2006, but my experience with entrepreneurship goes all the way back to the 1980s when my parents started their first business.

It wasn't an easy childhood.

There were years when money was incredibly tight, like being on food stamps and only wearing hand-me-downs from friends and relatives tight. My love of financial planning started all the way back then, when I'd collect and obsessively count all the change around the house and save (okay, horde) any money I received from birthdays or odd jobs for some unknown future need.

My parents' first business took quite a while to blossom, but it grew over the next 15 years, and by the time I was in high school, my parents had started a second business. It may not have been the smoothest ride, but my upbringing set me up to be able to relate to and connect with entrepreneurs like magnets being drawn to one another from across a table and buzzing with energy on impact. We see each other on a deep level, like a soul connection that instantly recognizes an aligned partnership.

And as the universe would have it, my very first full-time job out of college was at a local bank, which was five-year-old Hannah's dream job.

I get to count money all day long!

That particular bank attracted a lot of local business owners. I loved it when they'd come into the branch to deposit their cash and tell me how business was going, and it was especially fun to visit them at their own shops! When I moved away, I was sad to leave that job, but it was all on purpose.

My next job was at a large financial company, where I found "it"—My true calling.

Financial planning was the thing that challenged me, intrigued me, and combined relationship building with counting money and planning for the future!

The partners at the firm I worked for mainly worked with executives at big companies, but there were some business owners and entrepreneurs sprinkled throughout their client base. Like at the bank, I'd spend extra time with those business owners, researching everything I could about all the options they had to create stability and wealth for their businesses and their families.

By the time I became the lead advisor for my own clients, I had worked with enough people to know I desired to work specifically with entrepreneurs. They were the clients that lit me up! The partners at my firm were more comfortable with executives at large companies, though.

"Do you really want to learn so much about small business?" they said. "Why don't you keep focusing on these big companies? That's what we know best. You can't create your niche like that anyway, it finds you, and you just follow it."

First of all, that sounded like straight bull shit. *How could you think that you can't create your niche? That makes no sense!*

And second of all, I knew that wasn't right for me. Trying to get executive clients wasn't working. It felt heavy, difficult, and exhausting trying to get clients in that world—like I was convincing people to work with me through a slimy feeling sales script, always overcoming objections and getting through the icky sales part so we could get to the fun relationship-building part.

It felt heavy because I didn't desire to work with those clients. At all. I desired to work with entrepreneurs. I also desired to make more money and have a voice and a position of leadership that allowed me to steer the direction of the firm.

The more I allowed those sparks of desire to fly, the more I realized I couldn't create the business of my dreams at that firm.

I couldn't even go to another firm and be happy! My higher self knew, once again.

I have to create the business I want to see in the world. It doesn't exist yet.

It was a huge leap of faith, but my higher self was guiding me, and I knew I was following the right path. She never leads me astray.

Over the first year of owning my own wealth advisory firm, I was journaling non-stop. I wrote about the clients I desired to work with: who they were, what they did for a living, what their fears and worries were, what their goals and dreams were, what they did for fun, and what they cared about in the world. Doing this helped me create a specific model client to target all my marketing towards.

And I wrote about what I desired my own business to look like: Who I'd be helping with my work both in my firm and out in the world, how much money I desired to make, and the experiences and adventures I desired to provide for myself and my family.

As I was writing and writing (and writing some more) about exactly who I desired to help and what issues I desired to help them solve, the sparks started burning brighter. The clients that were out there for me started hearing me more clearly. As I wrote for Forbes, posted on social media, and gave presentations and facilitated workshops, I started calling in clients who were exactly the entrepreneurs I desired to work with! It felt like magic!

But it wasn't magic; it was the intention.

By intentionally writing out my desires for my life, business, and clients, I created a roadmap for my energy to follow.

My sales conversations became easier because I drew the right people to me. When I talked to people who were the exact right fit for the way I work, there were almost zero objections to overcome. The sales process felt easy and beautiful!

The revenue I desired for my business started becoming a reality. I replaced my income from my previous firm in less than nine months and was making well over six figures in my second year of business!

All of this happened and keeps happening because I took time to identify my desires and then had the courage to bring them out into the light. I decided to talk about them, write about them, share them in conversations with other like-minded business owners and supportive family and friends, and put them up on a vision board in my office, where I see them every day.

And as new desires come up, they get to take their place in my heart and my mind too. Being open to the evolution of desire and allowing new things to catch my interest is part of what creates innovation in my business and allows me to grow faster than I ever imagined. The more time I spend doing things that light me up, the more I enjoy my life and the faster my business grows!

As I walked back into the house with Leif, he curled up on his bed for a nap, and I sat down to prepare for a financial planning meeting with one of my amazing entrepreneur couples—the niche I desired, and then went out and created.

THE STRATEGY

The Light Up Your Desires journaling prompts are the exact same prompts I give to new clients to help them define their desires for their business and their life. Going through this exercise will help you define your desires so you can start pointing your energy and focus in the direction of your dreams!

You can find the journal pages here:
https://x2wealthplanning.com/light-up-your-desires-journal

STEP 1: DISCOVERY

To start, print out the journaling prompts! If you can't do it this second, grab some paper and a pen and start writing out all the things you desire. You may notice your initial desires are pretty surface level and might sound like:

"I want to buy a new luxury car."

Or, "I want to make $1,000,000 in revenue."

Those desires are wonderful! Write them down. In fact, write down every single thing that comes up. The more you write without filtering anything, the easier it will be to dig deeper into the heart of your desires.

If the desire "I want to buy a new luxury car" comes up and instead of writing it down, you say, "That's ridiculous, my car is fine," you've just made your desire for a new car wrong, and you've stopped your creative flow in its tracks. Whether you need the new car or not doesn't matter. What matters is your ability to say what you want without being the first person to shoot down your own ideas. The exercise of letting your desires flow onto the page requires a safe space without self-judgment.

Be kind and curious during this exercise. Write down every desire that comes to mind and if one seems surprising to you, let your curiosity take the lead!

If you want to make $1,000,000 in your business and it seems like a stretch from where you are today, be interested and curious about the desires that accompany your revenue goal by asking more questions:

- Who will you be helping if you're making that amount of revenue?
- Why do you want to help them?
- Do you have employees at that level, and what does that feel like?
- What impact do you want to make on the world?
- Why does it matter to you?

Making $1,000,000 in revenue is the surface-level desire. If you reject it out of hand and make your desire wrong, you'll miss the exploration that happens beneath the surface. As you stay kind and curious with yourself and keep asking follow-up questions, you'll start to reveal your deeper, more meaningful desires naturally.

Identifying your desires is an important first step, but don't stop there! Lighting up your desires is crucial. It's what brings your desires out of the shadows, out of your mind and heart, and allows them to be seen.

You may have heard about research saying if you tell other people about your goals and dreams, it lowers motivation and decreases your chances of achieving your goals. And that makes sense if you tell people who don't understand big thinking. If you tell someone that's only ever worked as an employee about your desire to make $1,000,000 in your business, hire a team, and change thousands of people's lives with your work, it might be too big for them to understand. And they'll tell you so.

"Why do you need to do that? Why can't you just be happy with what you have?"

But you know why. Your vision is so much bigger than you can even describe. Rest assured that pushback comes from the other person's fear or doubt about the situation and doesn't have anything to do with you! But if you're just starting to nurture those tiny sparks of desire, they can be stomped out like an ember if you're not careful about who you talk to.

To keep that from happening, when you've written out your desires, and you're ready to light them up by talking about them, you want to be in a safe and supportive space. Accountability and clarity are powerful benefits you can only get by talking about your desires with others, so make sure you bring those desires to people with whom you want to have accountability and who you trust to help you bring clarity to your vision.

The other turbo-charged benefit to lighting up your desires with people you trust is inviting collaboration! When you're with a supportive team, and you reveal a desire you want to go after, they may have connections and help readily available that you would never have known about otherwise.

Once your desire has been nurtured from spark to ember to bright burning flame, you'll be on your way to aligning your business and your actions with the money that's there waiting for you!

STEP 2: ALIGNMENT

Once you've discovered your current desires, you can start aligning your actions and your finances in the direction of what you truly want. This is where planning and accountability come in to turn your desires into reality and where the success stories at the beginning of this chapter started to grow from ember to flame.

The adage, "If I want to know what you value, I only have to look at your calendar and your check book," applies here. You have to align your time and money with what you truly desire and keep checking yourself against those measures again and again.

When I talk with my clients about their invested money, we go through the following questions:

- What is this money for? (Retirement? Education? A new home?)
- When do you want that to happen?
- Why does this goal matter to you?

Money is a tool to help you live a life you love and make the impact you desire to make on the world. When you align your money with your true desires, the wealth-building process feels easier and more joyful. And importantly, you feel a deep sense of satisfaction and accomplishment when your goals start becoming a reality.

When I talk to those same clients about generating income in their business, we go through more questions:

- What are your current expenses?
- What are your current revenue streams?
- Which of your revenue streams is flowing the best right now?
- Which of your revenue streams do you enjoy the most right now?
- How much time are you spending on the activities that will grow the revenue stream you enjoy most?

When we align your work activity with the actions that will help you generate more revenue in the way you enjoy, the revenue-building process feels easier and more joyful too!

STEP 3: EXPANSION

The most beautiful aspect of defining your desires and then aligning your actions and spending with those desires to make more money is that it works. You will start to bring in the clients you desire, the contracts you desire, the sales you desire, and all of that leads to more money in your business and your bank accounts!

And as you experience your business and your wealth growing side by side, you will naturally start to desire new and different things. Your target client might start to shift. Your goals for impacting your community might expand. Your desires for your work/life balance might start to change.

This is the expansion of desire!

When you start looking around and realizing you desire something new, the process starts again.

Discovery.

Alignment.

Expansion.

Over and over again.

It's a beautiful and virtuous cycle.

Defining your desires and building wealth with purpose is an act of love for yourself and for everyone who will benefit along the way. That includes your family, your employees, your clients, and the thousands of people that exist in your chain of influence. Light up your desires and be the flame helping others light their desires on fire alongside you. Because when you are living a life you love, it makes the world a brighter and better place for all of us.

If you are ready for that support team to help you discover, align, and expand your desires for the next evolution of your business and your wealth, I'd love to hear from you directly at hannah.chapman@x2wealthplanning.com!

Having lived through the entrepreneurial rollercoaster her entire life as a child of self-employed parents and as an adult, building businesses of her own, **Hannah Chapman** knows exactly how to help multi-passionate entrepreneurs build financial safety where they need it so they can continue to take bold action to build their businesses and personal wealth. Hannah is the founder of X² Wealth Planning and a wealth advisor helping abundance-minded, multi-business households find financial clarity and put the strategies in place that will allow them to live their wildest dreams. She's successfully guided clients through the world's financial ups and downs since 2006 and holds the Certified Financial Planner (CFP®), Accredited Portfolio Management Advisor (APMA®), and Chartered Retirement Planning Counselor (CRPC®) designations.

Hannah is also mom to three humans, one Labrador retriever, and lots of plants! She and her husband are both avid hikers, travelers, and classically trained musicians. When she's not connecting with other beautiful humans and helping them grow their businesses and wealth, you'll find her sitting in her backyard listening to the wind going through trees and songbirds chattering to each other, hanging out with her kids, reading, or creating art. Connect with Hannah to share your entrepreneurial story!

Connect with Hannah:
Website: https://x2wealthplanning.com/
Linktree: https://linktr.ee/x2wealth

RELATIONSHIPS

The relationship pillar of wealth for this section has been anointed with sacred water and divine generosity for healing whatever is ready to be purified.

Water can be soft and gentle, she is rhythmic in her unique ebb and flow, yet she's strong enough to cut through rock and find a way through any barrier with great purpose.

The spirit of water takes us deep into the emotional realm and invites us to swim amongst the shadows held in our subconscious minds. She may need us to be still or dance in sacred rage to release what has been suppressed within our bodies for too long.

She invites us to let go of internal turmoil with holiness and float effortlessly with soul-aligned purpose.

RITUAL: Have a glass of water within an arm's reach. Come into a sacred relationship with yourself by bringing your attention inward. Sit quietly while breathing through your nose and out your mouth. Continue with deep, spacious breaths until your feel relaxed.

Notice the power within your energetic center by placing your hands upon your belly just beneath your belly button. With both hands covering your entire lower abdomen, send healing love to this part of your body.

Take your glass of water, cupping it in both hands, and bring it to your heart. Enchant the water with this mantra by saying it out loud:

"All that I desire is now quenched. I release the past and am open to receiving an abundance of blessings now."

Take a sip of the water to anchor this into your physical body. Take your time with these sacred sips. Feel the sensation of water rolling over your tongue and down your throat. Intentionally receive it as it travels deep into your sacred center. Give yourself full permission to drink in this magic with healing intentions to activate change and transformation.

Allow any thought or feeling to come without judgment. Feel, sense, hear and know you are worthy of each blessing on its way to you now.

Receive a complimentary activation into the Wealth Codes at www.jenpiceno.com/resources

CHAPTER 6

HAPPILY EVER AFTER

EMBRACING CONFLICT FOR
HEALTHY AND RESILIENT RELATIONSHIPS

Kelly Cameron, Love & Connection Coach, M.Ed., CPC

MY STORY

Just breathe, I keep telling myself. *In. Out.* Hands clenched, staring at the dark corner of my overstuffed closet, with the door partially closed. I'm trying to hide, but there is no place to escape—ever.

I checked on the kids first. "Are you okay?" I held them tight in a fierce and protective mama bear hug, trying to infuse the energy of love, security, and calmness. "I will fix this, and we will be okay," I bravely proclaimed.

I didn't want to stay too long with the kids so as to not lead the angry one to them. I rushed over to the other side of the house into my closet, with too many bags and hats hanging on the door for it to close, giving me the illusion of safety and solace.

Breathe, breathe, slow it down. Every inch of my body, inside and out, was utterly taut. I was one big clench. *Think, think, think—what the hell do I do?* I promised my kids I would fix this, but I have no idea how or where to start?

He's looking for me so he can justify his actions, words, and aggressiveness.

"Why are you in the closet?" he asks.

I do not say anything. I'm still focusing on breathing and cannot formulate words.

"What are you doing in here?" He prompts again.

He knows I'm beyond angry, but I know he'll pretend to be surprised and taken aback at my over-the-top reaction.

"What is the matter with you?!" are the only words I can manage to utter.

As predicted, he feigns surprise at my visceral reaction. I know this pattern well now, and it'll somehow become my fault.

"What's your problem?" he readies himself for battle, all while holding himself in check. He wants me to lose it first, so he's justified in his counterattack.

I'm tired, mentally and emotionally exhausted, and at a loss of what to do. We've been in this place before, except this one was the worst—supercharged and traumatic.

I witnessed the entire scene between this man and my youngest child, and I was shocked into paralysis. I knew him to be an intense and challenging person much of the time, as well as charming, fun, and generous. But this—coming at my kids—is absolutely unacceptable. Nope. Not having it.

It didn't matter what his lame explanation was—his hollow shell of a justification of why he felt entitled to terrify my children with his aggressive and threatening words and behavior.

This is why I'm in the closet, trying to breathe and calm myself. There's no point in trying to resolve this issue. We've had discussions and arguments and heated conflict ad nauseam on the topic of my kids and how they take my time and energy away from him. There is no resolution. I've finally realized the conflict is pointless. My quest and work towards peace and harmony with the four of us in this house will never succeed.

I've repeatedly tried to appease him, explain my perspective, and try to find some common ground and agreements. *Ah, I think I understand some of the main issues here. Our goals and values are not aligned, and we are not on the same page. It's clear to me now that no matter how hard I try, we will never be working towards the same outcomes.* Therein lies the root of the problem.

I have to figure a way out now. My mama bear protective energy is in overdrive, and my planning brain is taking over. *I got us into this mess, and I will get us out. My focus is to build my business and find a way to be financially independent again, get help for me to stay focused and strong with therapy and coaching, and find a way to safety and peace for my kids and me.* It will take longer than I want, and there are many trials and tribulations coming that I can't avoid. I stay hyper-vigilant in protecting my kids as best I can. I learned later that I could not always be their protection, and the traumas happened anyway. This battleground was my most impactful teacher on this journey.

I grew up in a family that collected marriages and relationships like Tom Brady amasses Super Bowl rings. It was undoubtedly a unique feature of our family but seemed semi-normalized as I grew up. My dad is pretty legendary in this arena—heck, he's got Elizabeth Taylor beat. I keep reminding myself that I'm *not* in competition with my dad—I'm genuinely not vying for any titles!

Yet, here I found myself hyperventilating in the closet, in my third marriage. My two kids were navigating having a stepdad, I was trying to keep the peace, and we were all traversing trying to fit in and be a part of someone else's family.

Growing up, I was the quiet, shy, introverted kid flying under the radar and avoiding conflict at all costs. I did well in school and was usually the teacher's pet. I was also pretty socially awkward, so it was easier to keep to myself.

I was barely out of high school and still trying to figure out my college major when I embarked on my first marriage. At 20 years old, we were just kids with absolutely no clue about life, much less how to have a healthy and lasting relationship. I learned many things in those few years. I knew I wasn't ready to be a wife, and I had no idea how to fix our problems. It was much easier to go our separate ways—no kids, no harm, no foul.

I felt pretty darn good about my second marriage! It was remarkable for so many years. We got along so well, we were kind to each other, and we identified with each other's traumatic and dysfunctional pasts. We were a soft place to land for each other. We built a life together—homes, kids, careers, businesses. Life was good, on the surface, anyway.

We were both so kind and gentle that we avoided arguing and fighting at all costs for nearly our whole relationship. I think we both believed avoiding conflict was the goal that led to success in the relationship. Everyone thought we were the perfect couple, with fairytale level happiness and success. We thought so too.

As time wore on and life started throwing more at us, things got wonky. Big decisions, conflicts, and disagreements were all on the upswing, and sadly, we didn't have the skills or tools to navigate these storms together. We spent so many years avoiding the discomfort of difficult conversations and differences of opinion. We saw no way through the storm, and we were seriously unprepared.

In the end, the conflicts and disparities grew so big they overwhelmed our relationship. We didn't have the strong foundation, tools, or the ability to weather these storms together. The damage was done, and there was no coming back. It was heartbreaking and so sad. We ended our marriage amicably and have been successfully co-parenting our children with love and respect ever since.

We figured out how to muddle through and adjust to make life good again on our individual paths. My focus was on my kids and myself, just figuring out life as it came along.

And then I met someone. I wasn't looking. He was charming, Italian, and much older than me. My whole life seemed to be full of opportunities falling in my lap, so I didn't much question it. I realize now that nothing in my life had been very intentional, just letting it ebb and flow as it does. I allowed the relationship to unfold.

This man was strong, opinionated, full of energy, and he adored me. I quickly learned how to use my voice to express my opinions and wants. It felt safe initially. I realized conflict and disagreement didn't have to be scary. I was proud of myself and more than a little surprised I could go toe-to-toe with the high-spirited Italian.

It was a compelling change to the dynamics and pace of life. However, after the wedding, there was frequent and more intense arguing. I did not enjoy this level of conflict and discord. It was exhausting and took a toll on me mentally, emotionally, and physically. I found myself struggling.

I ended the marriage for my and my kids' mental and emotional well-being. I'm not in the habit of blaming others, and I believe relationships can end without placing blame or fault. My kids and I continue to spend time individually and together to work on our growth, healing, and intentionally being healthy and happy humans.

During this time of healing and reflecting, I dug deep within myself, working on my mind, body, and spirit and peeling the layers of the onion away—discovering who I truly am at my core. Choosing to be intentional for the first time in my life and not just letting it all happen. I've learned that I'm much more than a daughter, sister, or ex-wife—even more than my beloved role of mom.

I decided I wanted to create my new healthy life with healthy and happy relationships. I looked around at people I knew. Some have been married for a long time and are not content but choose to stay together. Others are fiercely and proudly independent and do not want to be in a serious relationship again. Still, many others are somewhere in between.

I sat with this topic of relationships for quite a while. What do I want? How do I feel about it? These were questions I never asked myself before, never intentionally and consciously feeling into *my* wants and needs in this world.

I made a choice: I want to be in a serious relationship; I do not want to be alone for the rest of my life. I want to find my person and, most importantly, learn what a healthy relationship means and create that together. I also want to show my kids what a healthy and happy relationship looks and feels like. I am my father's daughter, after all—I still believe in the fairy tale and the happily ever after—but I want it on my terms this time. I want true love and connection, which starts with me being healthy and loving myself. I spent much time and energy focusing on myself, deepening my connection and relationship with myself, and I will always continue this work on myself.

Then, out of nowhere, he walked into my life. Both of us were on our own conscious paths of self-discovery, healing, and personal growth for some time. We became friends initially and slowly got to know each other, with no initial thoughts of anything more than a friendship. At some point, something shifted, and we saw each other in a new light. *This man is doing his work and digging deep to be his best self. How refreshing!*

I'm happy to report I have full, direct experience and knowledge that creating a healthy relationship in a very intentional and conscious way is not only possible but it's also fantastically beautiful and fulfilling. My man and I have built this beautiful, living, breathing relationship from the ground up, laying a solid foundation built on dynamic communication and fearlessly diving deep into the roots of our conflict. We do not shy away from conflict or disagreements, nor do we come at each other like World War III. We have balance and moderation where conflict is concerned, and we are focused on the same goals and outcomes for our relationship.

We are kind, loving, and steadfast in our commitment to ourselves and each other to always show up as our best selves. We're also human, so sometimes we may not be at our best, but we're always our true authentic selves and owning our actions, words, and behaviors. With all of the tools we've picked up along the way, we've learned that how we approach and navigate conflict is the most impactful skill for greatly enhancing our healthy and happily ever after. There are always bumps along the road of life, and having the skills and tools to navigate these bumps and detours helps us create a healthy, happy, and resilient relationship with each other.

I frequently speak on the power of healthy conflict, which boggles the mind of the shy, introverted kid who would cringe and hide from a sharp tone of voice. From my experiences and observations of relationships, we as humans cannot completely avoid conflict, nor should we. I've found a way to incorporate healthy and respectful disagreement into relationships without causing trauma and power grabs. I'm passionate about teaching others how to learn healthy conflict skills and use them as tools to create happy and healthy relationships.

THE STRATEGY

It seems most people are not comfortable with or skilled in the art of conflict. Most people avoid conflict, arguments, disagreements, and confrontations. The thought of navigating these situations with another human being often sends waves of panic, anxiety, and just plain uncomfortable feelings. Avoidance is typically the end result.

With avoidance comes either a mountain of resentments and assumptions swept under the proverbial rug or the inevitable blow-up where we've reached our limit and find ourselves unloading everything, including the kitchen sink of things we're fed up with, tolerating, or a mixture of both.

How do we embrace the conflict without causing more stress and anxiety to ourselves, our relationships, and the people we are with? Admittedly, it's not an easy start. Embarking in uncomfortable conversations can feel impossible. The more you're willing to engage in these challenging interactions, the more you will gain.

Honing the skills of healthy conflict bring a wealth of enhancements to you and your relationships. Confidence, empathy, compassion, respect, understanding, teamwork, empowerment, connection, and love are some of the benefits.

Remember, conflict is not bad and doesn't need to be hard, and it's necessary for our relationships to build trust, strength, resilience, flexibility, and a strong foundation. Let's break it all down and demystify this conflict piece of our relationships once and for all!

I. WITHIN OURSELVES

Learning healthy conflict begins with being aware of ourselves. Where are we mentally and emotionally? Are we feeling triggered or heightened emotionally? How can we calm our nervous system down to come from a more grounded and calm place? Jumping into conflict from a place of heightened emotions will escalate the situation in short order.

1. Notice your mind and body. What are you thinking? What are your emotions? Is your body ramping up for fight or flight?

2. If you're not calm, take the time and space for yourself to ensure you're grounded and calm, so you can approach and engage with a clear mind and calm emotions. If you need to notify the other person that you need some time and space before continuing, honor yourself and the other person.

II. WITH EACH OTHER

Setting a container and structure for how to engage with each other is paramount. If we genuinely want to learn healthy conflict, these are the components to consider and practice:

1. Use "I" statements. Begin sentences with "I feel/think/want. . ." Do not begin with "You are/did/always/never. . ." Employing "I" statements helps us take responsibility for ourselves and ownership of our feelings, needs, and wants. When we lead off with "You. . .", we immediately put the other person on the defense, and they will likely shut down or go on the attack. A productive conversation will not proceed.

2. Schedule a mutually agreed-upon time and space for the difficult conversation to occur. This gives both parties ownership and agreement without feeling blindsided or surprised.

3. Remember not all conflicts will come to a neat and tidy resolution. Often, we're going for clarity and understanding of each other and our perspectives, not necessarily resolution. We're not trying to sway the other person and win them over to our side. Asking questions and being open to learning about the other person and their beliefs gives us clarity and understanding.

4. Find common ground with each other. Keep widening the view, like the aperture in a camera lens, to find where you can agree. Finding that common ground is a great way to start and realize you're on the same team, and you likely want at least some of the same outcomes.

5. Listen! Truly listen and hear each other. Do not just pause and wait for your turn to speak. Listen and hear to understand and learn.

6. Keep it as calm as possible, holding on to mutual respect and love. If voices are getting louder or more intense, take a break for a few minutes to calm them down.

These are the tools instrumental in navigating and resolving conflict once and for all. While we are mainly focusing on our primary personal relationships with our spouses or life partners in this chapter, we can utilize these healthy conflict techniques in all relationships. I firmly believe our kids need to know these skills and will benefit significantly in life. We can use these skills with family members, friends, and co-workers. The possibilities are endless!

Two things I love to dive into are personal and spiritual growth and relationship dynamics. These are the areas of life I geek out on! If you feel called, I would love to hear your stories of how you're embracing healthy conflict for the enhancement of your relationships and your happily ever after! Email me at kelly@connectedlove.us

Kelly is a Love & Connection Coach on a mission to teach others the tools for healthy and happy relationships, to ultimately help strengthen families and spread more love around the world.

Kelly has teamed up with her soul mate and life partner Scott to create the dynamic and transformational couples program Connected Love. By reverse-engineering their intentional and conscious healthy relationship, they designed the blueprint for couples to find clarity, connection, and deep love in their happily ever after. Connected Love programs include workshops and private coaching, with retreats and experiences coming soon.

With her university experience and studies in psychology, family studies, and education, Kelly expanded her view and experience by working in corporate settings as well as laying down her entrepreneur roots in multiple industries. Realizing her eclectic experience, education, and natural wisdom could be put to good use, she embarked on the journey of coaching and helping others.

She holds licenses and certifications from:

- Institute for Professional Excellence in Coaching (iPEC) - Certified Professional Coach
- The Awakened School ® - Certified Transformational Coach
- The Art of Feminine Presence ® and The Art of Masculine Presence ®

Born and raised in Phoenix, Arizona, Kelly enjoys life with her two teenagers, fiancé and love of her life, and their three entertaining fur kids. She spends her free time deepening her yoga practice, connecting with family and friends, hiking, traveling, and continually up-leveling her spiritual and personal growth experiences.

Connect with Kelly:
Website: www.KellyCameronCoaching.com
Website: www.ConnectedLove.us
Email: Kelly@KellyCameronCoaching.com
Facebook: Facebook.com/KellyCameronCoaching
Instagram: Instagram.com/KellyCameronCoaching

CHAPTER 7

UNCONDITIONALITY

EXPERIENCING TRUE UNCONDITIONAL LOVE IN RELATIONSHIP TO EVERYTHING

Amber Wright, Author, Speaker,
Transformational Business Coach

MY STORY

It's all you. If I could write an entire book in three words, those would be the words. This is the truth at its most basic level. You *are* everything, and you are in a relationship *with* everything. We know this. But since humans are such complex creatures, we tend to ask complex questions. What if the answer was simple? What if life could be so pleasurable it becomes euphoric? An expression of abundance in every area. Something you crave and embrace at the same time. What if contrast could be felt as simply as a tease towards what you want to experience? What if blockages are transmuted into catapults? And what if relationships could be easy, fun, and immensely fulfilling?

They are. So then, why do we struggle?

Enter the subconscious mind.

During childhood, humans are in theta or alpha brain wave states, which is basically hypnosis. We're open to suggestions which then become our belief system. Our subconscious assumes this is the way life works. We continuously recreate patterns from childhood in relation to everything around us, whether it benefits us or not. Our subconscious programming controls 95% of the decisions we make. There are even some claims this number is higher. This is why positive thinking alone only gets us so far. In truth, we will always stop at the subconscious blocks we built up to protect ourselves from perceived danger. This is unconscious, and ignorance is bliss, right? Until you're on your deathbed, reflecting back on so much love lost and blissed-out experiences denied—what a waste of the only life you have in this body. Something deeper is required to break these blocks down indefinitely. And if you learn the art of unconditionality, it can happen faster than you think. Can you let it be easy? Are you ready?

Growing up as an only child with an emotionally unavailable mother and a father who abandoned me and never looked back provided me with some awesome attachment issues. What a weird way to say that, right? But let me tell you, once you create harmony, you can't help but appreciate what made you who you are. You feel love for the experiences that created you and honor them because, without them, you wouldn't be here right now reading these words. Really feel that. It's true.

My mother is an amazing woman. We have a great relationship, and I honor and appreciate the expansion I received as I write about this experience.

When I was ten years old, I came home from school one day, excited to go ride bikes with my best friend Tim, who lived down the street. I walked into my room, threw my backpack on my bed, and called him on my pale yellow, corded telephone: "Hey Tim, what's up? Ready to go?" We rode every day up and down the same hilly road to see who could go the fastest without holding the handlebars. He said he was ready. I hung up the phone on the wall as the long twisted cord tangled and swung below. Suddenly, my mom opened the door and rushed past me, slamming it behind her. She didn't seem to notice me and was moving things around frantically. I asked her what was going on, and she said, "We're leaving. Now! If we stay here, Martin is going to kill us! We're gonna go live with your grandma in Washington."

Time stopped.

We lived in Tennessee. Martin was my stepdad. My third.

I loved him. He was the closest thing I ever had to a father. He didn't seem capable of that. I didn't understand. Everything around me slowed down. I was surrounded by white noise as my mother loaded the minivan. I don't remember what took place before we drove away. I dissociated. I wished he'd come home early so I could see him again.

He never did.

I didn't get the chance to say goodbye to Tim either. My mom let me stop and see two of my friends who lived in a different neighborhood. That felt safer to her. As we drove away from their house (they were twins), I stared out the window through wet swollen eyes and blurred vision, reminiscing. They were like sisters to me. I started to feel numb and like I was dying at the same time. I was powerless. My life just got ripped out from under me, and this wasn't the first time either. As we drove across the country, I stared out the window with my whole body away from her. I refused to speak.

I hate you. I want to jump out of this window so bad.

I imagined my body rolling down the highway.

Would she even care?

My young mind was sure the answer was no.

She doesn't love me anyway. I never mattered. She'd probably just keep driving.

I would go on to create incredible things from this trauma.

The next day we got stuck in an intense hail storm. My mom turned on the radio, and the announcer said there were three tornadoes that had just touched down. They were all over level three and whirling around us in a triangle. We were in the center. There was nowhere to go. Huge balls of ice hit the windshield. The sound was deafening. And again, I felt like I was going to die—a familiar feeling. Look what I created! How powerful we are. I manifested three tornadoes around us. Not just one, but three. Yes, I did that. And everyone else co-created it with me. I did not understand the laws of the universe at that time, of course. It was physics. But that, my friend, is for another book.

This pattern of extreme fear, betrayal, and flailing for security played throughout my life in cycles. I can easily identify these moments now that my eyes are open in unconditionality. When you become enlightened to the fact that you're everyone and everything, there is a massive shift in your life's path. Your world is a reflection of what's going on inside you. All the characters in your life are a mirror. No exception. Every single thing that happens to you is you. You are repeating a cycle that, for some reason, you believe to be true subconsciously. Some cycles are programmed into the very DNA that created you. They can serve you or hinder you, and it's not right or wrong. It just is. We must satisfy our deep primal need to follow our subconscious beliefs right off the cliff of relationships, over and over again. Remember when I say relationships, I don't just mean with people. I mean with everything.

After experiencing many tornadoes throughout adulthood, I avoided relationships for a long time. But I was done hiding. It was time to be in love! So, with the intention to clear everything in the way of the kickass relationships I desired, I fully opened up. I met everyone from that moment on with an open heart and full faith that I was safe—no more holding back. Things shifted in positive ways, fast. And then suddenly, every shadow I hadn't looked at rushed in. I let it happen. I allowed the pain and discomfort and kept going anyway. It was glorious. I felt it first, then asked myself: *Why did I create this? What need am I fulfilling? What belief is playing out?* The key was to remember whatever happened around me was happening for me. Whatever thoughts came creeping in were there to serve me in a release. I spoke my truth and expressed myself, even if it meant screaming into a pillow. When I allowed feelings without judging them or the other person, they magically disappeared. And my reality would shift a little more. What I didn't realize is I got to create harmony in the most important and difficult relationship in my life—the one I had with myself.

THE SUBCONSCIOUS DAM

You are water. Water knows there's always a way around perceived obstacles. When you have resistance to a situation or feeling, you feel pressure. Your subconscious created dams to try to guide your experience based on your paradigm. Paradoxically, you magnetically attract situations that fulfill your cycle, and you continue experiencing various levels of your own tornado.

Now that you've read that, this is where all blame stops. You create everything in your observation, including how other people show up for you. Unconditionality is learning how to love them and seeing them as the perfect aspect they are. If they get triggered, ask: "How can I support you as you move through this challenge?" Keep your heart open with compassion and forgiveness. When you're triggered, feel it and let it wash over you in gratitude because it showed you a piece of your own shadow. Yay! You may need to separate yourself from intense situations to recenter, but the important thing is to allow it to unfold and be a witness instead of a judge. As you do this, harmony is attained.

As we feel pressure against the dams we built, we seek relief in the form of substance abuse, abandonment, self-sabotage, blame, victim mentality, eating disorders, obsession, judgment, etc. Steeped in trapped emotions that gain control of our perception, we choose fear over love and close down our heart center. At this choice point, to avoid pain, even if it's unconscious, you reset the cycle. You'll gain temporary relief, reinforcing this choice was the right one and build the dam up a little more. The irony is that the dam itself is the very obstacle keeping you from the ultimate pleasure you seek. It happily and comfortably closes back up. And the cycle continues.

The beauty of self-awareness is that we see that our dam is holding us back from the bliss of a full life, and we become 100% responsible for our reality. This is true unconditionality. We realize that even accidents are a co-creation of our subconscious mind in concert with universal laws. In this moment of realization, we make the conscious choice to be unconditional in our relationships with others, ourselves, and our environment. Perhaps this is that choice point for you. Let's do it!

The most important piece of doing this work is to realize it's not about the story of what's happening right now. It's not the tornadoes, it's the feeling you're experiencing. If you can learn how to feel without attaching a story, then you become unconditional. The same goes for how others feel. Perceive, but don't judge. When you judge, you recreate. Just allow them to feel, understanding it's showing you something too. Maybe you feel overwhelmed. Feel that then. You'll notice your mind will attach thoughts to these feelings to try to explain them. Your job is to simply allow the feeling only and detach from the thought or situation. It just is. As you feel it fully, you have the opportunity to shift it into pleasure because you're allowing your subconscious to fully experience a cycle it's been trying to complete your whole life. There's pleasure in the contrast. Allow those around you the same compassion. You become fully responsible for this moment you created, and in this release, you transmute darkness into light—the ultimate shadow work. The dam releases an explosion of appreciation for your experience. Now you get to receive the flow of pleasure in that area of your life. Keep going!

THE STRATEGY

THE PROCESS OF UNCONDITIONALITY

Before we dive into practical application, I want to touch on the fear of feeling severe emotions. I can speak from my own experience of rape, physical and psychological abuse, and other trauma. This process worked for me when nothing else did. One day, I allowed the feelings around being raped to take over my body, and the negative charge was gone forever. But you don't have to do it alone. A counselor, coach, or therapist is helpful. If you're involved in abuse of any kind, I encourage you to seek support and focus on self-care. Allowing abuse to or from yourself comes from deep-seated unworthiness. I've been there. You truly deserve better.

First of all, if you don't meditate, now is when you will start. Every day for 15 minutes first thing in the morning, sit and be quiet. Whatever type of meditation you decide, the most important thing is consistency. This will help prime your self-awareness when faced with the dams you intend to break through. Secondly, trust the process. You can pick one topic or all of them.

1. Write down all the emotions you desire to feel in each type of relationship in your life. Do this in single-word bullet point format. Keep writing until you don't have anymore. Remember to stick to feelings and emotions. If you have a hard time thinking of some, you can look up a list online. Don't worry if your current relationships don't feel the same as what you want. Just be honest and know that this is the way to harmony.

Significant Other

Children

Parents

Other family members

Friends

Co-workers/Boss/Employee/Business Relationships

Neighbors

Acquaintances

Exes, etc

2. Now take situations and treat them as if they were a relationship. Because, in truth, they are. What emotions do you desire to feel around these topics? Single-word bullet point format.

Family/Kids/Home Life

Money/Finances/Wealth

Home/Space/Residence

Vehicle/Transportation

Job/Business/Career

Fun/Play/Hobbies

Body/Health/Vitality, etc

3. Reflection: Now, think about your desired relationship with pleasure and journal a page about it. Why pleasure? This is the basis of all life—the driving force of why we're here—to give pleasure and receive it. It's a word that makes us think of sexuality, and that is the truth. Sex is what drives the universe to expand. But I'm not talking about the simple act of penetration. I mean the marrying of duality—intertwining the masculine and feminine essence—the sensuality of that harmony that brings bliss beyond imagination. When we become unconditional, bliss can be felt when performing any action or receiving any reaction. And, yes, when two people are self-aware, this creates a whole different level of pleasure when it comes to intimacy. But yet again, that is for another juicy book.

4. Now write all of the emotions you desire to feel about yourself.

5. Once you have completed all of the above or the most important topics to you, highlight all of the emotions you're regularly experiencing in your relationships. The words that aren't highlighted give you a clear view of what you're resisting. As you move through this process of transmuting, you'll be able to highlight more of the words in each category. Celebrate that!

6. Now set the intention to become unconditional. To allow others to feel, be, and show up in the world as they will. To understand that what you're getting from them is directly related to what's going on inside you. Set the intention to become unconditional with yourself. To realize that the feelings you have and perceptions you experience are there to serve you in this process.

7. Write these words on a blank sheet of paper: "It is my intention to practice unconditionality in my relationship with myself, my relationships with others, and my relationship with my environment, to create harmony and true wealth in my experience."

8. Sign it.

9. Now be willing to see the "why" behind all those emotions you couldn't yet highlight. As you allow uncomfortable emotions to surface, remember not to look at the situation or the story. Just feel it and realize you wanted to create this on an unconscious level. Remember, your intention is harmony. Allow it to wash over you and reach for the pleasure of feeling it. If you need to, ask those questions: *Why did I create this? What am I getting out of this? When did this cycle start in my life?* Trust this process. And as you do, those unhighlighted emotions will become more apparent. Go back and highlight them as they show up. True wealth will follow.

The tricky part of this is letting go. You have set this intention to create harmony through unconditionality. The relationships you have already created will grow in different ways. As you shift, there will be negative feelings and limitations you don't need to experience anymore. You may decide to move to a new location, in which case your city is no longer needed. You may lose or gain friends. The majority will be able to create harmony within the connections they already have. But if a connection is deeply rooted to complete a painful cycle, it may not come with you. Know you are a magnet. What is a match to you will come to you. Be it positive or negative. Part of unconditionality is loving the endings too. Feel the pleasure of appreciation for what they are opening up for you, and let them go in gratitude.

The only thing you can control is how you perceive. Your reality is subjective. So is everyone else's. That means they can only see through their shadow too. When you perceive someone through the lens of unconditionality, they become clearer vibrationally, and so do you. You heal them as you see their perfection, free of judgment. And since they are you, that is the best gift you can give to that version of yourself. Now, just make sure when you look in the mirror, you're giving the same unconditionality to your reflection. Once you have managed both of these things, enjoy the bliss and pleasure now available to you. You've got this. You're perfect. I love you!

Amber Wright is a #1 international best-selling author and CEO of Stargazer Strategies, a business consulting company dedicated to helping entrepreneurs and large corporations clear stagnancies and create vibrational alignment through their staff, clients, vendors, land, inventory, marketing, and every other aspect of their business.

As a business consultant and speaker with over a decade of entrepreneurial experience, she loves teaching on topics such as employee retention, client loyalty, meditation, unconditionality, manifestation/LOA, and motivational topics, and will soon be introducing her new 5D Business Blueprint. With her own blend of bluntness and humor, she breaks through paradigms and opens a path to greater awareness, creating harmony within the audience.

She's a Quantum Reiki Master and certified in the traditional Hawaiian practice, Ho'Oponopono.

Amber lives in Hawaii with her four children. They moved to the island of Oahu in 2020, starting their adventure with only suitcases. They have two cats, two dogs, and a vegetable garden. She loves to snorkel and scuba dive and is also learning how to surf.

She is a lyricist and a singer and collaborates with wonderful people around the world.

Her next books are coming in 2022:
The 5d Business Blueprint
20 Steps to a Spiritual Awakening

Her previous book:
Jaguar Medicine - #1 best seller in 20 countries

Connect with Amber:
Website: www.stargazerstrategies.com
Email: amber@stargazerstrategies.com

CHAPTER 8

DISMANTLING THE PEOPLE PLEASER

THE JOURNEY BACK TO SELF

Morrighan Lynne, Intuitive Life Coach,
SafeSpace® Trauma Facilitator

MY STORY

There's a moment when you realize something isn't working. You may try to ignore it for a while, but in the back of your mind, you know—something's not right. It's a corner turning moment when your awareness ignites from the realization that you've existed for others and not yourself. Sure, you may have done your very best to go along with the hand that was dealt. You might have worked your ever-loving heart out to blend in with the environment and given it your best performance. Hell, you might have even fooled yourself into believing it was your purpose in life. Although inevitably, disillusionment comes knocking, and you see the truth behind the mask.

This story isn't about that one time I suddenly awakened to my burden. It's not about a single second of clarity that reshaped my life and rescued me from the darkness in a single swoop of a hero's embrace. No. This is a tale of what it's like to be in the middle of the ocean, fighting to keep my head above water, gasping for air, kicking against the strong current, and slowly drowning over a span of 46 years. It's a lifetime's journey of trying to fit, shrink, mold, and shapeshift into a form pleasing to everyone else's pallet.

The "pleasing" of others is a strong drug. It fed my soul in places where self-worth was null. It filled in the cracks of my wounded heart like spackle. I hoped that if I fulfilled the needs and desires of others, they'd give me love in return. Innocent enough in the beginning, that addiction festered and grew in my body like a disease. It shaped me into something unrecognizable—craving more and more attention—but always left me starving. Never fully fed, I was always hungry. It's a vicious cycle.

But it's also a powerful seat to hold. When you master being a people pleaser, you learn to manipulate your environment with simple gestures and silly gifts. You adapt to please, and in return, you have control. It's so addictive to be loved that we hardly notice the manipulation behind the innocence of seeking validation that we are worthy. Who's really the puppet master here? The people pleaser or the ones we're pleasing?

As a child, I learned the fawning skills of anticipating the needs of others before they asked for them. I would diligently scan the room, watching their body language, listening to their breathing, and picking up subtle tones in their voice just so I could spring into action with whatever I thought they needed. I sought their favor, and in return, I got a lifetime of shame for prostituting my value so willingly.

I didn't know I was a people pleaser. It wasn't until I saw myself in action, playing the role. At first, I didn't want to admit it—it was too revolting to witness. It is rare for people to willingly go into that level of honesty with themselves. Typically we are thrust into those deep places without warning, which is exactly how I came face to face with my shadow self.

Even though I saw clues of my people's pleasing abilities scattered throughout the years, I somehow missed it. However, one fateful day I knew I couldn't ignore this pattern any longer. My moment of disillusionment happened while I was smack dab in the middle of a yearlong program I was teaching. I tried my best to accommodate 42 individuals' wants and desires and over-extended myself to the point of emotional breakdown. I knew my students were just eager for more and excited to dive deeper, but the people pleaser within was triggered with the responsibility to make them all happy regardless of the requests.

Late one restless night, I lay in bed racking my brain to make all the puzzle pieces fit. For days I tried to maneuver class topics and activities that were requested. I added a curriculum I hadn't initially promised, adjusting schedules and trying to pack in more excitement. *What if I add this? What if I expand that? How much can I add before it gets overwhelming? And what if they get upset? Is this too much?* I lay there swimming in stress, thinking about an upcoming meeting and what I would say to hopefully satisfy everyone. But something felt wrong in my body. My stomach was in knots, my heart felt heavy, and I felt so bogged down in obligation I was nauseated. I felt the fight in my senses between my wisdom of what was needed and the desire to please them all.

Overwhelmed and consumed, I heard the voice of my spirit guide: *Careful, you're about to give over your entire class to your students. You are letting them be in charge by being overly accommodating. Are you sure you want to do that?*

A lightning bolt flashed in my body. Suddenly aware, I realized what he meant. The people pleaser wanted so badly for everyone to be happy that she was about to let them call the shots and take my course in a direction I had not intended.

I finally saw the pleaser in action! She was running the show and was about to sell out just to be liked! I was so angry with myself. *How could I have dedicated the past 16 years to building my business only to give it away so easily? How could I have been that blind? Was getting their approval more important than trusting that I knew where to take my course? Why was I willing to give away every bit of my boundaries, self-worth, and self-respect just to contort my existence for their approval?*

As hard to swallow as it might have been, I needed to see that pattern in action. I needed to see how the inner pleaser manipulates my awareness to conform to the acceptance of others. My whole life flashed before my eyes, and I saw all the choices, survival tactics, manipulations, and strategies I used over the years—every single time I gave in, even when I didn't want to. I saw all the ways I prostituted my value for the acceptance and comfort of others. Anger and humiliation ran through my veins like fire. The shame scorched through my soul with the knowing that I had been living a lie my whole life. I always made other people's feelings more important than my own. I was devoted to their happiness while betraying myself time and time again.

I did not like sitting in that awareness. To come face to face with this lifelong pattern was excruciating. My mind raced with questions and flooded with memories long forgotten. I knew avoiding this newfound insight wasn't going to help, so I decided to dive in deep for more clarity in the hopes of understanding who I was. *Was I born this way? Or was I made this way?* I needed answers, so I set aside time to explore them in meditation.

Settling into my chair, I closed my eyes and allowed my mind to ponder where it all began. Soon, I stumbled upon a buried memory. When I was four, my mom was a bartender at a little honky-tonk on the side of the highway, where she often worked the day shift. I would sometimes go with her when she couldn't find a babysitter. I'd sit at the bar, drink a Cherry Coke, and eat up the attention from the customers. Every now and then, my mom would slide a quarter over to a gentleman and say, "Play 'The Devil Went Down to Georgia,' and she'll dance for you." They'd hobble over to the old jukebox, make their selection, and it would fire up the familiar tune. My mom would give me a glance, and I knew I was on. I'd jump down from the barstool, get on the black and white tile dance floor, and dance my little heart out. I enjoyed the attention. It made me feel special. I knew everyone was watching, and I loved it. Now, as an adult, I cringe at how accommodating I was for attention. I fed them with my "yes." I gave the men what they wanted without a second thought. That was the birth of my people pleaser. If I gave people what they wanted, they gave me attention, and I was starving, so I gave everyone everything, all the time.

I sat there in my meditation chair, feeling waves of shame flood my nervous system. *How could I have liked that attention so much? Why didn't my mom protect me from that environment? Was I that expendable?* Emotions raced through my system as my mind tried to make sense of the situation. I felt so ashamed.

Eventually, shame turned to compassion as I saw that little four-year-old in my mind. She was so sad and confused. She looked up at me and asked, "Why don't they love me?" I replied, "Because they don't know how. They only know how to take; they don't know how to give." She laid her head on my chest and cried. So I held her. The four-year-old who just wanted love was seeking validation that she was a good girl, and unfortunately, the adults in her world did not nurture her appropriately.

As I sat with my hands on my heart, my eyes closed, and tears running down my cheeks, I told her, "I'm so sorry you weren't loved the way you needed to be. It's not your fault that you craved attention; it's very natural. It's not your fault that your mother exploited your little body to gain favor with her male customers. And from now on, you'll never have to be in that situation again. I'm here now. I will protect you."

She looked up at me with her tired eyes, seeking permission that it was okay to let go. I held her close, my heart aching from the wound, and I cried until I had no more tears left. Eventually, she faded away, and I fell into a deep sleep.

The next day it was as if someone had turned up the saturation on a color template. Everything seemed richer, brighter, and crisper than ever before. I was no longer living in the shadow of that wound, and it was time to explore what might be next.

As the days went on, I scoured my world, looking for signs of being a people pleaser. I found hundreds of places where pleasing others was so effortless I barely caught myself doing it. I was surprised by how easy it was to slip into that role. It was exhausting to see it all, to stay diligent. But, I knew these dark corners needed to be explored if I was going to move forward in a healthy way.

The more I allowed myself to sit in the space of taking full accountability while also looking at my past with kind, compassionate eyes, the more I was able to move through the darkness with ease. I didn't get stuck in the judgment or shame of those choices. I didn't stew in the resentment of what others did. I simply accepted it and allowed myself to witness the pattern in play.

Extracting the pleaser programming is not an overnight process. It took time to untangle my internal value from how others see me. It's a daily conversation within myself to remember what I'm doing this for. This is all for me and my inner four-year-old.

I just knew it was time to turn my eyes inward and ask myself if I was happy with myself—if I could accept myself for who I am, just as I am at this very moment. Deep down inside, I knew it wouldn't matter if others didn't. It's truly time to stop betraying myself, to choose happiness for me, and allow others the space to be disappointed that the people pleaser is dead.

THE STRATEGY

In my many years of being on a healing journey, I've learned one very important thing. We cannot skip over the process to get to the finish line. We must sit and be present with our experience, one step at a time. This allows the nervous system to experience sustainable change that is permanent and lifelong. If we rush through the processes simply because it's uncomfortable, we are doomed to repeat the pattern.

My intention with this practice is to gently walk you through each layer so you can discover what is keeping you stuck in the pattern and create a safe space to allow a gentle movement forward. This strategy is appropriate for any healing journey, regardless of the wound.

My loving suggestion is to move through them slowly, with presence and compassion for whatever might come up. You're healing spaces in you that have not been in the light for a long time. Be kind to yourself, stay aware, and always choose yourself.

STEP 1: AWARENESS

Having a clear awareness of yourself, your experiences, and the outside stimuli in your life are important. Spend time simply witnessing your day-to-day experiences and checking in with how you feel about them. What feels okay and not okay? How does your body react to those experiences? Can you dial in on exactly what isn't working for you?

My example: I noticed my body reacted with a knotted stomach, my heart was heavy, and I was nauseated. These indicators gave me the message that something wasn't right, giving me the chance to troubleshoot my experience. That's when I saw the people pleaser in action. I gave away my power for the acceptance of my class participants.

STEP 2: ACCEPTANCE

An important step is to be able to accept what is. Accept people for who they are rather than who you want them to be. Attaching to people and wanting to change them gets you caught up in the tug-of-war and traps you in a constant struggle of wills. Acceptance releases your attachment to any given situation. Judgment ceases, and there is space to move forward with the appropriate action. Sit in this stage of the process until you are aware that all struggles and fights have left your body. Resistance can look like judgment, shame, anger, or avoidance. Simply be in this moment until you feel the resistance wane and you're able to accept what happened, simply as just that. It happened.

My example: I had to accept that my mother is who she is and that no amount of love I could give would have ever been returned. By accepting her for who she is, I was able to cut the cord and let her simply exist without feeling the need to change, rescue, or fix her. It gave me the chance to drop the fight and allow her to be just who she is. Which, in turn, gave me the space to be who I am.

STEP 3: ACCOUNTABILITY

This might be the most difficult part of the process, owning who you were and what you did in the situation. We typically want to self-punish at this point. We see our mistakes and berate ourselves for not knowing, doing, or being better. It can be a precarious trap if we don't keep an eye on that habit. So be wary and alert. Navigate this step with the clarity of accepting your part in the situation without the added judgment. Sit in this stage of the process until you can see your part through the eyes of compassion mixed with a bit of clarity that you never want to go back to that behavior again.

My example: I took accountability for allowing this pattern to mold me. I enjoyed the attention when I was younger, and as I grew older, I was able to adapt that skill to continue getting love and acceptance, creating a toxic pattern in my life. It molded the people pleaser, causing me to search for acceptance my whole life. By sitting in the accountability of my part in it, I was able to feel at peace with my past and motivated to transcend that pattern moving forward.

STEP 4: ACTION

Once you determine a pattern that isn't working, it's time to find it in your life. Begin looking for times when you recognize the familiar habit. Watch yourself in situations that are favorable for the pattern to emerge. When you can see yourself slipping into the behavior, see if you can gently steer yourself in another direction. Create a pattern disruptor. Something you do disrupts the pattern and allows your awareness to choose a different outcome. This will take time, so be patient with your process. Eventually, you will disrupt it so completely that the old pattern will not be able to anchor, and you will be free from its conditioning.

My example: I made it my passion to see all the areas where the people pleaser lives. I watch for her addiction to please. When I notice those situations, I simply say to her, "Honey, we're not doing things like that anymore." And I moved forward with conscious boundaries and a clear focus on what is working for me. I continue to work the people pleaser out of my system and develop stronger boundaries around the energy I give others. This gives the message to that wounded part that she is safe and I will protect her from now on.

If you would like a supportive space to explore this conversation deeper, I have a video tutorial and guided meditation that takes you step-by-step into this process. Please visit www.morrighanlynne.com/wealthcodesstrategy, and we'll dive in together.

Morrighan Lynne is an intuitive life coach, psychic empath, clairvoyant, spiritual medium, artist, and author. With a fiery gypsy soul and an eclectic approach to spirituality. She supports the ever-evolving human with compassion, straightforwardness, and loving accountability.

Morrighan has received certifications through The Awakened School®, The Art of Feminine Presence®, and is a SafeSpace® trauma facilitator. Her style of coaching is intuitive and direct. Focusing on shadow work and trauma healing through somatic practices, she gets to the root of the problem and goes where many don't dare. A unique spiritual teacher, she has held hundreds of workshops, retreats, classes, and galleries over her 16+ year career.

Texas-born, she and her husband have laid down roots in Boise, Idaho. She spends her downtime romping through the mountain forests with her husband, meditating, camping, paddle boarding, and hunting for mushrooms. She dabbles a bit in photography, loves to garden, and enjoys painting mandala art.

To see what she's up to these days, connect with Morrighan at www.morrighanlynne.com and get the latest news. Plus, be sure to take advantage of the free gift offered to you in her chapter by visiting www.morrighanlynne.com/wealthcodesstrategy

CHAPTER 9

THE MOON AND ASTROLOGY AS A SACRED RESOURCE

MANIFEST CLARITY, CONFIRMATION, AND CONFIDENCE DAILY BY FOLLOWING THE TRANSITING PLANETS

Jessica A. Wolfe, Astrologist, Intuitive, Tarot, Divine Feminine

MY STORY

The depression pressed me so hard I burst into finite particles. I had no choice but to seek change. I was an unawakened soul craving the spirit world. After a series of challenging events, I moved into my own apartment in the middle of Atlanta, Georgia. I was done dating and being social. I needed alone time. I needed me. I decided to abstain from sex, partying, and toxic environments for nine months while I turned myself into a monk in my little one-bedroom apartment in the city. I signed a two-year lease, and my soul's intention was to learn myself again. Who was I? Where was I? What were my needs?

There was no way I could continue living my old life. I quickly made a new best friend, and we started having conversations about astrology, moon signs, magic, angels, Abraham Hicks, spirit guides, and Jesus on the daily.

The synchronicities began. I started going to Hillside Chapel and Truth Center. I felt safe worshiping Spirit and Jesus while allowing my esoteric curiosity to grow. Slowly, I became obsessed with astrology. I also became obsessed with Guru Mooji and his Buddist beliefs. Shiva and Ganesh came to me in my dreams. I found pure awareness by looking at my shadow side and choosing to love myself anyway. I was in the Dark Knight of the Soul.

Astrology became my number one. Astrology gave me clarity on why things were hard. Suddenly, I realized I wasn't a victim of life. Instead, the transiting planets just had a hold on me.

I found myself staying up till 1 a.m. with astrology books in my bed. I'd wake up and start reading again. This behavior hasn't stopped. Understanding astrology saved my life. Astrology gave me my power back and opened up a whole new world, just for me. God is good.

THE STRATEGY

MANIFEST CLARITY, CONFIRMATION, AND CONFIDENCE DAILY BY FOLLOWING THE TRANSITING PLANETS

You're walking down the hallway. You're alone, and the air feels unfamiliar. You're slightly nervous. You've got your backpack on your shoulder, and you're wearing your fresh new sneakers. You've got new jeans, and you've had a decent breakfast. You're walking down the hall looking for classroom nine. It's 11 a.m., and this is your last class of the morning—astrology 101. You're unsure why you signed up for this course, but you feel the pull. The tug. The call. You know to listen to this inner voice.

"Welcome," says a warm, joyful, natural beauty of a teacher as you enter the classroom. Her energy is light.

You notice there are no desks, only blankets, and pillows on the floor. The windows are big. There is stained glass art hanging from the ceiling, projecting rainbows throughout the space. The overhead lights are off, and the ceiling is covered in string lights.

What kind of course did I sign up for? You wonder.

"Astrology," says Ms. Wolfe in a gentle, nurturing tone.

Did she hear me? How did she know my thoughts?

"Welcome. Feel free to sit anywhere you like," says Ms. Wolfe.

Slowly you find a pillow in the back corner on a blanket. *This feels like a safe space.*

"That's my favorite blanket," says Ms. Wolfe. "It was a gift from my grandpa. He bought it in Pasadena, California."

Others slowly walk in, and Ms. Wolfe greets the students with the same greeting. "Pick any area," she says.

It's 11:11, and class begins.

"Good morning, fellow beings. Welcome to Astrology 101. Today we begin our journey into the ethers. Into space. The space of Spirit, God, Source, and Mother Nature. The space where we have zero control, yet all the free will in the world, Astrology. In this course, I will teach you how to use Astrology as a sacred resource to find clarity, confidence, and confirmation in your life. Please open your assigned book to chapter 9. Let us begin with two quotes."

Chapter 9
Astrology and The Moon

"Radin suggests that Einstein's Special Theory of Relativity proposes that matter and energy are different aspects of the same substance. Entanglement is a property of both matter (as in atoms) and energy (as in photons). This means that the bioelectromagnetic fields around our bodies are entangled with the electromagnetic fields in the local environment and with photons arriving from distant stars."

Quote from D. Radin, Entangled Minds: Extrasensory Experiences in a Quantum Reality (New York: Simon & Schuster, 2006). page 268

Ms. Wolfe then reads a quote out loud and asks us to close our eyes and allow ourselves to get lost in her words.

"Allow these words to soak into your soul," she says.

"Luke 21:25, "There will be signs in the sun and moon and stars, and on the earth dismay among nations, in perplexity at the roaring of the sea and waves."

Astrology is an element. Each planet in our solar system holds energy, a frequency—vibration. Imagine the Sun. The sun has rays projecting off of it that we can see. Each planet, even Earth, has energy expanding off of it. As our solar system rotates in space, we come into contact with other planets. These planets are energetically sending frequencies to Earth and then onto us.

By following the transiting planets, we can predict what energy is approaching. The definition of transiting is to pass through. Transiting planets are not your birth planets. Transiting planets is what's affecting you at the moment. By using astrology, you can watch the transiting planets and prepare yourself for what is to come.

We are going to focus on the moon. The moon holds a frequency that affects bodies of water. The rise and fall of the ocean tides are affected by the moon. Humans are made up of 60% water for the average adult. Because of this, humans are greatly affected by the moon as well. Every two to three days, the moon will enter a new zodiac sign projecting different energy onto Earth. This is important to understand. This explains why sometimes we wake up sad, and sometimes we wake up ready to complete tasks. If the transiting moon is in the zodiac sign of Scorpio, we may feel intuitive, psychic, or even obsessed with something. A Scorpio moon takes us to the underworld and may bring about beautiful darkness. If the transiting moon falls in Sagittarius, we may have a hankering to make travel plans or go for a run.

It's important to honor the moon in our everyday life. We are not a victim of this energy; rather, we may work in tandem with it. The female body might ovulate and bleed on new and full moons. Women used to get burned at the stake if their menstrual cycle linked up with a full moon. God forbid the stress of that could make a menstrual cycle disappear altogether. Babies are born on full moons as the placenta is a percentage of water. Full moons bring things to the surface as it draws things up and out. The full moon will show us what we need to see. Sometimes this is uncomfortable. When individuals don't want to look at the uncomfortable energy, they may overconsume alcohol, food, or other indulgences to mask what's being brought up. This is why hospitals, police stations, and service industry folks get hit hard on full moons.

Emotionally, if you've been avoiding an inner wound, the full moon and other transiting planets will bring it to the surface. This is a gift. Suffering is inevitable, but the Universe does not want us to suffer. God does not want us to suffer. Instead, the Universe wants us to heal. We are not victims of this world. No ma'am, no sir. There is an unconditional love that exists. That's the goal.

As the planets rotate in the solar system, they communicate with one another. This is called an aspect. Jupiter will be like, "Oh hey, Saturn! What's up?! What lesson will we teach today?"

The planets send us life experiences called karma. In this karma, we have the free will to decide how to behave. Then our free will turns back into karma.

By following astrology, you can spot what themes are approaching and prepare.

There is a new and full moon each month. They are two weeks apart.

To recap—a full moon brings light to the unseen in our lives. The strategy is to observe it—no need to act yet. Only look at what is popping up for you energetically. Give the moon permission to shine a spotlight on the things you need to see for your highest good and the highest good of others. Sit with this energy for two weeks until the new moon.

Let's talk about emotions for a second. In the book *Ashtanga Yoga, Practice and Philosophy* by Gregor Maehle, on page 13, he says, "An emotion is a conserved feeling that arises because the original feeling has left a subconscious imprint in the mind."

Healing is when we remove the imprints in the mind. Fewer imprints equal fewer triggers in our day-to-day. We can't heal what we don't know exists. A full moon is a part of this healing process. It's an opportunity to heal and clean up our spirit so we can advance in the game of life.

On a new moon, you want to set an intention.

I want to disclose there is never a right or wrong way to use the moon. Your soul knows best. You don't have to wait until a new moon to set an intention. This isn't the only way. In life, we try many routes to arrive at our destination. This is one of the many routes to enlightenment and unconditional love. Our sweet Universe is present with us at all times.

The moon cycle is a calendar for farmers and all of life. It's a tool for making decisions on planting and harvesting. When working with Spirit, you can plant intentions and harvest growth.

Here's how it works.

The full moon shows you something. Observe and sit with this energy for two weeks until the new moon. On the new moon, set an intention for the change you desire. Tell the new moon where you want to grow and what you want to manifest. Then sit back again. Wait two more weeks until the full moon shows you where you need to pivot. And then set intentions again on the new moon to achieve your goal.

Back to emotions. It's important we spend time learning emotions. They take up so much space in our life; it's important we know them and see them coming. If an emotion arises and we don't release it, it becomes stale energy in our body and will turn into a memory, an imprint.

Look at your rising thoughts from your higher mind. Don't get attached to the emotion, just look. Observe them passing through. Stay in your higher mind by breath, bandha (awareness), and vinyasa (moving the energy). Gregor Maehle also says in *Ashtanga Yoga, Practice and Philosophy* on page 10 that "Increasing our exhalation we exhale more toxins. The buildup of toxins and the simultaneous depletion of oxygen in certain tissues is the number-one cause of chronic disease. By breathing deeply, exhaling accurate toxins, and inhaling oxygen, we take steps toward returning the body to its original state of health."

These toxins include mental, emotional, physical, and environmental.

How does this relate to the moon? Moon energy gives us a chance to work with life experiences. It's the moon's job to show us these things. The moon is gifting us the opportunity to heal. Life is short, and your soul is aware of your dreams and the tasks you are here to complete while on Earth. When the emotion is depression, it can be a signal from your soul that it is time for a change. This is a message from your nervous system and the moon. Emotions are the element of water. The moon rules water. Are you depressed because of a mental, emotional, physical, or environmental toxin? What needs to pivot?

Each transiting moon lands in a zodiac sign and house.

When you're ready, pull a transiting astrology chart to find where the transiting moon falls in your natal chart. The app called Time Nomad is my favorite, and Astro.com.

Your natal chart is your soul's blueprint written in the code of astrology. It's packed with information on how you act, love, speak, work, etc. A transiting chart is a blueprint of what's happening in the collective. Pulling a transiting chart on top of your natal chart will show you where the moon is falling into your life and what the theme will be. (Add in aspects for more insight!)

If the transiting moon falls in your seventh house, it's asking you to look at relationships. If the transiting moon falls in your second house, it's asking you to look at desires, money, and resources.

What's the benefit of narrowing down the moon?

This prepares us. It allows us to work in tandem with Mother Nature. It helps us plan accordingly. Anytime someone asks me out, I look at the moon before I commit. Have you ever committed to attending a party, and the day of, you just don't want to go? Sometimes the moon is at play here. For example, when the moon is in Cancer or your fourth house, it's asking you to be a homebody and playhouse. Cancer and fourth house like to nest. This is an introvert's dream placement.

When the transiting moon is in Leo, it's time to go out! Take yourself out on a date! This is a transit when you may feel your best and want to be seen. Leo is the lion. It's loud and says, "look at me!"

Below are the themes of each zodiac house. Look at which house the transiting moon is in your chart. You should do this daily to gather insight. When the moon falls in any of these houses, this energy should be in the back of your mind. Ask the Universe to show you what energy you should focus on for your highest good and the highest good of others.

Cross-reference below to break down the theme.

1st House: House of the self. How do you come across to other people? Independent, self-identity, how you take care of yourself?

2nd House: House of worth, desires, and practicality. What you love, how you love yourself, self-worth, and abundance.

What you desire is often limited to your self-worth. Desire big. Think big for yourself.

3rd House: Communication, how you think, how you need to communicate, and how you process information. Also the house of siblings and short distance travel. Writing.

4th House: House of the home, private space, the heart chakra sits here. Maternal energy, domestic, cookies, and family. I don't like to play favorites, but this is one of my favorite houses. It is a sweet grandma energy.

5th House: Primal attraction, romance, children, playfulness, fun! Carnival energy, fairgrounds, kissing booth.

6th House: House of routines (not as fun), this house is the reality check after the 5th house funhouse energy. Bumps and bruises may live here if you don't like routine—health and working in the health industry. The 6th house sits across from the 10th house, which is the house of work.

7th House: Partnerships, platonic or romantic partnership, dating, relationships with other people, commitment. Relationships with objects, materials, habits, etc.

8th House: House of intimacy, sex, deep psychology, emotional patterns, control tactics, sexual fetishes, money, taxes, inheritances, other people's money, things you keep private and only share with those close to you.

9th House: House of intuition, third eye, psychic intuition, philosophy, higher learning (not to be confused with college. College is considered the 10th house due to lack of intuition involved.)

10th House: House of work-life, public life, education, college, reputation.

11th House: House of friendships, goals, memberships, social groups.

12th House: House of spirituality, house of the unseen, different dimensions, karma, psychic abilities.

If the transiting moon is in:

Gemini: Call a friend.

Virgo: Make a list.

Capricorn: Focus on work.

Aries: Start a project. Create.

Sagittarius: Go for a run, archery, or plan ahead. Look into the future. Sag can see the long game.

Leo: Go out! Be seen. Make yourself known.

Taurus: Take yourself out for a treat! Buy yourself a gift.

Cancer: Stay home in solitude or host a party.

Libra: Great day to schedule a counseling session.

Scorpio: Meditate and look inward. Call on psychic abilities.

Aquarius: Volunteer.

Pisces: Go for a swim!

Lastly, let's talk about what a ritual is exactly and how to communicate with the moon in prayer. First, all of the planets are made of finite particles from God, Source, Spirit, and Mother Nature. You may talk to the planets like you talk to God. Don't take it too seriously. Have fun! Laugh, and chat with the Spirit of the moon. I had intentions to share personal rituals with you, but I feel called to leave this out. You have the power to decide how you manifest. You're the magician. Ask yourself, "What do I need?" Moon rituals should feel like self-care. If you're too tired for a ritual, maybe rest is the ritual. That's perfectly fine. You don't manifest by doing—you manifest with your intention. What's your intention? You can't do anything wrong. When you don't do right, you're only doing a left. It's just another turn. All is well, my fellow beings! All is well! Until next time little humans. Big Love."

Says Ms. Wolfe.

Jessica A. Wolfe is an astrologist, Tarot reader, intuitive and Divine Feminine. She is the sole creator of MoonKith Astrology, an Esoteric Astrology Consulting Practice. She Offers Natal, Transiting, Solar, Synastry, Moon Readings, and more! At this point in time, she actively has 70+ clients throughout the USA. Her ability to read the stars is filtered through the love of God. Her Astrology readings provide insight into the soul with Divine guidance and positive, loving impact. She intends to lift you up and put you back in your power! She runs Moonkith Astrology authentically and follows the energy. She has lived many different lives and "Worn many different costumes," as Ram Dass would say. Because of this, she holds zero judgment. You are free to be you, as she is learning how to be a human too!

Jessica goes by the name of Jess, Wolfie, and Dreaming Sunflower. She's hiked the entire Appalachian Trail minus the state of Virginia. Her natal Gemini sun sits in the 4th house, house of the home. She loves being at home, working from home, and hosting from her home. Her natal 9th house Scorpio moon is devoted to intuition, education, and growing her spirit. Outside of Astrology, her new passion is Ashtanga Yoga. She is learning from the best in Atlanta, under Todd Roderick and Brice Elizabeth Watson.

Jess is old school and is slowly expanding via social media. She doesn't separate herself from Moonkith Astrology. You can follow her personal Instagram, where she actively speaks about the stars and her own thoughts. She's living in her truth. She asks you to enter her space judgment-free.

Connect with Jess:
Email: Moonkithastrology@gmail.com and jump in on Free Astrology newsletters! Mention 'Wealth Codes' for a free transiting Moon reading.
Instagram:@Emerald_In_The_Moon

CHAPTER 10

SPELLBINDING

USING THE POWER OF WORDS TO IGNITE DESIRE

Eirikah Delaunay, MFA, Somatic Sex+Relationship Coach

*"Admit to what you feel greedy about.
It will point to your most tender desire."*

~Danielle LaPorte

MY STORY

"Oh, yeah!" my husband exclaimed as he climaxed. One last thrust and he flopped over onto his side of the bed.

I snuggled up next to him. Still breathing heavily, he pulled me close. *Mmm,* I thought. *He smells so good.* I wrapped my leg over his and pressed against his hip, a slow grind to let him know I was still turned on and wanting his touch. I ran my fingers through his chest hair, up to his shoulder, and down his arm to squeeze his bicep as I arched up to kiss his neck.

He squeezed my elbow and pulled me just a little closer, then relaxed. His breath dropped into the slow, deep cadence of sleep. My hands on his skin slowed, then stopped. My body stilled, though I was still humming with the energy of my own arousal. The only outward betrayal of my desire was my feet rhythmically stroking the smooth cotton sheets, a motion too small to disrupt his sleep.

I slipped out of his grasp and eased over to my own side of the bed. *Why isn't my pleasure important to him? I hate that my body takes so long and needs so much attention to come, but that doesn't mean it isn't worth it.* I stared at the ceiling as I ran my hands over my own body, but my desire cooled as the gentle snoring began. *My own touch just isn't the same,* I sulked.

I tossed in the bed, trying to get comfortable, thrashing around in the sheets. Lee's snoring got louder. *I know he could tell I wanted more. I shouldn't have to ask for his attention. I love being part of his pleasure—isn't my pleasure hot for him, too? What's wrong with me? Or maybe he just doesn't care.* My mind followed its familiar litany of dissatisfaction until I was in tears. *I'm going to have to talk to him about this,* I realized. *It's only going to get worse if I don't.*

All day the next day, I tried to find the right time to talk about our sex life. I didn't want to bring it up when we were already stressed trying to get to work, and I didn't want to risk a fight as we were getting ready to meet some friends for a beer at the new brewpub in town. I also didn't want to talk about it right before bed, but I couldn't face another night of lonely disappointment.

"Hey, baby. . ." I began as we curled up naked in bed together.

"Hey, yourself," he responded as he pulled me close and kissed me.

I took a deep breath. "You know I really love how often we have sex, but I'd really like to have more orgasms. You come every time, but it seems we only take the time to get to my climax once a week or so. Could we do that more often?"

He pulled back and stared at me, then leaped out of bed.

"Unbelievable!" he exploded. "I can't believe you're keeping score in our sex life. Wow. You're a fucking bean counter."

I sat up and pulled the covers up to my chin, watching him pace in agitation. "I'm not keeping score," I protested. "I just want to feel like you care about my pleasure as much as I care about yours."

"Yeah. There it is again. Tit for tat. Whatever. I'm gonna go sleep on the couch. I hope you're happy."

"This isn't what I wanted. . ."

He slammed the door on the rest of my sentence, and I burst into tears. Again. This definitely wasn't what I wanted.

What I wanted was a stronger connection with my husband. I wanted to feel my pleasure mattered to him and that he enjoyed the intimacy and sex we shared. I wanted to feel like he could never get enough of me, just like I could never get enough of him. Sexuality is a powerful source of energy and vitality; it's the key to profound connection and ecstatic play. I wanted to share more of that with him. I wanted to feel like we were on the same team, giving and receiving delight and exploring the wide-open possibilities for arousal and satisfaction in life. I wanted to set every part of our lives on fire with the energy we generated between us.

I felt stuck. I couldn't expect anything to change by staying silent, but making him angry and defensive with words he perceived as dishing up a steaming plate of blame and shame wasn't helping us, either. I wanted so much more from him, partially because I knew more was possible. Sometimes our sex life was breathtakingly powerful, more than I could even imagine, but often it felt like just a habit between us.

The next morning, he was up and out the door before I was even dressed. At work, my best friend noticed I was quieter than usual.

"What's going on with you today?" she asked.

"Nothing, really," I deflected.

She quirked an eyebrow at me in disbelief.

"Okay, fine. I'm unhappy with my sex life. I feel petty talking about it, but I can't think about anything else," I confessed. "Sometimes it's great, but most of the time it's just penetration, his orgasm, then sleep. I know it takes a long time for me to climax, and that's annoying, but I feel so invisible and unwanted."

"Ah, honey. That sucks. Have you talked to him about it?"

"Yeah, and that just made it worse—I ended up sleeping alone. Besides, if he actually wanted to focus on my pleasure, I wouldn't need to ask for it. I don't want to feel like he's just going through the motions to make me happy when he isn't really into it. I don't see how talking about it can solve that problem."

She nodded. "So here's a secret they don't teach in sex ed: all of us want the people we love to feel pleasure and fulfillment during sex, but none of us are mind readers. There's so much misinformation about sex out there."

"I didn't even know the clitoris existed till a partner showed me when I was 19!" I interrupted.

"Exactly. Every body is different, and each body is different on different days, but we don't talk about that. The point is, we grow up believing we shouldn't have to ask for what we want, that it will just be magically delivered to us perfectly by our soulmate—who is totally set up to fail due to lack of information, and who then feels shitty when he doesn't live up to those ridiculous cultural expectations. Best case scenario, he can have general knowledge about what turns women on, but only you can teach him the specifics of what feels good to your particular body and heart."

"So how do I do that without making him feel like he's not good enough? That's clearly what happened last night when I brought it up."

"Focus your words and attention on what you want more of. What feels good already? Tell him that. Then actually ask for more. Think of it as a seduction. Try staying connected to your own embodied sexual energy when you share your desires with him. If you can tap into feeling sexy instead of hurt or guilty for asking, he will feel invited into deeper connection and intimacy with your tenderest parts."

"Are you sure he can't just read my mind? That would be so much easier."

"Trust me, I'm sure," she laughed. "But this is important. Staying silent means keeping secrets, and that's how bitterness and resentment grow. It's not easy, but it gets easier with practice. You can do this. I believe in you."

"Thanks," I said wryly.

"Oh, and one more thing. That thing you said about your orgasm taking too long? That's crap. Sex isn't a race. And it feels to me like you're projecting your own ridiculous performance expectations of your body onto him. Let yourself relax and enjoy yourself, and let him enjoy you, too."

She was right. I bought into some of the most dangerous lies of the relationship fairytale I grew up with: the belief that my partner could read my mind (or my body language) and know what I wanted and that if he really loved me, he would just naturally fulfill my desires. In a world where these myths were true, I didn't need to learn how to communicate my desires. And since I didn't need to ask for what I wanted in the first place, I certainly didn't need to learn how to take my partner's feelings into consideration when I asked.

It never occurred to me that he'd feel attacked or belittled by the way I shared my desire. I was so caught up in feeling hurt myself because I had to ask in the first place that I didn't imagine how Lee would feel hearing that I was regularly dissatisfied with our sex life. At the time, I felt I was the one making myself vulnerable by abandoning the fairytale and asking for what I wanted, but in a culture where masculinity is defined by performance expectations, he felt deeply criticized by the person he loved and trusted the most.

As a writer and witch, I knew how powerful words are in creating reality. What if I focused words on my own desire as a sort of spell to manifest more of the deliciousness between us rather than complaining about what I was missing? How could I turn asking for what I want into an opportunity to appreciate my partner instead of criticizing him? And could I connect with him from a place of my own embodied desire in a way that I could feel sexy in the process of asking instead of fearful?

I started by writing about our most recent sexual experience, where I felt fully inflamed by a desire for him and fully satisfied in the moment. I wrote down everything that made that experience so hot: how he touched me, how his body felt beneath my hands and body, and everything he said that pushed my arousal buttons. I cataloged how smell and taste added to the experience and considered the visual element of sexy clothes and lingerie that contributed to the moment's intensity. I described all the qualities about him that turned me on—his strength, his all-devouring passion, the way he never closed his eyes as if he didn't want to miss a single glimpse of our bodies intertwined.

Writing it all down helped me remember details and practice the exact words I would share. It also gave me a chance to see where I started slipping into the complaint, blaming, or shaming so I could shift those expressions with intention. These words were a spell to create the physical and energetic reality I wanted to live in, so I needed to pay close attention to getting them just right.

When I got home that night, Lee was watching baseball on TV. He didn't even turn his head as I came in the door. I dropped my purse on the table by the door and joined him on the couch.

"Hey, baby. Can we mute that for a minute?" He pushed the mute button, but he still didn't look at me. I reached out and took his hand. "I'm sorry about what I said last night. I was scared and clumsy and didn't communicate what I wanted to. I didn't mean to hurt you, and I didn't mean to make you mad."

"Whatever," he said, pulling his hand away.

I could feel myself getting shaky with anxiety that he would stay angry, so I took a deep breath and reconnected with the tiny flame of desire deep inside me. "Can I come sit in your lap?" I asked.

"Sure," he said, surprised but finally looking at me.

I moved to sit on his lap on the couch, and I leaned my head down to whisper in his ear. "You know I love you, Lee. And you turn me on so much. I love the way you smell, the electricity of your hands on my body, the intensity of having you inside me." His arm tightened around my shoulders, and his other hand started roaming over my legs. "I love it when you take your time to tease and torment me, building so much desire inside me that eventually it comes crashing down all around me. I love it fast and furious, too. I love all the ways we are together. I'm greedy for all the juicy hotness we can create between us." His hand slid smoothly under my skirt, and I gasped. "Oh, yes, please," I murmured in his ear. "Just like that. I am so very greedy for you."

Of course, communicating from my own desire wasn't a quick solution to the larger issues in our relationship, but developing a practice of regularly sharing mutual appreciation and arousal helped keep the flames of our erotic connection burning during our 17 years together.

Most importantly, however, learning and practicing this strategy (along with cultivating a smokin' hot self-pleasure practice) set the stage for the richness of my current life. Using words as intentional relationship magic—and being in a relationship with a partner who does, too—has created a sense of energetic ease and flow that is now the foundation of a life of simmering sensual pleasure and emotional wealth.

THE STRATEGY

Words are a powerful tool for manifesting an abundance of deep connection and erotic pleasure in your life. Being able to put your desires into words is the first step in transforming your dreams into reality.

Begin by settling yourself in a safe, comfortable place where you won't be disturbed for at least a half-hour. Breathe deeply into your heart, then your belly, then your pelvic floor, inhaling the clean, fresh air that will stoke the fire of your sexual energy and exhaling any fear or bitterness you might be carrying.

Use the prompts below to explore your own desire and pleasure in writing first. Reflect on the things you appreciate about your partner in both sexual and non-sexual ways. Consider your own fantasies, including those you may not have shared before. Even if you don't want to explore making those fantasies a reality, vulnerably sharing what turns you on can strengthen the intimacy of your connection with your partner and opens an opportunity to get creative together.

USING SEXY CONVERSATION TO BUILD CONNECTION AND AROUSAL

If you're uncomfortable talking about sexy times (the full range of sexual activities ranging from flirting to intercourse to snuggling and more), be honest with your partner about that. Vulnerability and empathy are powerful tools for both connection and arousal. Try starting your sentence with something like, "This feels a little scary (fill in your own true feelings) to share, but. . ."

- You are such a _____ lover.
- I love when you _____.
- It really turns me on when you _____.

- I think about you _____ to push me over the edge of orgasm.
- Oh, please _____. That's so good.
- I really want to feel _____ during sexy times.
- My favorite memory of sexy times with you is _____.
- I'd really love to try _____ with you.
- In my hottest fantasy, we _____. (Would you try that with me? Or I don't really want to act it out, but I want to share my secret turn-ons with you.)
- When I masturbate, I fantasize about _____ with you. Would you try doing that with me?

USING "BACK SCRATCH" INSTRUCTION SKILLS FOR TOUCH THAT LIGHTS YOUR FIRE

Think about a time that you had an itch you couldn't reach, and you asked your partner to scratch it for you. Odds are they didn't hit exactly the right spot with exactly the right kind of scratching the instant they touched you. You had to offer instructions: "Up a little, okay, over to the right, a little harder. . ." You had to think about their perspective as the toucher (their right, or my right?), neither of you took it personally when they didn't immediately find the itch, and you were reasonably patient with their efforts. And when they finally hit the spot just right, you moaned in pleasure and gratitude. Try this "low charge" technique for teaching your partner how to touch you for maximum pleasure in a specific moment, especially as bodies change over time.

- Experiment, follow instructions and practice patience on both sides.
- Avoid emotional charge around asking or being asked (slow your breath to settle your nervous system if you feel the charge rising.)
- Avoid anxiety about "doing it right."

USING MEMORY TO BUILD ANTICIPATION

Anticipation makes every experience better, and you can start building anticipation for your next sexual encounter anytime! Keep the pilot light of your sexual energy shining bright by using memories of your past experiences together as seduction toward the future.

- Verbally share your memory writing about your most recent sexy times to build enthusiasm and anticipation for next time.

- Mmm. . . last night/this morning/lunchtime/etc. was so hot! (Tell the story of what was so hot for you.)

- It's never too late to amplify memory into fresh desire: Remember that time we _____? That was so good. Let's do that again.

Sexy communication alone won't rebuild a connection where resentment has taken root, but weaving a spell from your appreciation and craving for more of the hidden treasures between you will ignite your shared desires and contribute to building a life that is blazing with abundance, connection, and joy.

For more sexy practices to heat up your relationship, visit https://desirealchemy.com/spellbinding/

The founder of Desire Alchemy, **Eirikah Delaunay** is an initiated priestess and trauma-informed somatic sex+relationship coach who shares her 30+ years of experience as a witch and sexual rebel with others who want to unleash their unique desires and generate connection and energy to fuel all their life's passions. Her mission is to re-ignite and strengthen stale relationships (including the relationship with Self) by encouraging true authenticity, practical skills, devotion, and delight.

A lifelong writer and academic with two amazing adult children, Eirikah discovered her spiritual path at 18, as she sought a tradition that held the feminine, sexuality, and nature sacred. She earned an MFA in Creative Writing and spent seven years as English and Gender Studies faculty followed by 11 years as a college vice president.

She has had the joy of more than a decade of connection and service in the Seattle sex-positive community, where she serves on the Board of the Center for Sex Positive Culture. Certified as a sex+relationship coach by the Somatica Institute™, she has served as a guest educator and facilitator on topics ranging from hands-on skills, D/s dynamics, sacred sexuality, and sexy communication.

Her erotic writing has been published in the Seattle Erotic Arts Festival Literary Anthology (2018-20, 2022). Her chapter "Light Your Fire: Ecstatic Embodiment to Fuel Your Dreams" was featured in the Amazon #1 bestseller *Sacred Medicine: Mystical Practices for Ecstatic Living* and her chapter "Turn Yourself On: Embodiment Practices to Jump-Start Your Day" appeared in the Amazon #1 bestseller *Ultimate Guide to Self-Healing Volume 5*.

She provides individual and partnered coaching for people curious and excited about using effective communication, magic, sexuality, kink, and/or power exchange relationships as vehicles for personal growth and bliss.

Connect with Eirikah:
Website: https://desirealchemy.com
Facebook: https://www.facebook.com/eirikah.delaunay
Linktree: https://linktr.ee/eirikah
Bonus resources are available at https://desirealchemy.com/spellbinding/
Email: eirikah@desirealchemy.com

FREEDOM

This offering of wealth aligned with the element of air to blow in the winds of change with the liberating breath of life we receive from personal and financial freedom.

This element invites us to get out of our heads so we can release the stress and anxiety that comes with overthinking. It kisses our skin with soft tickles and inspires divine intervention with a reminder that we get to live life on our terms.

There's an invitation to transformation, emphasizing balancing life and aligning with soulful integrity. The winds of change mysteriously swirl and dance within our hearts and souls to create freedom in mysterious ways. It refuses to be stagnant. It moves through us, around us, and within us.

As we receive the winds of change with an open heart, it flies with us into the mystical realms of non-ordinary reality to gaze upon life from a bird's eye view. It asks us to let go of the need to control and surrender to the unknown with spontaneous new abilities. It asks us to see what we have not yet experienced and heal what we may have not yet recognized.

RITUAL: Play soft, healing instrumental music that calms your nervous system. If you don't have a favorite artist yet, try my friend Ashana's Jewels of Silence Meditation CD here: https://amzn.to/3yDeAW5

Lay down and get cozy. Feel completely supported knowing you are safe, loved, and protected by celestial beings. Feel, sense, or know these guides lead you to liberated freedom.

Take deep, spacious breaths through your nose and out your mouth, inviting your stress to melt away with each exhale.

As you listen to the music, awaken your senses and allow the sound to wash over your physical body with sensual adornment.

Delight in the experience. Drift off into a spiritual journey and collect any messages your higher self or spirit guides want to share with you. Continue receiving this sound healing medicine as long as you desire.

When you feel complete, gently sit up and journal anything that wants to pour through you.

To tap deeper into the feeling of freedom, you may enjoy my online courses. Visit www.jenpiceno.com/academy to learn more.

To work privately or to accelerate your Wealth Codes journey, schedule a Wealth Codes support call here: www.jenpiceno.com/book_now

CHAPTER 11

THE BEAUTY OF THE END GAME

FINDING ABUNDANCE THROUGH ACCEPTING DEATH

Natasha Sharma BSc, CCHt, DipHB (KGH, UK)

MY STORY

I toss and turn in my bed; the sheets feel too hot and crumply. The darkness—is the same whether my eyes are open or closed.

He is playing a prank on me; tomorrow, we will both be laughing over this.

I cannot comprehend what happened even though I saw it with my own eyes. The person I love the most in this world, lying on the ground, eyes rolled back and tongue lolling.

I had no idea the human tongue was so long!

My tall, strong, handsome, larger-than-life grandfather was dead.

It cannot be.

I hear my bedroom door creaking slowly open. I see the outline of my father's form.

Be still. Pretend to be sleeping!

I regulate my breath and keep my eyes squeezed shut.

My father maneuvers himself between my bed and the wall, slumps down and cries—heaving sobs and raggedy breaths.

What is going on?

This is the first and last time I have seen a grown man cry unobserved. I know his dad just died; I saw it happen.

But my father crying like this?

It makes no sense to me.

He is going to be okay.

I want to reach out and tell him what I know, but I'm supposed to be sleeping. I stay still, say nothing, do nothing.

I think of my mother. I sat awkwardly on her lap earlier today. I felt her heartbeat on my back, her sweet, warm breath passing steadily back and forth past my ear—tickly but reassuring.

It's not enough.

I heave sighs and struggle to speak around unshed tears, "But today was the first time we fought," I mumbled to her.

"He understands, he loves you and isn't mad at you," she said, rocking me slowly back and forth and hugging me tightly.

I am a 14-year-old tall, gangly teenager, hardly a convenient shape and size for a mother's lap. I sigh heavily.

How would you know what he feels?

He's dead.

She doesn't understand!

I give up trying to find words, and settle into her comforting embrace for a brief moment.

On the day of his funeral, my mother fainted. I stood there and watched frozen, as a dozen people swarmed around her. If I thought my heart was broken on this day, I had no idea what was in store for me over the next few years.

Two months later, my mother was diagnosed with leukemia, one of the rare ones. She fought it valiantly for the next two years, leaving me in charge of the household, my father, and my siblings.

A sassy teen with that kind of power meant I was above the law of curfews and discipline. When she came home from the hospital visits, my teenage angst knew no limits, and the relationship with my mother was fraught with typical drama with no allowance for her, her broken heart, or a failing fight.

One dusky afternoon, she called me to her, sat me down, and said, "Now that you are grown up, I can tell you things."

I listened as icy fingers crept like tendrils around my heart. My mouth was dry, and my mind was numb.

"Your father is having an affair and has been for a very long time. He is a powerful man, and I have no support or money of my own. He will take you children away from me, and I cannot fight him. I want to leave him. Now that you're almost done with school, once you graduate, I can at least have you with me if you agree to come."

"Of course, I will," I mumble as my love for her surges up and eclipses any love I have for my father at the moment.

"Promise me you will keep this all to yourself."

"I promise," I say, looking into her eyes, willing her to believe me. I see a cloud passing over her face. Intuitively I know she regrets confiding in someone so young and unpredictable, questioning her judgment and faith in me. After all, I first and foremost fiercely loved my grandfather (who was now dead), and in second place, I loved my father, the apple of his eye, a daddy's girl. I was the one who was going to grow up and marry him, her hero.

How could she trust me?

"Mummy, open the door!" I yell over and over again, frantically pummeling the bathroom door, which she locked herself into after our conversation. I'm frightened; I know something is terribly wrong.

Finally, she opens the door, trying bravely to summon a smile to reassure me. I look at her in horror. She is pale as a ghost, hands trembling, standing limply in the ajar doorway, holding onto the frame for support, the room behind her dense with cigarette smoke.

My brain does not know what to process first. My mother does not smoke, but my father does.

Is he in there with her?

My heart races.

Don't be ridiculous; he is not home yet.

She looks like a ghost!

I know I have to reassure her, make her believe somehow that I'm on her side.

"If he ever finds out I told you, he will kill me," she whispers.

"He will never find out. I won't tell him, I promise!" I know she doesn't believe me.

I'm unable to convince her, and two weeks later, she is dead.

I sit outside her hospital room; the door is open, and I watch as the doctors charge the paddles and shock her. Her body is stiff, jerking up into the air, over and over. I arrived just a few hours before. "Who is there?" she asked.

I'm devastated and confused.

My own mother doesn't recognize me!

What is going on?

Her friends say, "Ranjit, it's Natasha. She has come to see you, it's Natasha."

"Who? Oh! My dear, come here, come closer, let me see you."

She peers into my face, trying hard to see past the descending veil of death; exhausted with the effort, she falls limply back onto the pillows, never to rise again.

I run, for the rest of my life, from person to person, often whispering, sometimes shouting out loud, "My mother did not die from cancer, she died from a broken heart!" I was looking for respite, relief, validation, or even understanding. In the end, the only person who could help me was me.

This download from the Universe, this knowledge that disease is linked to emotions, came to me so early, so clearly, and so surely. Yet, due to the unprocessed grief, I've been unable to do much with it until I healed, grieved, forgave, and embarked upon my journey of self-awareness.

Until then, the only stage of grief I allowed in was anger.

Anger became my constant companion for the next couple of decades. It fueled me and jettisoned me through life which I've lived on turbo charge, alone and aloof, so I never have to lose another person I love ever again.

THE STRATEGY

I've transcended and descended many times through my healing journey. Healing from grief is not limited to physical death. Any kind of loss, abandonment, or betrayal goes through the five (or seven) stages of grief. If you pause to wonder, it will make sense to you as it gradually has to me.

A friendship that no longer serves you is the death of that relationship. A divorce is the death of a marriage. A broken heart is the death of that romance, but it can also be the death of trust, love, or loyalty. The loss of a job is the death of the relationship with the company, accompanied by a myriad of other losses like routine, individual relationships with colleagues, even with the guy at the coffee cart, and emotive losses like self-confidence or self-worth. It can mean different things to different people in their individual experiences and circumstances. Each person is unique.

There are, however, common lessons to be learned and the same stages to go through. It's only the experience of it that's unique. We are all born, are alive, and will die. We will all go through the stages of grief whenever we face loss in our lives in one form or the other.

As a result, the stages of grief become a powerful tool at our disposal. Rather than it being a cross to bear, it can be wielded like a mighty weapon. Let us briefly visit what they are, and then I will dive into how you can use this very process as a tool to unlock the natural wealth and abundance that exists all around you, waiting to be invited into your life.

Denial

Even if we know with our logical conscious mind that someone has died, it can be hard to believe that someone important is gone forever.

Anger

Anger is a completely natural emotion and very natural after someone dies. Anger has several shades and ways of presenting itself, from irritation or short temperedness all the way to full-scale blow-ups. Death can seem cruel and unfair, especially when you feel someone has died before their time or you had plans for the future together. It's also common to feel angry towards the person who has died or angry at ourselves for things we did or didn't do before their death.

Bargaining

When we're in pain, it's often difficult to accept that there is nothing we can do to change things. Bargaining is when we start to make deals with ourselves, or perhaps with God. We want to believe that if we behave in a certain way, we'll feel better. It's also common to find ourselves going over and over things that happened in the past and asking a lot of "what if" questions, wishing we could go back and change things in the hope things could have turned out differently.

Depression

Sadness and longing are what we think of most often when we think about grief. This pain can be very intense and come in waves over many months or even years. Life can feel like it no longer holds any meaning, which can be very scary.

Acceptance

Gradually, as we move up and down through the stages, most people find that the pain eases, and it's possible to accept what has happened. We may never get over the death of someone precious, but we can learn to live again while keeping the memories of those we have lost close to us.

Shock

Numbness or emotional paralysis is the initial response when faced with loss.

Testing

Trying new ways of coping with the loss and rebuilding life after loss.

Dr. Elizabeth Kubler Ross shared the five-stage model in her book *On Death and Dying* that she developed while working with terminally ill patients. Later she revised this to the seven-stage model and extended it to the grieving process.

Important points to be noted, this is not a linear process. It's more like a sliding scale, and we can pass back and forth between stages repeatedly. There is no time frame, nor will everyone necessarily go through every stage.

There is a wealth of information and resources available on the subject if you wish to dive deeper into the subject. My objective is to share with you how I have transformed my understanding into the aforementioned powerful tool that it is.

By embracing and truly understanding the stages of grief, I'm now fully equipped to deal with any and all circumstances that I face in my life. It's one of the tools I use daily to check my alignment and to evaluate where I am emotionally at any point in time, like a barometer of sorts. Once I identify the stage, it brings me awareness, and that awareness gives me a choice.

The power to choose how I wish to process things at that point, what to do and how to do it. As a result, feelings can pass through and out of me fairly easily now and seldom linger long enough to cause harm.

The COVID pandemic presented many losses and changes in my life and the lives of those around me, as it did for everyone around the world. I truly learned the hard way that any change and loss cause us to go through the grieving process, as surely as does the death of a loved one.

What has had a tremendous impact on my reality during the pandemic has been the next level of grief—that is, death itself.

My own death.

The acceptance of the inevitability of it. To have looked myself in the mirror and accept without doubt or fear that I will die one day. Not someday, but one day. To feel bad about it, feel scared, all the emotions behind the loss, but not regret.

I vowed then to live my life in such a way that when my time comes, I go easily, happily, and with no regrets. I chose to embrace life and rejoiced in the fact that I'm not living in denial of death any longer. To realize that going back to any other way is a delusion.

It has allowed me to look at the people around me and know that everyone is going to die, some before me and others after me.

But die, we all shall.

It has been the single most transformative experience in my healing and self-awareness journey. Now, when I lose someone, I give myself permission to allow the stages to pass through me. I try to let go and flow and not hold on. I say try because it's an ongoing process.

After a lifetime of being socialized to fear death and deny both the reality of it and grief, reconditioning is a process.

Even now, it catches me off guard sometimes, the feelings that arise when I contemplate the moment I will die. The certainty that it will come to pass, coupled with the uncertainty of not knowing the how and when of it.

It can be overwhelming.

Then I remind myself that the moment of my passing is beyond my control. Total acceptance of it and that it's okay not to know, trusting it will take me easily to that point and beyond is the only reality that is real.

This has given me total freedom. I'm free to fiercely love the people close to me, to tell them, show them, and give them the precious gift of my time. I'm free to enjoy being alive to choose what I want to do with my life and how I wish to live it.

I welcome the wealth and abundance that flows so easily to me now that I'm no longer chained to the illusion that money matters. The rat race of chasing dollars and cents in an attempt to buy aspirational things and, therefore happiness ceases to have control over me.

My wealth is in my happiness, and my happiness is here now.

There is a very powerful verse in the Rigveda and the Yajurveda addressed to the Three-Eyed One, Rudra, an avatar of Lord Shiva. It's known as *The Mahamrityunjaya Mantra* (lit. 'Great death-defeating mantra') came to me during this stage of my life and has been an extremely powerful and effective tool in accepting my own death gracefully.

Understanding slowly and thoroughly each and every word of this verse and what it truly means is the death defeating part, not so much as mindlessly reciting it or having it play in the background on repeat.

Click the link in my bio and access both the audio and a video of *The Mahamrityunjaya Mantra* with English translations as a gift from me to you.

Welcome to your first conversation with your mortality.

For far too long, the human race has been embroiled in economics and power games solely driven by the need to prove that we can do things to be immortal by deed, lineage, or even name. Futile existences come and gone. Too many lives are wasted in enabling the seekers of that power.

You can take your power back. Work is necessary, and things are nice. You may be surprised at the choices you make once you deal with the fact that your time here is finite. When you contemplate leaving your possessions to people and actually comprehend you cannot take things with you.

Money matters, bills need to be paid, and lives need to be lived. Face your mortality, embrace the fact that you will die one day—maybe in a few days or perhaps in a few years.

You do not know when and that is what feeds the illusion.

Plan for your death. Put your affairs in order, no matter how old or young you are. Make a will, and update it regularly. Keep a note on your desktop or in your diary, so your loved ones are clear on what and how they should deal with your affairs. Leave them with clarity and not a mess so they can focus on the grieving process rather than sorting things out on your behalf. That is the last precious gift that you can give to them.

Face it, feel it, grieve for yourself, and once you pass out on the other side, you will be free. This freedom will allow you to make choices that make you happy now. To live life with infinite joy and appreciate every encounter and experience.

That is the beauty of the end game, and true wealth is to be found there.

Natasha Sharma was born and brought up in the United Kingdom. She has spent considerable time in Dhaka, Bangladesh, and now lives in Mumbai, India, with her husband, Rrajeev Sharma, and their two fur babies, Freyja and Isaac. She is a bonus mother to the beautiful Rewa Khare Sharma.

Her passion is guiding people to cure themselves of physical diseases by exploring the metaphysical connection of the mind-body-soul to the said illness.

Spreading awareness that the division of this trinity has encouraged ill health and malcontent. After all, there is no money to be made from peace, good health, and happiness.

The body has been taken over by modern medicine and the gods in white coats. The mind is elusive and undefined; maladies are given over to psychiatrists, psychologists, and counselors—the soul to religion.

Divide and rule, by those in power, throughout history continues to this day.

Imagine that power available to us once we align our inner trinity and embrace each and every part of us. Especially the broken bits. To be free of shame, guilt, and fear.

Her mission in life is to have conversations about death and use that inevitability to free people to enjoy their lives now.

She believes that death needs to be an easy day-to-day dinner table conversation. In that pursuit, she is starting the conversation here and will continue to write and speak openly and extensively about death until her mission is accomplished.

Reach out to her and invite her to speak to you, your family, employees, and anyone you feel will benefit from the reprioritization of their work and lives.

Connect with Natasha:
Website: https://www.bodyspeak.in/
Facebook: https://www.facebook.com/BodySpeak.in/
Instagram: https://www.instagram.com/bodyspeak.in/
Access your freedom from death toolkit:
https://www.bodyspeak.in/wealthcodes/

CHAPTER 12

TRANSCENDING THE PAIN OF LOSS

ONE GRATITUDE AT A TIME

R. Scott Holmes

MY STORY

*"Gratitude is not only the greatest of virtues,
but the parent of others."*

~Cicero

"Why is my life in shambles?" I asked the psychologist sitting across from me.

"Al-Anon," he answered.

Why is my life such a mess? Why can't I make any of it work right? Why do I feel so alone?

I froze with fear as I could not come up with a single answer. Life was a struggle. Emotions washed over me, drowning any rational thoughts. The darkness threatened to engulf me again.

"Step 4," I heard as I slid into the last row of metal folding chairs, hoping no one would notice me when the speaker asked, "Name three things you are grateful for."

Gratitude. Such a simple concept, such a natural state when you're in alignment.

At 13-months-old, Amanda, my youngest of three daughters, was stricken with herpes encephalitis simplex 2. This virus stopped just short of taking her life but left her multiply handicapped. My wife was amazing through this difficult time raising our three daughters, balancing the constant nurses, therapists, and counselors coming into our house, and keeping life on an even keel for my older two daughters. Life was work, exhaustion, tension, and definitely not the life we'd imagined.

Despite working two jobs, I took over care of Amanda when I got home from work and wondered how we would survive all of this for the next week, the next month, at all.

Walking into that church basement each week for Al-Anon, I found safety, understanding, compassion, and an island of peace for 90 minutes from the hamster wheel I ran on.

Most of all, I found the gift of gratitude.

I started with simple things when I went to bed: A roof over our head, a warm bed, and enough to eat. I woke up every day and was thankful for another day, that my family was safe, with my wife by my side.

Castle walls inside of me were built higher and broader so I could become the rock that would protect and anchor my family. Armor adorned my body thicker and thicker each day to fight through life, doing what I was taught a father and a husband should do—provider, protector, supporter. I continued my gratitude practice throughout those trying days, not truly believing what I was expressing but going through the motions—surviving.

The phone ringing at two in the morning is never good. "Mr. Holmes, I don't know any other way to say this, but Amanda has passed." We rushed to the hospital dozens of times, expecting the worst after getting a call from the pediatric nursing home that took care of her. Each time, Amanda would rally. Without fanfare or an ambulance ride and medics working on her as they had so many times before, Amanda stopped breathing quietly in the middle of the night with no warning.

How do you find gratitude in losing a child? Why would God choose to make her suffer for so long? How do you give comfort when you feel you have none for yourself?

That next year is a blur in my memory; going through life but not present. Zombies had more emotions than I possessed! I believe it broke parts of my wife. She simply could never get back to the person she was. The anchor I was supposed to be for her drifted away on the waves of pain and grief.

The only way grieving truly started was through gratitude. It became my mantra. No matter the circumstance, "What am I grateful for?"

When the fog lifted, change followed, as my awareness and presence became clearer through being grateful—grateful for the sun, for the rain, for those in my life, for a green light on the way to work, for my car starting.

My wife and I did indeed find gratitude in the number of people who took care of Amanda and cared about her. We got to keep her for 14 more years after she survived her initial illness. In the darkest of days, there was always something, however small, to have and show gratitude for. Her suffering was over.

Through the ups and downs of my wife's breast cancer journey, small slivers of happiness filtered into our world—family gatherings, grandchildren, summer nights on the screen porch. Gratitude was easier to see and feel even when chemotherapy called again, and vacations were taken at the oncology wing of Mass General Hospital. Whatever came along, the armor I wore was a smile. I allowed what needed to happen to happen, accepting what life threw at us and attempting to live with an open and giving heart. Moira often said, "No matter how hard life is for us, others have it harder."

The last years of my wife's illness were a succession of losses: Medical retirement from the teaching job she loved, the inability to drive, then unable to leave the bedroom where sitting or resting took up most of her days. Worst of all was when she changed from someone who had fought cancer to becoming a cancer patient. She fought hard, strength beyond measure, surrounded by love, family, and friends.

How can I keep on going? My partner has left me alone, and I don't know if I can live this solitary life. Where do I go from here?

Grateful for the love shown during Moira's last days; it carried me through those long days and much longer empty nights. My friends rallied around. My girls tried but had lives and families of their own. I was on my own.

Gratitude turned back to small things: Waking up every day, a roof over my head, having good food, the sun shining, raining, or snowing.

Much as the heavy fog dissipates through the course of the day to allow the sun to shine, by being present in life, being where I was standing, without mourning shrouding my sight, my heart slowly revealed what was a stripped-down version of myself. The realization came in waves—the 40 years I fought and struggled to accumulate things, what I thought I should value turned to just wood, metal, ceramic, and plastic. I had little attachment to all but those few items strongly anchored to my wife and daughters. I learned that much like the armor I carried every day, I was dragging along the burden of things.

"Joy is the simplest form of gratitude."

~Karl Barth

Brendan, one of my lifelong friends, lost his wife a year after Moira, so I convinced him to go on his bucket list trip to Ireland. As one of ten children of a strong Irish Catholic family, the pilgrimage to Ireland was a dream he thought he couldn't realize until we heard, "Aer Lingus flight 134 Boston to London now boarding," over the loudspeaker.

Ten days in England and Ireland wandering about with no one to answer to for the first time in our lives was liberating, exhilarating, and one of the first times in so many years that joy became present. The shoulds that ruled my life as a caregiver were shaken off and self-care—allowing my own journey to start—took over. Rediscovering long neglected friendships was heartwarming. Waking up to new adventures in a foreign land was expansive. The joy of seeing where the day would take us and what new places we'd see became a passion and opened me up to discover what else was in store.

I traveled to central Europe with Paul, the best man at my wedding. It was always a dream of mine to travel throughout Europe, and we made that happen. Seventeen days, 2500 miles driven, and eight countries visited. "Hey Paul, tomorrow I'm turning 60, so let's plan something big!"

We ate breakfast in Germany, lunch in Strasbourg, France, and then dinner in Basel, Switzerland. I couldn't have asked for a more incredible present: memories. Here I was, awakening to a new vista every day and finally understanding how my life was truly blessed.

A year later. Paul and I traveled with a tour group for 17 days through Thailand, Cambodia, and Vietnam. As close as we were, we became so much closer than brothers, as we lived in each other's back pocket for that entire time. The realization in traveling throughout Southeast Asia was that I was an accidental Buddhist. Understanding the culture and visiting Buddhist temples, I realized God was not something out there but very present within each of us. I had the feeling of coming home though I didn't know why.

Joy became ever-present in uncovering my relationship with my girlfriend; an empath, intuitive, and someone with the biggest heart I have ever met. She allowed (and allows) me to grow, journey, and explore. Sometimes she's beside me, sometimes she's waiting while I find answers, and she's always welcoming me home. She exposed me to mediums, healers, and true intimacy.

Samaha, a medium I worked with regularly, stopped in the middle of her reading and started conversing with one of my spirit guides. "Tell him he needs to go to Penang to the Burmese Temple!"

Samaha replied, "I don't know what that means."

"Tell him to go collect those parts of his soul left behind."

He then walked off without explanation. She shrugged and said she didn't understand. We googled "Penang" and "Burmese Temple." Sure enough, there was only one such temple in Penang, Malaysia. Also, there is a theory that soul parts get left behind when there is a violent or tragic death. They seek refuge in a place of safety.

Great to know, but what could I do about all of this? If she didn't know what to make of this, how the hell could I? Can life be any more of a puzzle?

Coincident or not, ten days later, an email arrived from the travel company I used to go to Vietnam. It was a ten-day excursion to Singapore and Malaysia, with the last stop in Penang, Malaysia, four blocks from the Burmese temple. My guides were clearing the way for me to follow the path I was destined for.

Nine months later, as I stood at the foot of the 40-foot gold-accented Budda, my arms outstretched and my heart open, I realized every experience, moment, and thought led me here. This was just one more path on my journey. I was transfixed.

I felt the full power of gratitude, joy, and abundance—the overflowing energy of unlimited possibility and being whole. *Is this what it feels like to be heart-centered?*

> *"Acknowledging the good that you already have in your life is the foundation for all abundance."*
>
> ~Eckhart Tolle

And that's when abundance started. I realized abundance was not a Rolls Royce or millions of dollars but was how I saw life, my mindset, and my perceptions. I truly had everything: A place to live, a job, love, my family, hot water, friends, Italian food, warm chocolate chip cookies, travel, and the endless possibilities life offered! And through all this, I found long-dormant passions that welled up from inside: To write, create, collaborate, heal, and teach others to heal themselves.

What is abundance but transcendence to a higher vibration in which to live our best life? That perspective allows you to act, not react, accept what is, not what is wished for, give without depletion, teach and not lecture, and allow and not expect, to work daily on this journey called life.

THE STRATEGY

Simple shifts in perception of everyday things can drastically change your feelings, mood, and understanding. True presence enables your heart to encounter the world you've created without the filter of your mind.

Wow, that sounds philosophical and not the reality you live in daily! The simple truth is that it can be. Look at the daily habits you've established and change those habits into rituals.

Rituals are practices you do regularly with presence, without distractions.

- Find the time that fits your day, even if it's only ten minutes
- Create a space that feels right:

  - Is it comfortable?
  - Is it quiet?
  - Bring your favorite crystal, oil, incense, blanket, or tea.
  - Find a pen and paper to record your thoughts.
  - Read a meditation or inspirational piece.
  - Listen to a guided meditation.

- Is there movement involved?

  - Yoga
  - Biking
  - Tai Chi
  - Breathwork
  - Walking
  - QiGong

GRATITUDE IS AN ATTITUDE

When life is a struggle, and we all have those days, use waking up to set the tone for your day. Do some daily introspection. Quieting everything around you as you listen to your heart center is like hitting the pause button on the movie of your life—clearing your mind to be present with intention.

How do we clear ourselves? It starts with learning, moves to a daily ritual, and becomes a belief. There is a simple energy clearing that, when practiced daily, leads to that quiet place within you. This is a fairly advanced guided self-clearing meditation from the book *RYSE, Tools for Life: Holding Your Personal Power and Life Force* by Nancy Risley.

- Surround yourself in the highest, most aligned healing, pure sparkling white light. Imagine it, feel it.
- Call on the highest knowing part of you that raises your vibration or that knows how to clear, repair, and align your energetic systems.
- Perceive in its perfection your crown chakra (pause), your third eye front and back, your throat chakra front and back, your heart chakra front and back, your third chakra front and back, your second chakra front and back, and your base chakra.
- Bring the light in the clean base, up the center of your spine to your crown, clearing the spinal column as you go.
- Go back to your third eye, back to your heart.
- Bring the light in through your crown, down your spine, past your base chakra, and out past your feet. Allow the highest light to extend out into your aura.
- Clear your aura from the spine outward, paying particular attention to the heart chakra layer, the beautiful pastel-colored sixth layer, and the beautiful silver beaded seventh layer. They are beautiful and shimmering, just raising your vibration and feeling good.
- Clear the Ida and Pingala (two tubes connected to each chakra) between the base and second chakra, second and third chakra, third and heart chakra, heart and throat chakra, and throat and third eye. There is high energy flushing through it.
- Activate the air pattern—a spiraling pattern around your torso, down to your base chakra, and up to the center of your spine.
- Breathe that highest knowing part of you into you.
- Feel everything click in.
- When you are ready, open your eyes and bring your consciousness back into the room.

We do this through intention and awareness. Daily practice of clearing, much like brushing your teeth or taking a shower, refreshes, cleans, and keeps us feeling better. No matter your belief system or religious practice, many find they become closer and have a better understanding of the faith they practice. A clear and present self allows understanding, shifting the chaos, confusion, and busyness of the mind to clarity.

A clear mind and heart are not the absence of emotion and thought. It's a happy place for your whole self. My happy place is an island beach in Florida—sitting or walking along the uninterrupted expanse of sand while the waves keep rhythm like a metronome. This is where I find peace within myself and the world. It is then I can see life from a different perspective. And that brings true understanding, true presence, being true to my soul's purpose, and closer to the Creator I envision.

How does this all relate to abundance? When we're clear in seeing all we have—physically, emotionally, spiritually, and energetically—we can be truly thankful. Gratitude becomes real. Living in gratitude brings freedom to be who you were put on this world to be. Joy comes along for the ride. Some call it the pursuit of happiness. I've always believed it's not the final destination but the way we experience life, our filter, and how we relate to everything in our world that matters.

Through joy, we lovingly see how much we have in our lives: A place to lay your head each night, enough food to satisfy your needs, your family—no matter how close you are at the moment, your friends' acceptance of the true you, the ability to sit in silence and allow.

When you're aligned, life becomes simpler, easier, and fuller. That's where abundance lies—not in acquiring the biggest, brightest, or best. It comes by being the best, brightest, most energetic you possible. Then you can live your abundant life, accepting it with gratitude.

Why is this important? This is you setting boundaries. Not only for yourself but for all those you're connected to. Feeling fatigued and overwhelmed? Set aside the time to see your life as full, as joyous, as what you've imagined through gratitude. Gratitude allows you to act and respond in a place of peace instead of in a place of fear, depletion, or anger in our old patterns of behavior.

Is it work? Damn straight it is. And as with all things, practice makes perfect. Don't wait to change. Don't put off feeling better. Give yourself the gift of you so you can show it to the world.

R. Scott Holmes is an energetic healing practitioner and transformational coach connecting on your vibrational level. No matter the emotional, energetic, spiritual or physical roadblocks you encounter, there is a path to healing and clarity leading to understanding and joy.

The Healing Journey uses Reiki, Polarity Therapy, RYSE, and Theta Healing and Find Your Voice techniques to clear your sublime energetic systems. Tools such as yoga, crystals, meditations, sound, journaling, and therapeutic oils are used to help you establish daily rituals. Finding the right tools and working with intention allows your body and spirit to heal and transform in miraculous ways.

If you want to live beyond the limits of human experience.

Seek and experience self-alignment to live fully.

Shift your values and focus on serving others.

Move through the fear that has limited your life, goals, and joy.

Find your voice for full expression.

Contact me and find that starting point.

Connect with Scott:
Website: Rscottholmes.com
Email: rscott_holmes@yahoo.com
Facebook: Find Your Voice, Transcendent Men
https://www.facebook.com/groups/355370599667931/
Instagram: r.scottholmes

Hosting Men's Group sessions via Zoom twice a month. Private client sessions by request.

CHAPTER 13

COME OUT, COME OUT, WHOEVER YOU ARE

YOUR WHOLE SELF IS THE PATH TO FREEDOM AND ABUNDANCE

Wanda Tucker, MA, LPC, LMT

MY STORY

5:17

Bolting awake, I see the numbers on the clock. My heart thuds and drops into my stomach. I roll up on my right elbow and look at Helen, my wife. She's gone. I knew it was coming but I can hardly breathe as I lay my ear on her chest. Silence. I pull out the stethoscope. I have to make sure. I hold my breath as I listen. Still nothing. I choose to believe her leaving is what woke me.

What will I do without you? Who am I now that you're gone?

If you ask the questions, listen for the answers.

Three weeks later on July 20, 2019, three things occurred: Helen's Celebration of Life, the birthday party for Jerry's one-year-old son, and my anointing. As I write this, I'm aware of the trinities for the first time. The Divine often reveals and confirms itself in threes.

Honoring, celebrating, and saying goodbye to my beloved of almost 19 years changed my world—changed me. The only thing I knew was I had to find my new normal. Helen was the love of my life. She was my rock. She showed me I am lovable and desirable. She mirrored my power back to me as she showed up fully powerful in her being. My mirror was gone—or so I thought.

My friendship with Jerry spans decades. When I taught high school, he was my student. Our birthdays are three days apart—and several years. Our astrological charts are eerily similar: Both Aries sun with Pisces moon and Pisces rising. He photographed Helen's and my wedding. Though we live in different states and don't get to see each other often, when we do our conversation continues from where we last left off.

Because they happened on the same day, Jerry couldn't attend the Celebration of Life. Obviously, I didn't attend the birthday party. We could only be there for each other in spirit. I say "only" as if it's a smaller thing somehow. Wrong.

Jerry put his son's birthday party on the calendar long before we scheduled Helen's celebration. Coming from the same hometown, he and I have friends in common and because the events occurred at the same time friends had to choose which one they would attend. Our celebrations happened in towns an hour and a half apart so timing didn't allow serial attendance.

Among the people who attended the birthday party was Devon, a man whom I saw for couple's work with his wife, Kristi. Devon now has ties with Jerry's family. While working with him and Kristi, I knew in my gut something was organically wrong with Kristi. I encouraged them to seek medical evaluation and treatment. Fortunately, they followed my suggestion. Unfortunately, my intuition was correct and Kristi had a condition that led to her early death.

Jerry messaged me after our celebrations. My name came up at the party, surprising Devon.

"Wanda? Kristi and I saw her together. She was the one who knew Kristi had a physical problem and sent us to get medical help," Devon said. "Her ability to see it was so helpful and I am grateful."

Jerry replied, "Of course! She's a fucking shaman!"

"No," Devon said. "She's a licensed professional counselor."

I laughed when Jerry recounted the conversation. I felt seen. Jerry saw me.

At the time, I thought, *Yeah. But how do I market that? What do I put on my shingle? Wanda Tucker, Fucking Shaman?*

Spirituality is my highest value. For 30 years the Enneagram has been my map. Spiritual teachers and guides from many different traditions use this ancient tool. "Ennea" means nine; "gram" means figure. The nine-sided figure represents spiritual gifts and sins or vices. For centuries no one was allowed to write about the tool. Instead, teachers orally transmitted the energy knowledge to students. Now books and audio teachings are available.

I immersed myself in the teachings. Initially, I narrowed my type down to five of the nine possible numbers. Clearly, discovering who I am promised to be a journey.

One day, after months of study, my entire life unfolded before me. I *knew* my number. However, identifying my type was just the starting point of knowing and understanding *me*.

Richard Rohr, a renowned Enneagram teacher, says of my number, "They can't not say 'fuck.' They look for opportunities to use the word." Jerry nailed it. He mirrored me.

Playfully, I started to call the intuitive energy work I do "Fucking Shaman Magic" or "FSM" for short. I offer FSM to support friends. Sometimes they ask me for it when facing a difficult situation or struggling with low energy. I text the message, "FSM on its way to you," and do an inner ceremony. I love being able to support my circle of people and be of service but my inner critic managed to keep my shaman self in the closet.

What will people think? I tell myself I don't want to offend anyone, but the truth is I fear rejection and judgment. I fear being misunderstood.

When the lockdown of 2020 occurred, intuitively I knew this as an opportunity. "An enforced spiritual retreat" is how I framed it. Synchronicity led me to enroll in and complete a course to become a spiritual director. A friend told me about the program she planned to take and I *knew* I had to do it.

"I want more Godde and the joy of Hafiz," I told Father Jim who runs the program. The course materials included reading books from all traditions and opening one's mind and heart to whatever Spirit offered in whatever form—or not-form—it took. For years, the teaching and training I received in nondenominational, evangelical Christian churches lacked the Truth for me. I loved Jesus then and I still do. Twenty books later, I changed. My theology transformed.

In October of 2021, I attended a spiritual retreat. The second-day exercise looked like this: "Walk in nature and see what you see. Be aware. See what the Divine reveals to you. What messages do you receive?"

The sun shone and the air was crisp, a typical October day in Oregon—typical when it isn't raining. Menucha, the retreat center, sits in the Columbia River Gorge outside of Portland on what used to be the estate of a wealthy merchant of a bygone era. Trees lined the walking paths and the fallen leaves emitted an earthy smell with each step. Earlier in the morning, a staff member spied a mama bear and her cub on the road. Nature surrounded me in her raw beauty, bombarding my senses. Fortunately, mama bear did not make another appearance.

I saw woolly worms—black-yellow-black fuzzy caterpillars everywhere. Not knowing much about woolly worms, I researched. I needed to know and wanted to share with the group.

"The woolly worm transforms into the Isabella Tiger Moth after an average lifespan of 10 years as a caterpillar. Ten. Fucking. Years. As a caterpillar."

I admit to having difficulty processing the information and understanding the Divine message. Not until the end of the retreat did pieces fall into place.

"Write your new story in the third person. Name the protagonist. What new call are you experiencing? What are the obstacles?" The leader gave instructions for the closing exercise. "And what is the title of your story?"

So I began writing.

A Woolly Worm Emerges

Once upon a time, a Fucking Shaman knew it was time to reveal herself and claim the fullness of who she was and what she could do. She realized others had stolen some of her gifts by hurting and judging her when she had previously opened to possibilities within herself when she was most vulnerable. She knew the gifts, talents, and possibilities still existed, but those "others" had effectively silenced her. Nothing more came out of her mouth. As she traveled from that place she found new companions and fellow travelers. She found a Beloved Partner. Some of them continued beside her for a short time. Some still walk with her—and she continues to find new companions along the way. She now knows the time has come to break out of the chrysalis and learn to fly, revealing herself to those who have eyes to see and ears to hear. She now knows she must open her mouth and sing again. She must move her body and dance the choreography that is still being written. She knows she must be open to the fullness and completeness of who she is—the gifts she has to share—the talents bestowed upon her. She knows she must emerge into and through the anointing she received to share it with the world. She knows she must claim her title: Wanda, the Singing, Dancing, Fucking Shaman. The End.

Only then did I realize Jerry *anointed* me. I knew I must accept the title and use the gifts I have been given.

During goodbye hugs, Jim M. wrapped his arms around me and said, "May this be your tenth year."

"That is the best blessing I could receive! Thank you!" I laughed heartily as I received and returned the hug.

Because I came to my anointing in an unusual way, some people will think I have no right to call myself shaman. Some will think my claiming the title is insensitive, cultural appropriation. *Wait! Can shamans be anointed?* One path is to be apprenticed to a recognized shaman. Another is to go through a major trauma or near-death experience, transforming the person who emerges as a shaman in the healing process. Some are born shamans. Members of the community recognize the individual and bestow the title. Jerry recognized and named me.

When I started writing this chapter, I thought coming out as a shaman was the point. My body told me there was more. Agitated and nervous, a low-level electrical current running through me let me know the story was incomplete. My transformed Christian theology had to be part of the story.

"What is a fear you are ready to release?" Jen asked in writing support group. After three minutes of speed writing, she gave us opportunity to share keywords or phrases from the exercise: "Impression management, misunderstood, no control."

If I call myself a Christian, some people will think they know what I mean by comparing me to their understanding of Christianity. Others will call me a heretic if they ask and listen to my beliefs.

In the early 90s when I learned the Enneagram, I did a deep dive in my personal work to discover my soul mission: "Love as Jesus loved." *What the eff does that mean?* I hoped for something more concrete.

"Washed in the blood" grosses me out. Repeatedly, Jesus said, "Follow me." He didn't say, "Just believe in me and go on about your business. I've got you covered," but *be like me.* Be fully human and fully divine. Live the path of love. Be the son or daughter of Godde. This is being a Christian—a little Christ.

As I struggled to release my fear, once again synchronicity brought what I needed to hear. The daily reading told the story of Jesus when Pilate questioned him before the crucifixion. "You are the king of the Jews?"

"You say," Jesus responded. *Your words, not mine.*

These perfect words showed up for me as I wrestled, worrying about how others might see me. *Even Jesus went through this?!* He didn't accept or correct what others called him. He *knew* himself. I AM.

Socrates condensed all philosophical commandments (and I say "all spiritual growth") into one sentence: "Know yourself." Studying the Enneagram, I can find and *know* myself, both human and divine. Our type describes the operating system we are born with. Our type never changes; however, we can upgrade our system to manifest the completeness of who we are meant to be. When all types are integrated in one being, that person reflects the face of Godde. Identifying my number is an event in the lifelong process of becoming the reflection. "Love as Jesus loved" mirrors the Divine.

Jesus lived fully human, fully divine. In the tradition I grew up in, Jesus was the only one who accomplished this. In my new theology, he was the first.

Coming out as my whole self requires knowing who I am. Now I get it. I choose the freedom and abundance Jesus modeled in being fully who he was. Hiding my self and gifts in the closet? Well—that is the antithesis of what he modeled.

Bringing my whole self out into the open puts me at risk for attack. Showing up fully, I am naked and vulnerable.

I don't know how caterpillar years translate into human years. If it's anything close to dog years, I'm right on track. Transformation can't be rushed. It takes as long as it takes. Perhaps breaking free from the chrysalis is sweeter for the wait. Once transformed, going back inside the cocoon is not an option. Flying is.

Who am I now that Helen is gone? I'm the same person I was before, yet always changing. *What will I do without her?* Instead of staying hidden in the closet, cozied up with her, I will come out into the world. Stepping into fullness, what once seemed like a dream feels possible. Owning my whole self and my gifts brings abundance. Freedom belongs to me now.

I am a Fucking Shaman Who Loves Jesus. Make of it what you will. The words mean what they mean to you. As for me, I AM.

May it be your tenth year!

THE STRATEGY

Self-knowledge and healing are processes, not events. Let yourself continue on the path and open to all that reveals itself. It is okay to change, transform, or do an about-face. Not only is it okay, it is necessary.

1. Introduce yourself to the Enneagram. The path to discovering your type is *"Know Yourself"*. Two keys: What is your native energy center (head, heart, or gut)? And what motivates you? Several typing tests are available, but be forewarned: Every test I have taken gave me the wrong result. If you choose to take a test, use it as a starting point. Read books. Listen to talks on YouTube. Take a class. You can find the classes I teach when you check out my website or Facebook page. Email me if you can't find what you are looking for. This rich tool can take you on a lifetime's journey.

2. Ask the question: "Who am I?" Over the next several days or even weeks, listen and watch for answers. You might get signs in nature as I did from the woolly worms. You might overhear a conversation. Perhaps the answer is in the next song on the radio. Maybe the Jerry in your life will tell you about his conversation with someone who knows you and you, too, will receive an anointing. Look for synchronicities. Journal about whatever you notice, even if it doesn't make sense at the time.

3. "Who or what is Spirit?" "How am I related to Spirit (Godde, the Divine, or whatever you resonate with)?" Get to know your connection. You need not believe in Godde. Everyone has a spiritual life. Journal your thoughts, feelings, and impressions. Meditate. Let this dimension reveal itself to you. Having a sounding board or spiritual director helps some people to clarify. Writing is good, but having a person who can ask clarifying or deepening questions expands awareness.

4. Be still and close your eyes. Go inside and ask, "What do I know about me that I am afraid to tell anyone else?" Be honest. You don't have to do anything about it yet. Notice. Write it down. What do you fear will happen if you tell others? How might your life become freer and more abundant if you do start telling and show up as that?

5. Find a mirror. A human mirror. Who knows you? Who loves you? Enemies and frenemies can be mirrors, too, but start gently. If you don't have someone you trust, maybe you need a "paid-for" friend—a coach or therapist. Find someone who will see your best self through their eyes of love. Ask them, "What is my greatest strength?" Or "What do you see as my gift to the world?" Take it in. See if it rings

136 | WEALTH CODES

true for you. Only you can know for sure if what they see is true of you. If it is not, reflect on what you are putting out there. Consider the freedom of being truly yourself instead.

Each of these can be used individually or use them in series. Revisit the questions from time to time to remind yourself you are looking for the answers.

Use your imagination. Imagination is a shamanic tool. It's not fantasy or make-believe. Imagination originates in other realms within us where we create, dream, learn, and transform. We find power in those realms to bring forth into everyday reality what our soul desires and what the Divine desires for our soul.

If you decide you want a coach, spiritual director, or paid-for friend, I would be honored to walk with you on this journey and hold space for you to explore. Connect with me through my website and Facebook. If you want a mirror, I'm polished and ready.

Wanda Tucker is a contemporary shaman, energy healer, certified spiritual director, and coach. She is also a licensed professional counselor and licensed massage therapist in Oregon where she has practiced for 40 years. As an ordained minister in the Universal Life Church, she loves performing marriage ceremonies.

Her work with individuals and couples addresses the whole person— mind, body, soul, and spirit. She has extensive training in energy therapies and trauma treatment. Working with the Enneagram brings depth to the emotional, psychological, and spiritual work she facilitates. Exploring dreams and the dreamtime further expands the work. Spirit taught her a method of dreamtime meditation to share.

You can access her services from anywhere in the world if you have Internet access. Conventional psychotherapy is available in Oregon only. You will find information about Enneagram classes she teaches on her virtual pages.

Wanda hangs out at home with her three-legged Manx cat. She hopes to make the Big Island of Hawaii her home in the near future. Wherever she travels she finds a labyrinth to walk, deepening her experience of spirit in that locale.

To make an appointment, email or call the phone number listed on her pages.

Connect with Wanda:
Website: http://wandatucker.com
Resources: http://wandatucker.com/resources
Facebook: https://www.facebook.com/wandatuckermalpclmt
By email: wanda@wandatucker.com

CHAPTER 14

STOP OVERWORKING AND START OVERFLOWING

USING HUMAN DESIGN TO CREATE FREEDOM AND ABUNDANCE

Kristi H. Sullivan, Human Design Expert, Author, Speaker

MY STORY

Six months. I had less than half a year to figure out what to do with my life, whether to continue with a career I'd built for nearly 20-plus years or determine if I was going to take another path—and figure out how to make money. The pressure was on, felt from all sides. Co-workers asked, "Do you need help finding another job?" My family wondered, "What's your plan?" Friends inquired, "What will you do now?"

It started on what I thought was a typical day at my office, except for the fact that I was scheduled to have my annual review. But that didn't happen. Instead, I walked into a meeting room, was invited to sit down, and immediately knew something was off. I told myself, *Breathe*—as I did in so many yoga classes over the last 20 years, while I was delivered the unexpected news that my job was being eliminated. Although part of me was excited for the newfound freedom and space to venture into something new, I also felt the typical disappointment, anger, and rejection that usually accompanies a layoff. Not to mention fear—of the unknown, change, the future, responsibility, and especially of the risk of failure or the results of success.

Luckily, a few years earlier, I discovered Human Design, a system that explains your unique energetic blueprint based on your birthdate. I sometimes call it "astrology on steroids" or "the owner's manual of your operating system." Imagine you're traveling along your life path—Human Design is the unique car transporting you along the journey. It goes much deeper than other personal self-assessments and helps you understand who you are at your core versus who you are not or who you might be programmed to be (influenced by the conditioning received in your upbringing and during life experiences.)

Learning about my unique Human Design helped me understand that responding to opportunities (as a Generator type) would provide me with the next steps in my life path and align me with success and abundance more easily than if I tried to initiate, push, or force things to happen. This was very different from my conditioning to work hard and then harder if needed. While this created success in many ways during my early life, there were also plenty of roadblocks, learning curves, and uphill journeys that sometimes created chaos and confusion. I sometimes felt like a square peg trying to fit into a round hole.

Once I began using my Human Design to navigate my path, things seemed to align differently. I started honoring my specific energy and practiced responding and using my unique decision-making process. I also focused on doing the inner work to clear old programming, shift self-limiting beliefs, and heal past trauma, including ancestral trauma. And I became mindful of how I make decisions, which opportunities to choose, and what the right work is for me to be doing. It was work that paid off.

Shortly after that fateful day at my office, I was having lunch with my friend Robin at a local Indian restaurant, sipping a warm cup of chai (my favorite). After explaining my recent turn of events, she graciously offered me a spot in her upcoming writing program. "But I'm not thinking of writing a book," I told her. "But my guides tell me you should be part of it," she replied. Truthfully, I didn't think of myself as a writer (as much as the editor I became during my marketing career), and journaling was not a typical routine for me. But I decided to say yes, following my gut.

Soon after, a few other opportunities came to me. First, invitations to be part of two masterminds, which helped me explore some ideas for my soon-to-be new business. And then an offer to join a program to hone my speaking skills, definitely an activity I enjoyed and wanted to cultivate more. And then, within six months of my unexpected job news, I learned about an opportunity to write a chapter in a book collaboration (my first of three books I co-authored that year). Those eventually led me to produce my own book a year later, be interviewed on numerous podcasts, speak at various conferences and events, and ultimately create a business following one step after another that arose on my path.

Looking back, I can see the effortless transformation through my Human Design lens. I simply responded to opportunities that felt right in my gut, paid attention to my mindset, beliefs, and thoughts, and focused on self-care to keep me energetically aligned in mind-body-spirit. That was the most important work to creating success and allowing abundance to flow easily.

In recent years, with the experience of the pandemic, work-life shifts (like The Great Resignation), and the acceleration of our human evolution and innovation, abundance is not defined by just money anymore. Our value is no longer designated by our productivity. Fitting into a formula no longer validates our true unique gifts. I believe we're all seeking true freedom and abundance to reflect a more authentic lifestyle.

I continue to use my Human Design to guide my success and freedom in alignment with my uniqueness, and I hope to inspire you to make similar shifts in your life. I'm on a mission to help you *Stop Overworking and Start Overflowing!*

THE STRATEGY

Human Design is called a rabbit hole for a good reason. It's complex and can take years to study. Mastering your design is an ongoing process. I recommend peeling back each layer carefully, and my mentors suggest experimenting with the information to allow time to integrate and embody the unique aspects of your true nature.

I often get asked, "Where do I start?"

I have identified five initial steps to help you navigate the rabbit hole with ease and flow:

1. Explore Your Design (Type, Strategy and Authority)

   First, I recommend going to MyBodyGraph.com or Google a similar website to look up your Human Design. In your chart, take note of your energy type (Manifestor, Projector, Generator/Manifesting Generator, or Reflector), as well as your specific strategy and authority. These are perhaps the most important, life-changing aspects of your unique blueprint, which, when followed correctly, can have transformative effects.

   There are many valuable resources online to help explain the numerous elements of your design and provide a lot of information for self-study. I also suggest engaging with a Human Design practitioner who has studied the system and can provide you with guidance and interpret your chart.

2. Evaluate Your Conditioning (and Decondition)

   Your true nature is how you were encoded at birth, but there are layers from life experiences and generational/cultural programming that affect the expression of our Human Design. We want to understand these layers, particularly the ones that may have an adverse effect, and identify the shifts that can help us become more authentically ourselves.

   This process is very important in helping express your true nature. Do your inner work to decondition any not-self programming, including self-limiting beliefs, negative effects from past traumas, and ancestral and cultural blocks. The more you can heal, shift, and release, the more your design will naturally align and bring you energetic ease and flow.

3. Expand Your Self-Care (and Inner Work)

In addition to making it a priority to follow your Human Design strategy, authority, and understanding of your conditioning, it's also equally important to prioritize your self-care. I believe self-care also has to be unique to you, based on your needs and what feels nurturing.

In some of my other books, I describe self-care in three categories: Occasional (temporary, time-bound, or sporadic actions), Daily (everyday practices with commitment), and Spiritual (deeper activities to evolve and heal, including inner work, mind-body-spirit practices, and self-love). Follow these tips as you expand your self-care:

• Make It a Priority

Put your self (care) first, create a schedule and block times, take frequent breaks, say "no," and set boundaries when needed.

• Keep It Simple

Don't make self-care overwhelming, time-consuming, or expensive, do it in small increments, maybe several times daily, or bookend your day with a few minutes.

• Make It Essential

Don't treat self-care as a luxury or a reward and not even a task. It's a necessity, like the oxygen mask.

Receive my free PDF to create your customized self-care plan on my website: www.KristiHSullivan.com

4. Experiment with Your Design

Understanding the elements of your chart is just the first step; the next is living in your Human Design. Bring awareness to how you're living in alignment, or not, with your energy type, strategy, and authority.

Let's look more closely at the Generators, for example. About 70 percent of the population are Generators (including a subset called Manifesting Generators). While the majority of people are this type, the general advice here also can apply to other types.

Generators have consistent life-force/work-force energy because we have a defined Sacral center (whereas other types are non-sacral beings). This makes Generators ideal for being the busy worker bee. We're designed to get things done and feel satisfied when we're doing the right kind of work that lights us up. When we're not doing the right work, we usually feel frustrated or burned out and are out of alignment with our design.

Be aware of functional burnout. This may look like overworking/ overdoing, being too busy getting things done, or feeling chronically overwhelmed but still continuing to function on a daily basis. This misalignment can lead to frustration, potential health issues, and even doing work that is not aligned with your life purpose and path.

In alignment, Generators feel healthy, sleep well, are rested and energized, and thus, are a magnet for opportunities—and have clarity and wisdom to decide about responding to those opportunities that feel right—and saying no to those that don't.

5. Experience Consistent FLOW

Use the first letters of FLOW to remember these steps as your continue on your Human Design journey!

- **F**ollow Your Strategy and Authority
- **L**ove Your Self (Care)
- **O**vercome Conditioning
- **W**ork In Your Design

For more information about Human Design, I invite you to take my self-guided, 60-minute mini-course, which introduces the energy types and strategies. The course also includes an interactive exercise to help you develop your personalized self-care plan, plus tips and handouts for creating daily rituals. The course is available at KristiHSullivan.thinkific.com.

I also offer monthly Introduction to Human Design webinars and workshops, which you can learn about in my Facebook group: Kristi's Human Design & Self Care Community, or by joining my email updates at www.KristiHSullivan.com.

Please reach out and connect, and may you find the FLOW in life!

XO

Kristi H. Sullivan is a Human Design and self-care expert, author, and speaker on a mission to help busy women stop overworking and start overflowing! She hosts a virtual community for female personal development junkies (like herself) to create better wellness, improve relationships, shift mindsets, and manifest more success, wealth, and freedom—to live their best life by design.

Kristi is the lead author of a best-selling Amazon book called Stop Overworking and Start Overflowing: 25 Ways to Transform Your Life Using Human Design, published in October 2021 with Brave Healer Productions, in collaboration with 25 other Human Design practitioners. She also is co-author of three best-selling collaborative books that were produced during the 2020 pandemic: {The Ultimate Guide to Self-Healing, Vol. 2; The Great Pause: Blessings and Wisdom from COVID-19; and Transformation 2020}, in addition to her latest books, {The Ultimate Guide to Creating Your Soul-Aligned Business, and Wealth Codes}, launched in 2022.

Kristi teaches internationally, both in person and virtually, and has been featured on dozens of podcasts, workshops, and conferences, including the Women in Business Summit, Women Future Conference, Wealthy Healer Conference, Coping with Trauma Summit, Forgiveness Summit, Awakening to a New World Summit, and EmpowerConn.

Her journey for mind, body, and spiritual development began nearly two decades ago as a certified yoga teacher (RYT200). During the pandemic, she retired from a marketing communications career and became a full-time solopreneur, developing her business online, where she connects her community to resources and support for transformation. She encourages her clients and students to be inspired and empowered to authentically align with their true selves to manifest abundance and live their best life.

Kristi is a 4/6 Generator with a passion for connecting with like-minded, inspiring souls and sharing her experiences and lessons as a role model to other life-long students.

Connect with Kristi:
Website: KristiHSullivan.com
On Facebook: Facebook.com/groups/KristiHSullivan
Or follow @KristiHSullivan
Amazon author page: http://www.amazon.com/author/kristihsullivan

CHAPTER 15

BEYOND SORRY!

COMMUNICATION MASTERY FOR
EXPANDED RELATIONSHIP JOY

Lulu Trevena, Quantum Healer, Soulful Living Coach

MY STORY

"Sorry!" She screamed at me through the phone.

I felt the assault hit my ear and vibrate in my head with a hot sting.

She is clearly not sorry, shouting s-o-r-r-y at me. Ouch! You've got to be kidding. That is not the way to show compassion or to make this right. I soothed myself by holding my hand to my heart and earnestly slid the phone onto my desk, aiming for some distance between her and me.

I wriggled my chair back along the plush rug—a little more distance still needed.

I turned my mobile phone to speaker. *At least now, whatever her follow-up would be, I won't allow it to enter my body up close, with bitter force.* Instead, I intended to let it float around in space before allowing it in—a little more radius.

My pause seemed to give rise to her anger. "Did you hear me? I said I am sorry. How many times do I need to say that?" Huffing at the end for emphasis. My whole office now felt cloaked with the heaviness of unrequited care via the speaker amplification. Sting intensified. Kindness absent, hostility hitting me again. I felt tears welling from a deep pit in me.

Feeling the tightness in my jaw, I took a long slow deep breath, unclenched my teeth, and with my heart pounding, in as even a tone as I could muster, I offered, "I can't believe you think shouting sorry at me would work. That does not feel sincere and does not create a feeling of reconnection for me; you are not showing me you're sorry."

Click. The phone went dead before I finished my sentence. She hung up on me! I think I accurately translated her action to mean, "fuck you." Historically the slamming of a phone was abrupt. With mobile phones, it's like a silent cavern.

I slumped back in my chair, lifted my knees, and hugged them tightly. I allowed the heaviness to encourage my eyes to close. This was a position I often used as a child, and it was still reassuring in my 50s. I found my equilibrium. What was not reassuring was her rancor and unwillingness to acknowledge her actions, address my hurt, and now her belligerent phone disconnection!

I think it's important to seek space to reflect and take a time out if you feel triggered or emotionally flooded. Relationships require kindness. Hanging up on someone is unkind. It's important to state that you need the time out; otherwise, it's a dramatic severing in our often-fragile human connections. Having empathy and humility is important. If possible, it's best to respond to your need for space and not react to a trigger of anger. Psychology calls it disrespectful and abusive. I believe we ultimately want to care for each other's hearts and create safety as best we can.

"We all seek honest, deep connections and need to feel safe.
Unkindness, side-stepping, and wishy-washy just won't do.
A sincere apology can transform your life and the lives of the
people you care for and love."

~Lulu Trevena

Let me touch on the overuse of the word sorry by stating that it's flung around all too often with no energy of care or kindness, diluting its meaning. Facilitating women in groups for years, I've noticed women say sorry like a standard response to anything and everything, in essence, all too often, for their existence. Please stop that, ladies.

I intentionally left it a day and sent her a short, sincere text message: "Let's chat soon. The other day finished a little abruptly. You are important to me."

As children, perhaps we weren't taught how to be sincere in our apologies. To repair, take responsibility, restore, and re-nourish through our clear and kind communication. I remember all too well saying sorry and not meaning it or crossing my fingers behind my back to naively make it invalid many times as a youth. As an adult, I've felt the sting and fracture when others aren't willing to make amends, or the absent-minded throw-away sort, a sorry tossed in the air hoping it lands and acts as a salve, yet void of sincerity. We need to offer each other the big, juicy, nourishing apologies—because it matters.

I believe it takes consistent self-awareness to be fully responsible and accountable for our actions, especially when we've hurt others. When we're sincere with our apologies, we accept responsibility for our actions and behaviors. We seek to make amends to the offended person directly. We meet on the bridge of reconnection. This is heart and soul work.

Our own personal healing and transformational work require us to be honest—unwaveringly honest *with* ourselves and *to* ourselves. Over the years, I've had to lay down my righteousness and feelings of low self-worth, often loosely depicted as stubborn pride. Even when my inner dialogue was protesting: *Come on, you know they are in the wrong!* On one occasion to a family member, with remorse, I said, "I intentionally said that to hurt you, after you hurt me. I am sorry. I ask for your forgiveness, please." This was a humble attempt even though it was laced with some justification, but it was sincere and transparent. Like a breath of fresh air, this was kindly met with, "Thank you for your honesty, I appreciate that," opening the door to create a richer connection.

Many might say we also were not taught how to clearly ask for our needs and get them met without some tactic or manipulation. We all know how that feels; yuck! Relationships require each person to show up—the more intimate, the more we need to show up, share our vulnerabilities, express our feelings, and clearly ask for what we need. It begins with communication and continues with actions that show others they're valued and important. Learn each other's love languages. We cannot operate as we always have and get different results!

It's time to grow up our apologizing.

When we're asking to be met fully by another, we're entering a different galaxy, and there will be turbulence on entering this new atmosphere. Our willingness, capacity, and love are required, as are some navigational tools, which I will share in the strategy section.

Mistakes, misunderstandings, and hurts are a part of life. How we meet them in ourselves can hinder or enhance our lives. When we address misunderstandings, mistakes, and hurts with another sincerely, whether as the recipient or the donor, this is character gleaming. No one is perfect; we all have our failings. When we show willingness and flexibility in our capacity to be responsible and accountable for our actions, words, and behaviors and attempt to unravel the messiness of life with a high measure of sincerity, we meet ourselves and others with loving communication—communion.

We build safety and trust. We feel met completely. We ignite mastery.

If we truly want great relationships, we must meet each other—heart naked. Be courageous and vulnerable, which means not quite knowing how to do that at times, and not assuming or thinking we do. Be willing to learn to unpack your baggage and build a container of safety with the sometimes unhealed parts of yourself.

Stay curious. Each individual is unique and requires different things to be met amiably. Ask heartfelt questions. This is how we honor, respect, and love each other. How someone shows up to sincerely heal a hurt or an experience of pain that fractured the relationship also shows you the degree to which they're seeking love, connection, and joy with you. When someone brings hurt to another, they embody courage and maturity and show value for the relationship.

"You know how important you are to me," is how I wholeheartedly entered the call. She said, "Yes, I do."

"The reason I came to you with this hurt is because I don't want it to be in the way of our friendship—and it is for me at the moment. I need to know I can trust you in the future, to listen to how your actions hurt me." I let the words glide from my tongue with calmness. "I ask that you please not hang the phone up on me. I feel uncared for when you do that in frustration." I imagined a spaciousness around me that I hoped extended through the phone and directly to my friend. "Will you be able to do that?"

She blurted out, "I am so sorry, Lulu. I value you and our friendship. I see where I overstepped your boundary, I am truly sorry I hurt you, and I am sincerely sorry for hanging up on you when you tried to address that with me. I have a lot happening in my life at the moment." I heard her words verging on tears, release imminent.

I embraced her apology with, "Thank you for your apology; I feel your sincerity. Is there anything you need from me to support you around this?" Tissues on hand for us both.

There was more to this healing conversation that was possible after the sincerity was present. It was healing for us both. People only feel the sincerity when it's sincere. If in doubt, ask. "Please let me know if you need anything more to support me in healing this with you." People need to know you care—really care. When we move on haphazardly without clearing the air or mending the fractures, we create a breeding ground that'll weaken the relationship. I have experienced this too.

In our follow-up telephone conversation, we recommitted again to what we both need and want and how important our friendship is. This is not rehashing; this is love in action—showing up, actioning our commitment.

Every part of our life is about relationships. Our challenges and celebrations happen in relationships with others. Each one of us needs to feel safe and sincerely cared for. We need communication, especially difficult communication, to be like a meeting at a round table—equals and allies, givers, and receivers, wholeheartedly willing and less like two sides in battle, with weapons just out of sight.

"When we give, we lose nothing."

~Unknown

THE STRATEGY

COMMUNICATION MASTERY FOR EXPANDED RELATIONSHIP JOY THROUGH SINCERE APOLOGY

Much of our personal healing work is an inner journey. While it's helpful to be supported by practitioners in the therapeutic field, we must take the actions ourselves. From this place of our own healing, unraveling, and reclaiming, we have a greater capacity to do the deeper healing that happens *between* places, one to another—rich work indeed, where interpersonal abundance can flourish.

When we show up for ourselves, we build self-respect and tend to those places where we held parts of ourselves at bay, unacknowledged, hidden, in shame, guilt, mistrust, or even disgust.

When we show up for others, we're making a declaration to deepen that relationship, build a bridge, expand our love together, and allow evolution in our intimacy and connection.

There is much written about forgiveness; the essence is present here. I'm offering to support removing the elephant in the room by creating spaciousness with communication mastery through a sincere apology. May each of us learn the art and skill of apologizing wholeheartedly and build trust in our relationships to bring hurts and grievances to each other to repair with tender and bold, courageous hearts.

"When one forgives, two souls are set free."

~Unknown

I want you to think of apologizing as a repairing and restoring gift to another and yourself. Think of it like a formula or recipe, one which requires certain elements always but where you can add some garnishes to compliment.

Unfortunately, too readily, people's conscience has been trained to shift the guilt to someone else. This shows a lack of sensitivity and an inability to look at their own actions and behaviors.

"A sincere apology needs to be at a higher caliber, bringing
forward unquestionable care to the person and the relationship.
It must supersede the pain or hurt experienced. The receiver is the
acknowledging barometer of this."

~Lulu Trevena

Start small. Don't try tackling that gnarly, historic, betraying red-hot situation quite yet. You need to build trust, especially with yourself, in this process. In-person apologies are best; on the phone is the next best. Texting or emailing an apology is not suggested.

THE APOLOGY ELEMENTS

Awareness

Commit to facing situations fully, address them bravely, and seek repair and restoration. Always keep a tender heart for yourselves and others. It is just ineffective to stuff it down, bypass, avoid, pretend it didn't happen, or numb out with any addictive substance or activity.

"The person who refuses to recognize the need for an apology will
have a life filled with broken relationships."

~Gary Chapman

Intention

Be embodied and grounded in your intention to repair and restore. You're meeting with gifting the other. No justification, no thinking someone will win, and someone will lose, no pointing out the other person's misgiving or mistakes in the process.

Timing

Create time to speak: Not on the go, but a time when both people can be fully present. No distractions, no phones. Commit to doing it promptly, but not when triggered or flooded. Our bodies somatically have a way of leaving energy in the body that can get blocked; ideally, try to restore and repair it within 72 hours.

Listening

Commit to listening from your heart to theirs. If someone brings you a hurt of theirs to be addressed with you, have compassion. Their feelings need to be validated—no shaming how someone feels.

Stay on One Situation, State it Clearly

Share the incident and hurt clearly. While it is tempting to bring in the whole historic weighted argument, resist—no guilting, no ammunition.

Show Remorse

Acknowledge Their Feelings

Own Your Part, Embody Accountability

Remorse, empathy, and compassion are essential elements.

Sincere words to use:

I was careless, thoughtless, insensitive, out of place, or rude.

I know I hurt you deeply, I am sorry I caused you pain.

I know what I did was wrong, you have every right to be upset.

My actions were unacceptable, and you did not deserve that kind of treatment.

I will rebuild your trust; I realize I will need to show with my actions.

Can you forgive me?

Acknowledge Their Relationship with You

Speak words that show your commitment, your unwavering care, and their importance and value in your life generously.

Ask For What You Need

Make requests, not demands. Find a meeting happy point. Ask for an agreement, and ask them to say what they agree to. Stay with this one situation.

Ask What They Need From You

Offer support, let them know you want to work together, support them with their agreement and show that their needs are valuable to you. Stay with this one situation.

Reconnection Confirmation

People only feel the sincerity when it is sincere. If in doubt, ask. "Please let me know if you need anything more to support me in healing this with you." People need to know you care—really care.

The receiver needs to feel heard, understood, and valued and sincerely have the relationship restored.

The apologizer needs to be calm, humble, sincere, responsible for the hurt caused, and active in repairing and restoring the relationship.

"Expanded joy is a freedom available to us all. Human connection can be so exquisite; be the type of person that adds to and enhances that."

~Lulu Trevena

Sincere apologies and restored hurts are a new frontier for emotional, relational, generational, and spiritual healing. May we aim to be wholeheartedly courageous and always willing to learn and grow.

I want you to have a handy copy of these apology elements. You will find my resource, Communication Mastery for Expanded Relationship Joy, here: https://livelifewithwonder.com/collaborative-books/

I have found giving wholehearted, sincere apologies and receiving them has restored and repaired relationships and connections, which has deepened them sweetly. I carry the blessing of these to support other relationships or challenges. It is the gold, treasure, and abundance, allowing for something richer to grow or bloom.

Which I believe is what we all want. I do. I want that for you, too.

Unhealed hurts get in the way of joy and joyous connections—we can choose today to intentionally be the gift to each other's healing. Return the elephants to the jungle and create spaciousness in our hearts, relationships, and all areas of our lives.

"To give and to receive are one in truth."

~A Course in Miracles

Please reach out to me for soulful coaching and communication mastery for expanding relationship joy: www.livelifewithwonder.com

Lulu Trevena is an award-winning author of the stunning hardcover art and poetic prose book, Soul Blessings, winning the 2018 Silver Nautilus Book Award. She became a published author after age 55.

She is a women's workshop leader, quantum healing practitioner, soulful living coach, Art of Feminine Presence®, licensed teacher, speaker, artist, and mother. Lulu is passionate about shifting the societal narrative about women and age. She believes now is the time for the rising consciousness of the planet and for women to live their purpose and passions unabashedly.

She is the creator of the card deck *"Moments of Transformation,"* and the hardcover journal, *Epiphany Journal and Playbook.*

Available at: www.livelifewithwonder.com/shop/

Lulu is the founder and Creatrix of *Live Life with Wonder*

In 2021 she was the lead author of the international Amazon bestseller

Wholehearted Wonder Women 50 Plus: Courage, Confidence and Creativity at Any Age.

In 2020, 2021, and 2022, she became a collaborative author in Amazon bestselling books, *The Ultimate Guide to Self-Healing Volume 3, Find Your Voice: Save Your Life, Sacred Medicine: Mystical Practices for Ecstatic Living, The Ultimate Guide to Self-Healing Volume 5,* and *Strong Mothers: More than a Survival Guide.*

Connect with Lulu at:
Website: www.livelifewithwonder.com
Email: lulu@livelifewithwonder.com or lulu.trevena@gmail.com
Facebook: www.facebook.com/livelifewithwonder
Instagram: www.instagram.com/livelifewithwonder

VITALITY

This section of the book brings you into enhanced vitality which pairs perfectly with the element of fire.

The divine spark of fire lives within us all. Its warrior-like energy activates, takes action, protects us when needed, and burns away anything not serving our highest good. Its life force energy ignites sexual power with passion and purpose and invites us to savor life without shame or judgment.

By harnessing our power, we illuminate our spiritual path and reclaim the lost pieces of ourselves. Fire symbolizes alchemical transformation, like turning lead into gold. Its heat will transform anything you offer to its dancing flames.

With that in mind, you're invited to alchemize your life. It's time to rejuvenate and increase the vitality within you by transforming whatever is not currently working.

An ecstatic pleasure comes after we burn away our limiting beliefs, fears, and worries.

Feel the burn move through you, for you, and with you so you can ignite your sacred flame and divine essence with confidence.

RITUAL: Have an unlit candle and matches, a fire-safe bowl, paper, and pen nearby. Set the space with additional lit candles for ambiance to activate sensations and desires you want to draw into your life for this ritual.

Take a moment to be present with the element of fire. Gaze at its dancing flames and let it awaken the fire within you. If you have multiple candles, give them all your attention individually with appreciation and connect with their fiery center.

Take the unlit candle in your hands and bring it to your heart. The candle symbolizes the mind, body, and Spirit connection. Place your desires into the candle with intention. When you're ready, light the wick. Gaze upon it for a moment with the question, "What shall I release today to bring more vitality, passion, and purpose into my life?"

Listen carefully, paying attention to your thoughts, feelings, and emotions. Write everything you think and feel down. When you've received everything you need to know, rip the paper into several pieces and place it in your fire-safe bowl.

Say, **"I release this and anything else I hold intentionally or unintentionally, consciously or unconsciously that's blocking my life force energy and vitality."**

Light the fire and watch it burn. Feel it all release from your body as you surrender everything to the fire with love and appreciation.

Receive complimentary resources to support your expansion at
www.jenpiceno.com/resources

CHAPTER 16

HARMONIZE YOUR DIVINE MASCULINE AND FEMININE ENERGY

GET SHIT DONE AND FEEL GOOD DOING IT!

Kelly Myerson, MA, OTR

MY STORY

Feeling into the ease of a free Saturday after the holidays, I sat mindlessly scrolling on Instagram and sipping my coffee. Opening up the shared album again, I perused the smiling photos of my siblings, cousin, and families from New Year's. Four years felt like too long to wait to be together. I clutched my heart feeling the gratitude for our time together.

I was suddenly pulled out of my musings by a text message which popped onto my screen for my sister and me.

Mom: I fell last night, and Daddy hurt his back helping me up.

Shit. My heart began to race, and my mind tried to keep up. *How badly are they hurt? Did she hit her head? Should I be calling an ambulance? Why didn't they call an ambulance?*

I was interrupted by a text from my sister, "Call me."

Dialing her number, I walked upstairs to my bedroom and gently closed the door.

She picked up before I even heard it ring.

"What the hell!" She barked. "Kelly, this is the second time she's fallen in the past couple of weeks! I'm really worried."

"Me too, Jill," I went on, "I'm going back up there today. Yesterday, I cleaned the heck out of the kitchen sink. It was the top priority on her list."

We both laughed, more out of exasperation than humor.

"Jill, I think I should take the next week off work. Mommy has a couple of appointments, and I want to go with her to talk to the leukemia specialist." I was surprised to feel conviction in my choice. It was a quick, intuitive choice—no overthinking involved.

I sighed. Just a few days before, Mom texted us both, "Can you both call me later?" The words felt like a sucker punch to the gut.

I flashed back to our conversation in September 2021 when she sent much of the same text.

"Girls, I have a pre-leukemia condition called MDS. The doctors told me it's secondary to the chemo and stem cell transplants from when I had multiple myeloma." Jill and I launched into asking all the questions about the myelodysplastic syndrome, and I took copious notes.

"They're just watching my numbers for now. There's no need for treatment." I hung onto those words—clung to them, actually. I desperately prayed for a miracle. She was nearly 14 years cancer-free.

But cancer came back.

So, on a cold Saturday in January 2022, I headed back up to my parent's house to see what I could do to help. Placing a KN-95 on my face, I knocked on the door and stepped inside. Immediately, I was met with two little furry faces barking and whining at me.

I stooped down to pet them. "Hi, Cookie and Gus," I cooed. They pushed at each other in an effort to be most in contact with my hands—*sweet little pups.*

"Hello?" I called out.

"I'm in here," my mom softly called from the living room. My footsteps creaked as I walked down the hall and into the living room. As I rounded the corner, I met her eyes. Her face worked up a smile.

"How are you, Mom?" I asked while removing my coat, hat, and scarf, placing them on the back of the folding chair deliberately across the room.

"I'm okay, a little sore. The damn pain in my throat is making me miserable." On the coffee table in front of her, several bottles of medication for her throat were lined up.

"Have you been able to eat today, Mom?"

"Not really. I had a little protein shake. It just hurts so bad."

"I can imagine it does! Have they figured out how you got ulcers in your esophagus?"

"No! The doctor said they're like what they see in AIDS patients!" I could tell from her response, the comparison to AIDS patients was not encouraging.

"That's crazy, Mom." The floor above us creaked, and I could hear my dad slowly making his way down the stairs. "Hi, Dad, how are you?"

"Hello, Kelly. I'm a little sore." He moved stiffly, reaching for his lumbar cushion, and sat gingerly in his recliner.

"I'm taking this week off work to be with you guys. I want to help you with all the appointments and getting the house in order."

With a look of concern, my mom responded. "Can you afford the time off?" Even in her current state, my mom was more worried about me than herself.

"I'll figure it out. It's more important for me to be here right now." The look of relief washed over both of their faces. At 45 years old, I couldn't pass up the opportunity to be a support for the two people who always put my siblings and me first.

"Tuesday, I have an MRI. Wednesday, I see the urologist. Thursday is the appointment with the leukemia specialist to go over my numbers and find out what's next." I entered each appointment into my digital calendar as she called them out.

"What do you guys need most today?" Their faces looked so tired. I wanted to take away any extra burdens. It also felt good to get busy and not allow my mind to wander too much. *Take one moment at a time, Kelly. Don't get yourself too deep into thinking about scenarios.*

On Monday, when I returned to help my mom take a shower, she seemed less steady on her feet. "Isn't it easier to use the shower chair, Mom?"

"Not really. It's helpful to sit on when I get out of the shower." The poor woman put two daughters through degrees in occupational therapy. No way she was going to get by without us recommending durable medical equipment!

"And, you should really have the bedside commode set up bedside."

"I know," she stopped me by raising her hand, "Jill told me." I let it go for the moment. Once she was dressed, I took her under her right arm and helped her stand up. We walked slowly to the bedroom, and she sat on the ottoman, breathing quickly, her face reflecting the pain she was experiencing.

"Okay, Mom, what can I do for you here?" She sighed as she looked around the room. "Well, you could start by putting away the baskets of folded laundry."

We worked together for the next hour or so. I tidied her bedroom, following each of her instructions completely and without question.

For the next few days, we went to appointments and I stayed by her side at home. My dad and I tried to encourage her to eat.

On Thursday, my dad, sister, mom, and I arrived at the hospital to meet with the oncologist. My dad went to park the car.

Entering the lobby, we were informed only one of us could go with her to her appointment. There was a momentary twinge of people-pleasing in my head, but I ignored it.

I pushed my mom down the hallway in the wheelchair, Jill trailing several steps behind us. We rode the elevator feeling like criminals. Once we reached the floor, we found seats and waited for my mom's name to be called.

"Miriam?" Jill and I looked at each other. We moved to the doorway, and a nurse glared at us. He looked more like a bouncer.

"Only one of you can come in." He folded his arms.

"Can you please ask the doctor if my sister can join us?" I pleaded with the nurse holding back tears. "My mom's finding out about her leukemia treatment!"

"You shouldn't even have been able to come up here!" He paused. Then he seemed to resign, "Alright, you can come in," he said, pointing in my direction, then gesturing at Jill, "You wait out here, and I'll ask the doctor."

I followed the nurse to the examination room with my mom. I carefully moved her wheelchair forward and back to get it neatly between two chairs. Moments later, Jill slipped into the room. We smiled at each other with our eyes.

Although my mom had been crying out in pain on and off all day, when meeting with the doctor, she seemed more herself. She answered questions and asked for clarification on the chemotherapy she'd be receiving starting Monday.

"My daughters are both occupational therapists, so they probably have lots of questions for you." We all chuckled. Leaving the appointment, we had a stack of literature and a schedule for chemo the next week.

The next morning, when I went to her house, she struggled to hold a conversation. She was crying and moaning. She wouldn't eat. We couldn't get her to walk much.

I pulled my dad aside in the kitchen. "Dad, I think we have to do something. I don't feel like we're able to help her here." We both began to cry. I hugged him tightly. I knew no matter what, I'd be sticking by his side.

I called her oncologist, and we made plans to have her start treatment as an inpatient, but we needed to get her to the hospital.

"911, what's your emergency?"

"My mom is sick, and we've already talked with her doctors to get her admitted into the hospital, but we can't get her to the car. We need an ambulance."

"Okay, we're sending someone to you."

Tearing off my mask, I wept, watching her leave on the stretcher alone. *What if she doesn't come back?* But in my heart, I felt grateful I was there, despite the painful decision we had to make.

I took off work to sit by her bedside in the hospital. I prioritized her even as my heart was breaking. It became apparent during her hospital stay that the cancer had already rapidly progressed.

We brought her home from hospice on February 17, 2022. My brother Chris came in from California, and the five of us were under the same roof for the first time in years.

In her last moments on Earth, we sat around her hospital bed in the living room. Chris pulled back the curtains as the sun rose. "There are two blue jays out there."

He looked at Jill and me, "Some believe they symbolize loyalty." He didn't need to say what he thought as he began to cry. Our parents spent nearly 47 years together.

Jill and Chris stepped out of the room. I sat on my mom's left side. Her breathing was erratic, and she looked unsettled. *How can I ease her mind and body?*

Immediately, I recalled nights with my son singing him to sleep. Leaning towards her and holding her hand, I steadied my voice and began to sing.

"Blackbird singing in the dead of night, take these broken wings and learn to fly."

A few minutes later, Jill came into the room with no knowledge I had been singing and said, "I want to play *Blackbird* for her." We were feeling the same pull to soothe her passing. The synchronicity confirmed she needed music.

Chris and I quietly nodded in agreement. My mom was a huge music lover. As *Blackbird* played on Jill's iPhone, a single tear slipped out my mom's left eye. I gently wiped it away with the side of my pointer finger.

"What should we play next?" I asked.

Jill played some of her lifelong favorites, *"God Only Knows"* by the Beach Boys, *"Here Comes the Sun"* by the Beatles, and *"Teach Your Children"* by Crosby, Stills, and Nash.

Chris then played *"Pigs on the Wing"* by Pink Floyd. Jill followed with George Harrison's *"Give Me Love."* We ended with *"My Sweet Lord."* Over the last couple of songs, her breath slowed to seemingly once a minute until it stopped, and she was gone.

My mom left us Sunday, February 20, 2022. We weren't ready to let her go. She was our voice of reason and who we sought out for advice. She left a legacy of love.

It was in this dark time I realized how far I had come in my own healing journey. I used my intuition to guide me even though much of my life was spent on perfectionism, overthinking, and people-pleasing.

I trusted my heart, my voice, and my gut. I got out of my head. I lived my life in flow.

There was no greater evidence of my vitality and my abundance than the capacity to drop everything and shift into caring for my mom. I became the rock my family needed, and I didn't sacrifice my own well-being.

THE STRATEGY

Is your vitality lacking? Perhaps you've also been through, or you're currently facing dark times? Maybe it's divorce, overwhelm from overworking, or health struggles of your own? Maybe, like me, you're caregiving for others?

How do you go from the masculine energy of getting it all done and infusing the feminine energy of ease and flow?

You need to prioritize yourself, mind, body, and spirit for optimal vitality. Let's begin with your mind.

Silence the noise. Mindset is everything. My greatest weakness used to be an overactive mind. I lost so much energy stuck inside my head. These are strategies I use to free my mind. They are simple and potent magic!

Stop overcommitting. Just because you can, doesn't mean you should. Reserve your time and energy for invitations for which you feel a whole body, "hell, yes!" This can be a "hell, yes" with joy or, as I felt with my mom, a "hell, yes, I believe this is 100% what I should be doing now."

Silence your inner critic. She's sneaky. She'll show up unannounced and trigger your inner child. Call her out. I tell her, "Not now, darling." If she stirs up your inner child, be prepared to pause and nurture your inner child.

Engage in activities that nourish your mind and spirit daily. The more time you spend intentionally feeding your mind, the more aware you are when unhealthy thought patterns arrive. Choose to nourish your mind based on joy. I love meditation, podcasts, books on tape, and finding uplifting memes on Instagram.

Silence the outer critics. Sometimes they are actual people in your life with strong opinions about who you should be and what you should do. Don't "should" on yourself, and don't let them "should" on you.

Sometimes the outer critics show up when you mindlessly scroll and get into comparison mode. Be a conscious consumer of social media. Put limits on how much you digest other people's energy. Get crystal clear on who you are and where you're going.

On my own path, my biggest growth has happened when I'm learning more about myself and how I operate best. Two of the most impactful practices have been entering my Akashic Records and delving into Human Design.

I'm a mystic nerd. I love to geek out on science and all things mystic. I'm not for everyone. But I know the clearer I see myself, the more magnetic I become for the exact people I want in my squad. If you're interested in who they are, check out The Mystic Nerd Squad Podcast, https://www.beingwellwithkelly.com/podcast.

Get organized. Clutter and mess aren't literal noise, but if you've been in a chaotic space, it screams at you. What's worked for me is a fine balance of masculine disciplines, keeping my spaces and processes organized mixed with the feminine energy of devotion to beautifying and using my creativity. For example, I use Trello for project management. It serves my need to be organized, and the utility is fun and whimsical. I keep a monthly whiteboard with my calendar and appointments, but I use colored markers to make it pretty. I clean up my kitchen at the end of the day while listening to classic rock or a podcast.

Be honest with yourself about what you need. Let's get real. Vitality will elude you if you're not taking care of your health and well-being. Be honest, babe. Where are you falling down on the job of radical self-care? (I'm re-reading this piece of advice for myself!)

Self-care is all abuzz these days. Let's keep it simple. Begin with the basics for humans. We need to sleep well, eat well, exercise, and cultivate a healthy, toxin-free environment.

The foundation for radical self-care is the cultivation of habits. I've created my own model for shifting into better habits, starting with sleep. If you're struggling with sleep, reach out. I'm a sleep specialist, and we can get you your best sleep ever. Check out my resource page for more info on fostering better habits and getting great sleep, https://www.beingwellwithkelly.com/wealthcodesresources.

I spent most of my life great at getting shit done while simultaneously treating my body and mind like crap. It's not a sustainable model for humans, especially when you're driven by purpose.

My vitality is dependent on freedom in my mind and heart, an overflow of energy in my body, and a deep connection to purpose, spirit, and my people.

I hope you're feeling empowered to improve your vitality. We've got big work to do on this planet. Get clear on who you are, silence the critics (within and without), cultivate a self-care plan for optimal well-being, and go get shit done and feel great while you do it!

What's your first step in your journey to optimal vitality? I love hearing about the first steps, and it's a great way to build accountability! Send me an email and share your first step at kelly@beingwellwithkelly.com. Be sure to visit my resource page for more tips and some beautiful pictures of my mom https://www.beingwellwithkelly.com/wealthcodesresources

Kelly is an author, podcaster, and sleep specialist who will cultivate space for you to emerge from stress and overwhelm to lead and savor the life of your dreams. As an occupational therapist, Kelly has over 20 years of experience specializing in sensory integration techniques. Her background in occupational therapy provides a unique perspective on development and the human condition. She values personal power and inspires all of us to build our capacity to surpass our potential by living in alignment with our true selves.

With a master's degree in Strategic Communication and Leadership, she brings data-driven techniques leading to lasting change. Over the past 15 years, she has experience teaching topics including self-care, leadership development, outcome measurement, sensory processing related to anxiety, and sleep. Kelly is a holistic entrepreneur bringing a wealth of experience and fun science to the table, whether speaking to engaging guests on The *Mystic Nerd Squad Podcast* or supporting women in revitalizing their lives.

You can check out her four chapters in the Amazon Best-selling books, *Sacred Sleep: Cultivating the Best Sleep of Your Life in The Ultimate Guide to Self-Healing, Volume 4,* and *Courageous Self-care: Putting Myself First to Serve Others in Find Your Voice Save Your Life Volume 2, Radical Self-care for Caregivers: Nourishing Yourself Through Grief"* and *Loss in Sacred Death,* and *Sacred Rest: Be at Your Best by Doing Less* in *Sacred Medicine.* All available at https://beingwellwithkelly.com/books/

For additional resources related to Kelly's healing journey and to connect with her, please visit https://www.beingwellwithkelly.com

CHAPTER 17

CRACKING OPEN

USING MUSIC TO UNLEASH YOUR VOICE

Kelli Murbach

MY STORY

Have you spent your whole life shutting yourself behind walls for safety's sake, only to find yourself feeling disconnected and nearly dead? Isn't it time to experience your life?

On my fifth Christmas day, I laid the first brick in my fortress of solitude. Twenty-two of us sprawled around my aunt and uncle's basement in that food-and-present coma you get. I surveyed a room littered with wrapping paper, ribbons, bubble wrap from our sleigh bells, and each person's pile of gifts. I couldn't help but notice my little brother's pile of presents was way bigger than mine.

"That's just not fair," I blurted loudly.

Loud enough for my mother to hear, which wasn't the world's best idea.

Mom got up, grabbed my hand, and marched me across the basement, up the stairs, across the length of the house, and into an open bedroom. There, she swung me around in front of her, looked at me, and said, "Hey. I get it. Life isn't fair. Your attitude sucks. Fix it before you come back downstairs." Mom believed in telling the truth to power, and at that moment, she thought I had power. Then she walked out of the room, half-slamming the door. Only to reopen it long enough to say, "And, don't touch the waterbed."

She left me there.

Stunned, frustrated, and scared, I stood alone in the dark bedroom with my pulse beating at my head and the sounds of Christmas filtering through the floor. Yeah, I noticed the different-sized piles. Yeah, I was mad. My brother had been around for a while, but *he still kept taking up all the stuff. He got all the presents and all the attention. It just isn't fair.*

I didn't know what to do. I knew I couldn't crawl into the waterbed and hide among the coats. Mom expected me downstairs with a better attitude. I laid down on the floor and tried to fix the churn inside.

At that moment, the fortress of solitude began to take shape.

Mom wanted me to be only polite and supportive. I could do that. I covered my mouth with a bit of figurative tape from the opened presents. Crying silently now, I began to build the shell. To soften the blows, I wrapped myself in discarded bubble wrap and wrapping paper.

Eventually, I hauled myself off the floor and into the bathroom, where I washed away the tears but not the puffiness. Before I left the bathroom, I checked for presentability. Feet solid, shoulders back, and a calm face—the checklist would soon become part of my standard operating procedure. Then I headed back across the house and down the stairs, where I pretended to have a good afternoon because that's what you're supposed to do.

This small starter of a fortress was reinforced over the years. I applied a new piece or layer for each seemingly insignificant thing—like who gets paid for grades (not me), who my parents would've driven to the magnet school (not me), who had homework help available (not me), and I could go on. By the time I left high school, my walls had contained my feelings and limited intimacy. You would only know if I was having a difficult day when I was sick enough that I should've stayed in bed. Even when I couldn't control the flood of emotions, I did what I could to hide. So if you ever saw me cry, you never heard me cry.

That's the girl who showed up at college. I arrived on campus knowing I'd have to poke a hole in the outer walls and do some reaching to make friends. I remember that first afternoon in Norton Hall bummed because my roommate and I didn't click. *You have to try,* a small voice inside me whispered as I knocked on my neighbor's doorframe.

Luckily, they welcomed me, and soon our crew was about 24 people. We did all kinds of things together in the first six months. We figured out you could shower 11 people in the girls' stall, you could fit 12 people in a two-door Pontiac Starfire if you put two of them in the trunk (I wasn't there that night), and around the north side dining hall tables, you could fit ten people. That wasn't big enough for us, so pushing three tables together was common.

If you'd shown up to the north side dining hall for dinner on the second Thursday in April that first year, you'd have found me wedged into one of those pizza slice-shaped spaces made when you connect two round tables together. In a conversational lull, my best friend tossed, "Kelli's dad just died."

Crap. I didn't actually mean to tell anyone else. She spoiled that plan. I have this fortress of solitude, you see. I shouldn't share an attitude that sucks.

I spent the next week finding paper to patch up the leaks I kept creating in my fortress of solitude. You see, I cried a little bit that day when Mom called to tell me Dad died. I cried that night when I got home. I cried a little bit at the church during the memorial service. I cried on the way back to school. With every tear I cried, I found another little bit of something to reinforce the fortress walls.

In the 18 months that followed, I patched those leaks so well that I didn't cry again (disregarding Hallmark movies) for another decade. I discovered small new places to find wall reinforcement. Rolled eyes become a bit of tissue paper that covers my left flank. Flat-out rejection makes for sturdy cardboard that protects my chest, so I know nothing is going to hit.

Eighteen months after Dad died, I dreamed about a former suitemate moving back into the suite. Her presence tripped some switch in my dream, and rage overtook me. Without compunction, the dream version of me took off her head with the chainsaw that'd become my arm (I really shouldn't watch The *Evil Dead* before I go to bed). I bolted awake, heart-pounding and believing I was someone who could decapitate a person because they annoyed me.

To say the least, I doubled down on the walls, adding layers of steel plate and concrete, determined not to release any of the bad stuff within me.

I lived like that for, about, I don't know how long. People who knew me before the lockdown became frustrated because they couldn't reach me. There were no holes left. New people didn't try because there were no obvious entry points. I spent years containing all the feelings inside my fortress of solitude. So many emotions were packed in there that I couldn't identify what I felt unless rage exploded all over. Life became nothing more than time filled with work, books, television, and eventually a church.

To be fair, the construction and maintenance of the fortress gave me what I needed to survive a childhood of being seen and not heard. I felt safe blending into the woodwork, being unnoticed, and feeling unbothered. My interactions with the Bossman seemed to be the only thing causing any ripples in my life.

It was all well and good until one Tuesday morning on I-85 south in front of the Lucent Technologies building. The radio broke in, "A second plane has hit the Twin Towers in New York."

I'd contained feelings for so long that I didn't get mad. I didn't get sad. I didn't get thrilled. On that morning, I didn't feel anything. *My God, they really should stop taking Tom Clancy novels so literally,* was the only thought in my head.

As I took the ramp to the perimeter, I knew I fucked up. My insistence on keeping all of myself encapsulated within the fortress left me emotionally dead. I'd given up my freedom for a sense of safety that left me numb and detached. Knowing all of this, I did that one thing I was really good at. I found a paperclip and half a stick of gum and Macgyvered that crack, so I couldn't see it anymore.

Remembering those days locked inside this metaphorical fortress, I realize that though my structure had many rooms, I'd filled each room so well that I lived in one corner of one room. I surrounded myself with rigid expectations, perceived slights, and fear of who I would be without the walls. Just thinking about it, my chest constricts, and it hurts to breathe. I hear how much time and energy I spent pushing against all the fortress stuffing as I reach to connect to another living human.

I was lonely and bored and ultimately afraid of expressing any tiny bit of myself. In that darkness, occasionally, bits of music caught my attention. There's nothing like Bette Midler crooning *"The Rose"* to remind you how much your life was not about living.

Then came a trip to the beach. While sandy beaches don't float my boat, I managed to drag myself there one early Saturday morning to watch the sunrise. Primed by Pat Green's *"Wave on Wave"* and Evangeline's *"Love Ain't Always Pretty,"* the tide approached as I took off my blinders. Sitting there with a cold, damp butt, I accepted my responsibility for the disconnection between myself and the world. *The fortress is mine. I built it. I maintain it. If I want out of this darkness, I'm going to have to unload and aerate it. I was the one I was sent to save, and it ain't going to be pretty.*

I stood up, brushed the sand off, set my feet, and said to the surf, "I commit to learning how to actually live my life so that I can be more than building to be acted upon."

I wanted to be in the world. I showed up to all the things the church asked me to do. I befriended my coworkers and ended up with an unintentional office husband. And, at the suggestion of my mental health professional, I took an improv class.

Okay, so Mike's suggestion was to take a class. Like most things, I took the advice a bit farther than expected. That one class became four classes. Over eight months, the fortress cracked enough for me to be a reliable member of an improv team. Improv required me to locate my feelings at the start of the scene and do my part to make my partner look awesome. Given how bound-up and locked down I was, improv demanded my trust; I had to trust that even if I screwed up, the scene would happen the way it needed to. I was angry in almost every scene, and nobody died. I started to feel emotions in my body, and I began to believe my feelings wouldn't kill me or anyone else.

These are the first steps I took toward being alive, alert, and awake. Luckily, I believe in the long game. Just as creating an impenetrable mobile fortress required decades, opening and accepting visitors and new tenants calls for a regular recommitment to creating and maintaining doors and windows.

Since that morning on the beach, I've educated myself about the connections between mind, body, emotions, and spirit. Those connections and being honest about the pain of my childhood helped clear out much of the debris within the fortress itself. Removing all that clutter made room for me to do the things needed to get the life I wanted. Action, even from within my fortress, scares me spitless. I do it anyway. Now, with cleaner rooms, I have the freedom to soar and the freedom to fall on my face. I've done both.

Admittedly, two decades later, I still carry around the fortress. However, the emotional crack created by improv has become a full-fledged set of operable windows. The reckoning with my lived childhood experiences spawned a door or two. I still get overwhelmed and find myself figuratively running around, closing all the windows, and locking the doors. Today though, they stay open longer and reopen faster than ever before. My progress blows me away.

People continue to show up in my life, even as the ongoing fortress renovations mean I'm not the person they initially befriended. Their continued friendship allows me to exit the fortress more easily, even as my circle of people grows. Today, I breathe, feel emotions, and actively participate in my life.

THE STRATEGY

Make Noise

Given that music served as a one ray of light penetrating the depths of the fortress, I offer a tool using music as its foundation.

STEP 1: CREATE A PLAYLIST OF YOUR LIFE.

Using your music app of choice, create a playlist of your life. I call mine "Theme Songs," It includes all kinds of music and, quite frankly, doesn't make a lot of sonic sense.

Some things to think about when creating the Playlist of Your Life:

1. What songs pump you up?

2. Are there songs you sing/hum along to every time you hear them?

3. Are there songs that hold your deepest longing?

4. Are there songs that make you cry every damn time you hear them?

5. Are there songs that make you smile or grin?

6. Is there a song that channels your anger?

7. Are there songs that embody how you walk in life?

8. Are there songs that echo some part of your experience?

9. Did you have a song of summer? Or another season? All three of the summers between my college years had a different theme. They're all on my list.

10. What songs get stuck on a loop?

As of this writing, my list is 40 songs long. It represents moments and swaths of my life. I listen to it when I need to reconnect to who I am and who I want to be.

You want to keep this playlist under 50 songs to be intentional about what's there and make the next step easier.

STEP 2: CREATE A TEMPORARY PLAYLIST

At that moment where you're stuck, create a temporary playlist. Populate it with at least three songs from the Playlist of Your Life.

These songs speak to what you're feeling right now, the tweaked past, or what you wish you were feeling. Or they're just what you really want to listen to right now.

STEP 3: LISTEN AND MAKE NOISE

The last step is to find privacy if you can (or need to). Crank your volume up as high as you can stand it.

And sing, holler, or speak along as loudly as you can. Let the feelings flow through into your voice. Be as with the music as possible.

For those who have walled ourselves away and quieted our voices, this activity can help jumpstart that bit of yourself that needs freeing.

I usually do this step in the car. I have what has been described as a one flat note singing voice, a tin ear, and an unconventional sense of harmony. So, I sing in my car rather than scare my cats or subject anyone to my joyful noise.

And here's the why:

1. It's breathwork without being boring. You must breathe to sing, holler or speak.

2. It's a fun way to check in with yourself. Sometimes I pick songs at random from the big list and get an insight into where I'm at from what I chose.

3. It's parasocial—so while you're not directly connecting to another person, you are connecting to the musicians and the writer. If you're deep in your own, lockdown can be a way to not feel entirely so alone.

If you'd love to have more simple, practical activities to support you along the path of becoming alive, head on over to https://secularshepherdess.life/wealth-codes/ for some of my favorites.

Kelli Murbach is a modern-day secular shepherdess and life reclamation coach who believes in the power of stories to move and change us. She has 22 years of experience with the work of healing from the silent trauma of emotional neglect. She's called to create safe and inclusive spaces allowing her clients to find the internal order they're missing so that they may be present and alive to the wonders of life.

Kelli retired from structural engineering four years ago to help others be seen, have their truths acknowledged, honor their choices, and share the possibility that tomorrow can be different. As your coach, she'll help you examine your stories, discover where those stories knot up, limiting your ability to be present, live in life's flow, and meet every moment alive and whole.

When she's not holding space, you can usually find Kelli with her nose in a book, trying to avoid being bossed around by her three cats. She's also known for absurdly long conversations with her friends, her love of modern fountain pens, and saying "Good morning" at all times of the day.

Sitting (or standing) with others as they experience their emotions, make significant commitments, or experience personal breakthroughs are Kelli's favorite moments of this work. Whether you need space to do the work necessary to move forward or need someone to hold space while you honor a change in your life, she would love to hear from you to see if the two of you could take the next steps together.

Connect with Kelli:
Website: http://secularshepherdess.life/
Facebook: https://www.facebook.com/SecularShepherdess/
Instagram: https://www.instagram.com/shepherdesskelli/

CHAPTER 18

AWARENESS

THE ROCKET FUEL FOR AN AUTHENTIC LIFE

Jamie Lee Murphy M.Ed., SC-C, CECP, Shamanic Practitioner

*"Your playing small does not serve the world. There is nothing
enlightened about shrinking so that other people won't feel
insecure around you. We are all meant to shine, as children do."*

~Marianne Williamson

Awareness comes in many forms, and it *is* the rocket fuel for an authentic life *full* of vitality. Authenticity is living in integrity and listening (being aware) of your soul's voice. Vitality is pure life-force energy; it's feeling alive in each moment of your Earth walk. The relationship between authenticity and vitality is intertwined and correlational.

The less authentic your life is, the less vitality you channel, and the more authentic your life is, the more vitality you harness.

Some signs you have been living an inauthentic life accompanied by low vitality include disconnection from intuition, addictive habits, lack of life direction, feelings of shame and guilt, feeling unworthy, lack of trust in self and others, shutdown energetic system and chakras, low physical energy, anxiety and depression, and chronic illness. What does an authentic life accompanied with thriving vitality look like? Read my story below.

MY STORY

I sat on the porch, a light breeze invigorating my soul as I took in the dawning of a new day—the dewdrops glistening on the blades of grass and melodic birdcalls dancing in the air. The sun coming up over the horizon dared to set the day ablaze with passion and opportunity. My heart began to fill with anticipation of what this day could bring. My thoughts began to swirl around in grateful reflection: *I feel excited about all of the possibilities of today. I am connected in mind, body, and spirit with my purpose, the world around me, and who I truly am. I am honored to have the opportunity to live this beautiful life. I am abundant. I am worthy of the life I have and my purpose on this Earth. I am in gratitude for my health and clarity of thought. How did I go so long not living this way?* I chuckled as I thought to myself. Now, especially in the most mundane of moments, I felt alive, vitality seeping from my pores.

Amazing, right? It wasn't always like this.

"I can't do this anymore." Exasperation fell from my lips.

"What do you mean you can't do this anymore?" She stared at me with a look of disbelief.

What do I mean? Am I blowing up my life? All I knew was that I could no longer live this way.

"We're on different paths. You refuse to heal, and I refuse to hold myself back anymore to be close to you," I said. My heart sinks at the gravity of my words.

This was one of the most difficult conversations I ever had in my life. It was years in the making; we'd been together for almost a decade. We had a life together: a family, pets, vehicles, and a brown picket fence. To the outside world, we were the picture of the perfect couple. In reality, I was suffocating, not to mention mentally, physically, and spiritually exhausted. I stared at myself in the mirror, realizing that the "me" looking back was a hollow version of myself. My eyes were lackluster, and I lost the ability to see the beauty in myself and the world around me. I felt broken, disconnected, and lost. Tears streamed down my face as I reflected on the conversation from earlier, how I got here, and what this meant for my life.

The swarm of voices began to fill my head: *You're a failure and a bad person for breaking up the family. What kind of loyal person can't make it through the hard times? You should always put others before yourself. You fought so hard for this relationship and your ability to be proud of your truth, and now you are just going to give it up? This relationship is no longer serving you or your greater purpose in this world.*

I stopped for a moment, and clarity began to trickle in. I realized some of those thoughts had voices that didn't belong to me, and I did not necessarily believe them. *Whose voice is that?*

You're a failure and a bad person for breaking up the family. What kind of loyal person can't make it through the hard times?—Grandparents. This voice stemmed from the family and religious beliefs passed down on divorce and commitment. Both sets of my grandparents stayed married their entire lives even when there were times that called for divorce.

You should always put others before yourself—Mom. This voice stemmed from my mother always putting the family's needs above her own, even when it was to her own detriment. This is also known as being a martyr.

You fought so hard for this relationship and your ability to be proud of your truth, and now you are just going to give it up?—Ego. This voice stemmed from the amount of effort and bravery it took to come out and live my truth as a part of the LGBTQ community. I linked my truth with this relationship because I was in this relationship when I decided to come out to my family as pansexual, which is someone who falls in love with the person and their soul, not their gender.

This relationship is no longer serving you or your greater purpose in this world—100% me. There is my voice! I finally found it sifting through all of the noise. This was my authentic voice guiding me toward my truth, purpose, and vitality.

My belongings felt heavy in my hands as I packed the moving boxes. My adopted son was so brave throughout the whole separation. He looked at me with those big, shiny green eyes and stated, "Momma Jamie, I know that you love me and always will." My eyes filled with tears, and my heart ached in my chest as I pulled him in and held him close. "I *will* always love you and be there for you," I replied.

The drive to my Aunt Stacey and Uncle Ron's house (who graciously invited me with open arms to stay with them) felt like a funeral procession. Flashes of my previous life illuminated before my eyes, emotions coursing through my body, and exhaustion set into my soul as that version of myself was laid to rest. My new life began that day. My entire body ached with fatigue as I entered my new room and flopped down on the bed. I stared at the ceiling, numbness encapsulating my mind and emotions, as I drifted off to sleep.

The next six months of my life was a rollercoaster of peace and enlightenment paired with pain and despair. I spent each waking moment re-evaluating the essence of my true self and purpose for this lifetime. The layers began to shed away. Some of the layers included "shoulds," fitting in, adhering to expectations, being too much, making myself smaller to hold onto relationships, agreeing with others against my integrity to keep the peace, fitting everything into boxes of right and wrong, and feeling like a victim. Other layers ripped and held on for dear life on their way out; these deeper layers included what I deserve in life, numbing my emotions with emotional eating, cigarettes, and diet pills, believing that others know me better than I know myself, being an overachiever, and choosing other people's happiness over my own.

As the layers of the false self burned away, the blossoming of my authentic self emerged from the flames. My life began to take form like a sculpture whose excess was chipped away, finally displaying the beauty that was there all along. My inner voice happily sang songs and spoke clearly as she guided me on each step to my new life. I learned how to protect myself and turn the victim into a survivor by learning Krav Maga. I flew to Mexico by myself to go on a spiritual retreat at Teotihuacán. I reconnected with my childhood sweetheart, now my loving husband. I followed my inner guidance to let go of my professional counseling licensure and become a shamanic practitioner, spiritual counselor, and energy healer. Now, I have a thriving business that is growing every day. Following these breadcrumbs on the path to authenticity led me to feel more alive than ever before. As my vitality flourished and electrified my being, my health improved, old behavior patterns fell away, and fear of embarrassment and rejection diminished.

Now, I allow, feel, and process my emotions, including receiving their messages. I maintain healthy boundaries while respecting others' opinions. I no longer pretend to be anyone other than who I am. I'm comfortable in my skin, and I don't feel the need to apologize for that. I believe in myself and my purpose. I acknowledge that I'm doing my best, and that changes daily. I *love* myself. I'm in gratitude for each and every day I live and every experience I have. I see the beauty all around me as the sun rises, and I look forward to what the rest of my days on this Earth will bring.

THE STRATEGY

WHOSE VOICE IS THAT?

Often, there are times when it feels like words come out of our mouths that don't belong to us. The same thing happens internally when we have thoughts of criticizing ourselves. Who *is* that person? Have you ever caught yourself saying, "Whoa! I sound like my mother/father, boss, ex-lover, etc." Well, you're probably right. As we grow up, we begin to internalize voices and beliefs from loved ones, friends, teachers, significant others, society, culture, and the media. We hear the same message over and over, and the message quite literally sticks in our brain! Once it's in our brain, we begin to deliver messages to ourselves and others that we do not actually believe.

LIVED EXPERIENCE

Use a journal or the reminder/notes list in your phone to keep a tab of the habitual thoughts and messages that you tell yourself about yourself and the meanings you assign to situations. Be sure that this list includes both positive and negative thoughts and messages so that you are not solely focused on what is wrong. At the end of the day, make a quiet sacred space to review your list.

First, take some time to decompress from the day. Get centered with deep breathing, meditation, body movement, grounding exercises, or mindfulness—dealers choice! When you feel centered, it's time to re-evaluate each habitual thought and ask yourself, "Whose voice *is* that?"

This experience will help you identify and become aware of which habitual thoughts you've internalized from someone else and which ones belong to you. Some ways this information may come to you is by hearing a person's voice in your head, someone's name popping in your head, or seeing an image of a person who uses this language. When you discover who the phrase belongs to, write down the name next to the habitual thought that belongs to them. When you're finished, look at the list and see how many habitual thoughts belong to you and how many belong to other people.

CEREMONIAL RELEASE

What you will need: Paper, writing utensil, match or lighter, burning bowl or fire pit, and shovel.

Congratulations! You've uncovered the beliefs that do not belong to you. These habitual thoughts no longer serve you, and it's time to release them from your life to make space for the true you to emerge. On a separate sheet of paper, write down the habitual thoughts that no longer serve you and the true owner's names. Send gratitude and compassion to everyone on the list.

Reminder: Someone who harms you is typically in an immense amount of pain themselves.

Next, place your paper in the burning bowl. Say your intention out loud, "I now lovingly and willingly release to the sky all thoughts and beliefs that do not serve me or belong to me. I am in gratitude for the lessons, and I fully step into my true being." Light the paper on fire and watch it completely burn out. After it has cooled, take your shovel, and dig a small hole in Mother Earth. Place the burnt paper into the hole. Say your intention out loud, "I now return this energy to Mother Earth. This energy has come full circle. I ask her to transmute this energy into healing for the planet where it is needed the most. I am in gratitude." Fill in the hole with soil. Blessed be. You are free!

Jamie Lee Murphy an Atlanta, Georgia native. She is the founder and owner of Vessel of Divine Wellness. She started Vessel of Divine Wellness because she believes that everyone deserves the opportunity to live an authentic life and shine their light into this world while feeling safe and empowered. She believes that personal growth, integration, and freedom to live the life you have always dreamed of are possible with a little courage, an open mind, a smile, and a compassionate guide to help you along the way. She is available virtually and globally.

Jamie is a spiritual counselor with an M.Ed. in Professional Counseling. She is a shamanic practitioner, ordained minister, certified emotion code practitioner, certified angel intuitive, registered yoga teacher-200, and an energy healer. She loves to utilize these different skills and support individuals in overcoming the chains and boxes of their past and flourish in a purpose-driven, authentic life. Jamie is passionate about helping authenticity seekers see their inherent worth and live an authentic life. Her other passions include LGBTQ rights and animal rescue.

When she is not empowering authenticity seekers or writing books, you can find her spending time with her loving husband, hiking with friends, dancing at concerts, enjoying family dinner/game nights, or snuggling up with her pup, Murphy Lee and reading a good book.

Connect with Jamie:
Website: http://www.vesselofdivinewellness.com
Facebook: https://www.facebook.com/vesselofdivinewellness
Instagram: https://www.instagram.com/vesselofdivinewellness/
LinkedIn: https://www.linkedin.com/in/jamie-lee-murphy-527795152/

CHAPTER 19

CLAIM YOUR VITALITY

HOMEOPATHIC SECRETS TO LIVING A HEALTHY LIFE

Kristina White, Certified Classical Homeopath (CCH)

MY STORY

I'm 53 years happy! I find pure joy and peace when in the presence of animals and nature. I can't help but smile when around them, and there is a lightness that comes over me even from a simple bird's call, especially the crows when I'm out for a daily walk with the dog in the woods. I'm so thankful that I've created a life where I can live in this space of joy and peace, both personally and professionally.

I have always known my strong connection with animals and nature since I was young; my sanctuary and escape in my previous career of banking was at the barn with my beautiful horse Harley. Harley was very intimidating to many, as he stands just shy of 18 hands. That's about six feet tall. He is a Clydesdale thoroughbred cross. He's big, beautiful, kind, and fast. I can still remember the power and quiet strength in his canter, our absolute favorite pastime when we rode together. Sadly, in 2010 I experienced a serious fall from Harley after he bolted, which is ultimately how I found homeopathy!

The bolting started about six months before the accident. I had been in denial about the training we were receiving. I enjoyed the barn, friends, and the community we shared, but I intuitively knew Harley wasn't happy with the trainer for some time. I was not happy either, as I would often raise questions about the changes I observed in Harley's personality. My trainer would always respond with, "Don't question this, you are not the expert here." *No, I am not, but I am his owner and have the connection with him, don't I?* This was a very big red flag, but I was new to this type of riding, and at this point in my life, I didn't trust my intuition or my own abilities fully. I was afraid to lose my sanctuary and the horse community I was part of.

If you ride with any frequency, it's not uncommon to come off the horse. Let's not forget the quote, "Get back on the horse." I had no fear, and I was no exception to the rule. But this last time was very different. Harley didn't return to me after I fell.

Instead, he continued and ran to the far corner of his field and turned away. He always came back and welcomed me to get back on him, usually reaching his head down to nudge me—not this time. The strong connection we shared for years changed at that moment and has taken time and remedies to reclaim.

So, what does this have to do with homeopathy?

I came to find homeopathy because I literally could not, "Get back on the horse!"

The accident left me with severe headaches, back, and leg pains. I was not able to sit on a horse or a chair for any period of time due to the pain. I was unable to stand or drive for an extended period of time. I was forced to run my business remotely via a laptop propped on my belly. I was miserable. I was someone who enjoyed being on the road and with my clients working on projects. I rarely stopped and was typically restless when I wasn't doing something. *Isn't that normal?* I've come to find out it's not, but that's a much longer story!

During the same year of the accident, I was also going through a divorce and lost my father to a heart attack. The combination of the three events was the tipping point for me. The people, places, and animals that were my sanctuary were gone in my mind, and I was heartbroken.

In homeopathy, we often look at such events as a catalyst to people's health challenges and refer to them as "The never well since." I'll touch on this in the strategy below, and I'll share how you can look at such events and how they impact your vitality.

Over the months following the accident, I met with many talented conventional and complementary providers and had X-rays, MRIs, and more. There were no clear findings or diagnosis, and I continued to have severe random back and leg pains, bladder difficulties, headaches, and depression began to quietly set in.

Before this time in my life, I was someone that woke up happy and always felt pretty upbeat. I wanted to be up and out, whether it was for work or fun. My vitality was strong! Not during this time. I could barely drag myself out of bed. As someone who didn't want to disappoint people, I did a good job of masking what I was really feeling.

The physical complaints were tiring, and the lack of answers was unnerving, but I had no concept of what depression was until this period of my life. It was alarming and very humbling. I realized just how connected our physical, emotional, and mental symptoms, or what I have come to call "messages," are. I realized I needed to stop looking to the experts to fix me and become my own advocate if I wanted to get back on that horse. And I did!

As we know, the universe always provides when we're ready, and along came my solution.

My chiropractor recommended I see her homeopath. So, I booked my appointment with Dr. Linda Levine—a homeopath, chiropractor, and a medium. This magical lady is a true healer and an amazing, loving human being. She became my mentor and friend and eventually encouraged me to study and become a homeopath.

Linda started the phone session with, "Tell me everything, honey."

"Everything? Everything about my accident? Everything about the pains?"

Linda replied, "Yes, and tell me how you felt after you came off the horse."

"How did I feel or what did I hurt after flying off my galloping horse?" I asked.

"Yes, tell me what you hurt, about the pains, and I also want to know how you felt emotionally. Were you mad at him, at yourself? What were you feeling? Did you cry? What else was going on in your life?"

I was puzzled and fascinated by her questions. We continued our first session for almost two hours, and it was the most detailed and gratifying conversation I ever had about my health. The healing began during that conversation. Linda explained why certain questions were important and how my complaints were related to all three events, not just the accident. Here is the "Never well since." In my case, it was three events: The fall, divorce, and the death of my father.

The answers to the questions created a profile of who I was mentally, emotionally, and physically during that time and as an overall person. The questions were not only about the three events. Linda wanted to know what food I liked and disliked. She wanted to know about my digestion, sleep patterns, fears, dreams, and other relationships. In homeopathy, you often hear the analogy of each of us having layers similar to an onion. The events and our responses to the events are seen as layers. Our goal is to remove or process these layers and return the being to a balanced, vital state!

After answering all the questions, I felt such a profound relief. There was no judgment, just questions, observation, and compassion. I was hooked! We went on to work with several homeopathic remedies over about six months, and I found my physical, mental, and emotional symptoms not only resolved, but I shifted my perception of several beliefs and resolved even older painful events in my life.

To boot, I was on my way to becoming a homeopath!

One of my favorite aspects of homeopathy is observation with compassion and without judgment. If we applied this concept to everything in our lives, can you imagine the peace and tranquility we'd all share? It has taught me to value and honor my intuition and abilities fully. I've found my most successful cases with people, animals, and even plants are rooted in being present and truly listening and observing. I follow my intuition about what I feel from the being, questions to ask, where to delve deeper, and what direction to look for remedies. The messages and answers are there, and within us, we only need to hold them sacred and trust ourselves.

One of the reasons I shared this particular story is because it prompted me to recognize just how detached I had become from my true self and the physical, mental, and emotional messages my soul was sending. The messages were there; I only had to listen, or in my case, fall off my horse!

By studying homeopathy, I've come to understand how integrated our physical, mental, and emotional messages are to each other and how frequently they're shared across many events. The importance of the "Never well since," and the layers of the onion become clear.

The strategy I offer will provide insight into the impact of your life events, the unique physical, mental, and emotional messages created from our life events, and the connection between them. With this strategy, you can create your own homeopathic timeline of events to better understand the connections and move closer to understanding how homeopathy can provide remedies accessible to you and beneficial to your vitality.

THE STRATEGY

Through homeopathy, I've come to see each of us as a unique puzzle of sorts where all pieces are of equal importance and needed to have a whole vital being!

Grab a pen and a few pieces of blank paper, and let's explore your unique puzzle!

First, you want to find a space where you feel calm, centered, and grounded, and take the time to practice any ritual you enjoy that will help you with this. Your goal is to be able to write from your heart more than your mind, as we know how biased the mind can be!

Don't worry about what you're writing, what anyone may think, or how others may feel about the same event. It's important not to minimize your pains, emotions, or reactions to events that have occurred in your life. Just go with it as if you're writing in a diary and use the real words that come to you, not clinical words or diseases.

Remember, we're categorizing the messages as physical, mental, and emotional.

1. Let's begin by asking yourself what physical messages you feel daily or periodically? You're not tying the messages to any specific event yet; however, you're looking for things that have some frequency, not a first-aid type symptom such as a bruise or cut from a fall. You're asking yourself what messages you periodically receive and experience. Remember, you'll be digging deep in this exercise, so take it slow, be compassionate with yourself, and only go as deep as you're comfortable doing so at this moment.

   a. Start with the physical messages. For example, I have:

      • headaches

      • stomach pain

      • chest tightness

      • neck stiffness

      • tingling in arms

      • nausea

      • joint pain

      • skin eruptions

      • sensitivity to temperature, light, noise, smell, and taste

      • dizziness

   b. Move on to the mental messages that occur. For example, I am:

      • forgetful

      • confused easily

      • indecisive

      • easily distracted

      • suspicious

- apathetic

- very talkative

- quiet

- shy

- unable to finish things

- easily startled

- fatigued

c. The final category is the emotional messages you experience. For example, I feel:

- like crying

- angry

- sad

- alone

- abandoned

- hurt

- jealous

- fearful

- resentful

- vindictive

- anxious

At this point, you have a list of the messages and some of the pieces of the puzzle. Take a moment to scan your list, and here are some questions you can use to prioritize: What is the frequency? What is the intensity? Does it have a negative impact on my health and vitality? Select your priority messages from each category and move to the next step.

2. It's time to think about your life events and the possible connection to these messages. Keep in mind these events aren't always negative. They may have an intensity or be a pivotal

event such as a career change. For each message, ask yourself the following questions: When did this begin, or have you always (to the best of your memory) been this way? If you've always been this way, simply mark the message as "Just me."

For the remaining messages, ask yourself, "What was going on in life when this first started?" Typically, we look at a six-month period of time in relation to the message. Some examples are marriage, divorce, deaths (people or animals), accidents, home moves, caregiver responsibility, school changes, family or friend health events, etc.

3. Your final step of this exercise is to create your own timeline of events and the related messages. You will likely find many of the messages share the same event. You also may find some of the messages started with an event from a very long time ago and show up in other events growing in frequency and intensity. A sample of a homeopathic event timeline is:

December 2010: Death of father to a heart attack.

- Physical message – I have heart palpitations

- Emotional message – I feel anxious

- Mental message – I am fatigued

For the messages you marked as "Just me," we refer to these as constitutional characteristics, and you will find as you learn more about homeopathy they're helpful when selecting remedies for both acute and chronic care.

Through this exercise, I hope you are closer to becoming your own compassionate homeopath and advocate with a deeper understanding of just how unique your messages are and the connections they share. Explore more in homeopathy and live a healthy lifestyle and enjoy your vitality!

If you'd love to learn more about homeopathy, join me for a private session or one of our workshops and bring homeopathy into your home for your family, animals, and yes, even plants! Visit www.yourlifeandland.com. Please enjoy our free content page at https://www.yourlifeandland.com/freecontent

Kristina White, CCH, is the co-owner of Emerging In Health and Your Life and Land. She is a certified classical homeopath and educator with over 25+ years of experience working with people and animals. Her daily goal is to educate people on the value and benefits of natural health options in the home and hands of the individual. Through homeopathy, she has learned the valuable lesson of listening to the unique messages our body, mind, and soul send and trusting in our own abilities and intuition. She is dedicated to homeopathic research and volunteers at multiple farms and sanctuaries to expand the presence of homeopathy for our animals and plants in our communities.

Kris offers homeopathic education and vitality assessments for individuals, groups, pets, farms, and agricultural resources who want to explore and implement homeopathy and other natural resources into daily life for the health and vitality of people, pets, plants, and nature.

When not working on homeopathic cases, you will find Kris in her greenhouse growing herbs and vegetables, hiking in the woods with her dog, enjoying a sunset sail with her partner, or possibly at the barn with the horses. Homeopathy is how Kris reclaimed her own vitality and maintains her everyday health and happiness!

Connect with Kris:
Website: https://www.yourlifeandland.com
Website free content page: https://www.yourlifeandland.com/freecontent
Facebook: https://www.Facebook.com/YourLifeandLand

CHAPTER 20

YOUR BODY REMEMBERS

RELEASING TRAUMA
TO LIVE A FIERY, SELF-EXPRESSED LIFE

Damaysi Vazquez

MY STORY

I am fire!

I was born and raised in Havana, Cuba. I'm a mix of salsa, rebellion, humor, and love. And this lifetime, since I was five years of age, I had to learn to control my emotions and be resilient as a survival mechanism.

Between the communistic regime paranoia and the severe childhood trauma, I grew up to be a pretty anxious, outspoken, strong woman with a permanent sadness in my heart that would never go away.

When I turned 22, I had an unusual opportunity. Someone offered to hide me in a boat that had a destination from Havana to the United States.

"Mom, tomorrow I get on that boat, and I sail to Florida. I don't know exactly what awaits me, but I know I will see you and my siblings again soon," I said.

"Please be careful. I'm going to be praying until you call me," she replied.

With tears in our eyes (I had to be strong to not get hysterical), my mother and I hugged and kissed goodbye. I vividly remember hugging my siblings, not being able to tell them I was leaving Cuba. If anyone found out, the government would've stopped that boat and put me in jail for trying to escape.

The boat landed in Fort Lauderdale, Florida, 36 hours later, and I started my new life in America. A few years later, I brought my sister, mother, and brother.

Fast forward 18 years, I was at one of the lowest points of my life. I always struggled with depression, anxiety, and distrust, but at this point in my life, I was extremely depressed and hopeless, and I felt one of the worst feelings anyone could feel—I felt like I did not matter.

I tried many healing modalities throughout the years to heal whatever was causing these symptoms. I refused to take anti-depressants or anti-anxiety drugs. I spent tens of thousands of dollars trying to find the modality that would take the pain away. Some of the tools I learned helped a little, but nothing was getting to the root cause. No one could tell me why I was *still* feeling depressed.

Then I heard about ayahuasca, an ancient medicinal brew originating in South America and used by shamans to heal their patients' minds and bodies from past trauma. I decided to register for a weekend of psychedelic transformation.

I traveled alone to this retreat place in Orlando because no one from my family wanted to come with me. I was curious, scared, and desperate to find healing. Before I drank the shamanic medicine, I asked "Mother Aya" to show me the trauma I must have experienced in my childhood. I had no idea what I was about to learn.

When we experience extreme trauma as children, we block the memories as a coping strategy. It's called Motivated Forgetting in psychology. We do it because we have to keep living and go to school the next day.

As I sat there after drinking the medicine, I waited for the moment of truth. And I waited hours. I didn't see anything. All I experienced was extreme discomfort in my body. I was already distrusting as it was, so I definitely did not surrender to this process. I was stiffer than a corpse.

The following morning the shaman told me this happened because I was too afraid to see the truth.

"Well, no kidding," I said. "This entire experience is frightening, to say the least."

"Tonight, you will see what you came to see," The shaman assured me.

Hesitant and terrified, I drank the medicine the second night. I sat on my mat, and then the moment came. I saw a familiar face cross my mind, but it quickly eluded me. I was too deep in the medicine to even ask why I was seeing him. About 30 minutes later, the medicine presented this man's face again, and I asked, "Why am I seeing his face again?"

Suddenly, and before I could even choose to avoid it, the entire scene of that afternoon came rushing to me. I kept crying, "No, no, no!" I was only five years old, and I re-lived the horrible experience with all its details and emotions all over again.

Then the famous ayahuasca purge came. I was purging memories from my body living in me since the time I was five, causing depression, anger, and anxiety to be present in my everyday life.

This night changed my life. I learned there was inherently nothing wrong with me, that my innocence was taken as I was abused, and that even though my conscious mind forgot, my body still remembered.

I understood the importance of accepting the past and forgiving, even though I had no strength to do so at that moment. I understood the reason every adult who was supposed to protect me didn't was because they didn't know what was happening.

I cried for weeks and then began to forgive everyone, including *myself.* Children conclude that intense traumas like these must be their fault, and then they grow up to be codependent adults that struggle with guilt, shame, low self-esteem, and mental illness.

I went on to participate in ten ayahuasca ceremonies over the course of one year. I wanted to know it all.

One of the most important lessons I've learned is that there is immense peace in surrender. I used to think surrendering was for the lazy. I've always powered through everything in life, and I had no patience to surrender to Spirit. But through the most painful moments where I ran crying to the medicine, I saw a team of loving guides and angels working with me and that I was making their mission close to impossible with my stubbornness. In one of the ceremonies, as I had anxiety, they said, "Let us kill you, so we may bring you back to life. Surrender and trust us." Meaning: Allow us to take over, so we can actually help you. Then they repeated over and over, "You have to be willing to die (surrender) every day, so you can live."

You also have a team of loving, powerful guides and angels assigned to help you with your mission on Earth, and you'll make everything a lot easier on yourself and your spiritual team when you learn to trust them and surrender to your personal process. Whatever you're going through, know that your spirit guides and angels are waiting for you to ask for help. Listen to their guidance and trust them.

With each healing ceremony, I continued to do the integration work, which is the most important part. When we work with plant medicine or any tool that reveals trauma, those tools are the gateways, but *after* the tool is when the real work begins. For instance, one of my core wounds is "I do not matter," so my work has been to make my entire life about how much I matter to myself. I put myself first, and I actively love myself moment to moment.

We give meaning to every experience. And the *meaning* we give to things creates our perception of the experiences and of ourselves. The healing is not about what people did to us; it is about what we made it mean.

For instance, something traumatic happens. We can make it mean we're unlovable and unworthy, and now we have to heal from that erroneous core belief, or we can make it mean this person must have had a horrible childhood themselves and that what they did to us was not about us at all, and we do not need years in therapy to heal it.

THE STRATEGY

Nothing other people do to us means anything until we give it meaning. It definitely does not mean we are unworthy, stupid, or unlovable. People project their pain, and we don't have to make it mean anything. What our parents, teachers, and friends said or did is *not* a reflection of us; it's a reflection of them.

Our emotional intelligence grows as we learn not to give meaning to things. We learn to observe our lives as a witness to what is happening without losing our joy or our feeling of safety. However, for this to happen, we need to remove traumatic memories from our bodies.

Unfortunately, many of us were victims of some form of child abuse or trauma still stored in our cellular memory. No matter how many healing modalities you've tried, the healing work is never finished. So, I'm willing to bet this tool is really going to help you live a more peaceful, healed life.

When our bodies hold severe traumatic memories, we do not handle stress like everyone else. Our ability to cope with regular stressful situations diminishes to a great extent. Even if we consciously do not want to, we get immediately overwhelmed, anxious, and afraid.

We *freeze, fight, flight,* or *fawn.*

Since I can't tell you to participate in a plant medicine ceremony, I will give you a tool you can use in the comfort of your home that has a very similar effect.

This tool will work in your body at a cellular level, and it will remove childhood trauma (and any other trauma) from your energetic and physical body, layer by layer. It'll also regulate your nervous system.

You may release trauma by crying, laughing, screaming, toning, or stomping.

It's a very powerful breathwork technique. If you're pregnant, experience cardiovascular problems, epilepsy, or have any other physical limitations; please consult with your physician before doing this exercise.

Play upbeat shamanic music with drums to move the energy if you wish to. Have a light stomach, and find a comfortable place to lay down. Bring a blanket and a journal in case you receive an insight or memory you want to write down.

You will rapidly inhale through your mouth into your stomach, and without exhaling, you'll inhale again into your chest. Then you will fully exhale through your mouth, and as you do, you will make a sound of "Ahhh."

Do this exercise for about 30 minutes. If you need to pause a few seconds in between, do so, but do your best to keep breathing.

Allow yourself to release the emotions. If your hands get cramped, it is called tetany in medical terms, and we call it "the lobster claw" in the spiritual community. If it happens, it's your ego not wanting to let go of trauma and emotions. Your body does this to keep you safe because it doesn't know who you'll be without those traumas and beliefs. Don't worry about this, as you're not doing anything wrong; just continue to breathe and remember to surrender.

You're guided, protected, loved, supported, and you are not alone. As you see moments of the past brought forward while you breathe, ask yourself what meaning you gave it, and work on re-framing and healing that. Also, remember that the people who hurt us, although they're not justified, were also hurting and replaying their own childhood. Forgive them and set your soul free. They might not deserve it, but you deserve the freedom and beauty that comes from forgiving.

This technique has changed my life. Not only do I release trauma every time I do it, but it has given me insight into myself and my life, it has sharpened my intuition, and psychic abilities, increased my emotional intelligence, and made me a much happier woman.

Visit https://damaysi.com/breathe/ to watch me do this breathwork technique and do it with me.

My name is **Damaysi Vazquez,** and I am a mindset coach. I help women get over emotional blocks, so they can perform better in their businesses and make more money. I knew I was good at helping people when I was in my early twenties. My friends started to come to me for support, and my advice would change their lives.

I became an entrepreneur in 2006 when I discovered the Network Marketing industry. It was then that I began to attend seminars and read personal growth books. I also started to train my sales team to increase their performance, which led me to coach full time.

My zone of genius is to get to the root of the problem, pluck it out, and get the person to take action from a new mindset. The root of the problem is usually a fear of some sort, and I get the person to understand that the problem is not the fear, it's what they believe about themselves in correlation to that fear.

I am humorous, empathic, wise, and intuitive, and I have a direct approach to my coaching calls and my content. I find that most people appreciate my boldness, so I bring blazing fire and power to everything I do.

When it comes to marketing, I have an eye for details, and I create beautiful graphic designs. I started playing with graphic design a few years ago when I developed a passion for Pinterest marketing. With time I became a Pinterest wizard and started an agency to help celebrity coaches and business owners to get traffic and sales from that platform. I became so good at it that very renowned celebrities hired me to grow their Pinterest accounts to millions of views per month.

O

SPIRITUALITY

We now travel into spiritual wealth, sacred connection, and trusting our divine path. This, of course, has been paired with Spirit.

The spiritual realm brings divine transmutation, expected and unexpected transformations, the seen and unseen, celestial intervention, and a beautiful connection to all things.

We are students on an adventure of a lifetime. This is a quest back home to ourselves. The journey gets to be whatever we need it to be.

I live life in everyday ceremony cloaked in spiritual richness and drenched in sacred wisdom. It takes mundane tasks and transforms them with deep magical intentions that hold sacred purpose.

Spirt speaks to everyone in unique ways and at their level of awareness while lovingly dropping divine clues leading to expansion.

Unseen mysteries unfold with each new spiritual ah-ha. More clarity will reveal as you move forward through life, trusting your intuitive spiritual gifts, higher self, and guides. Life comes into alignment with newfound understanding.

We're invited to embrace the full spectrum life offers, stretching through our edges. With this philosophy (and lifestyle), we must accept all the pieces of ourselves with love (the light and the dark). As we evolve, life takes us through growing pains that our human mind may see as setbacks or challenges.

These obstacles are simply part of the adventure and enhance our spiritual quest for embodied wholeness. Once we receive these lessons as sacred medicine, things transform on all levels of consciousness. It propels us forward with the knowledge we could not receive in any other way.

Even with life-changing trials and tribulations, we are meant to live ecstatically, fully expressed, and so alive that simple pleasures feel orgasmic. To claim such pleasure, we must stay open to the creative twists and turns we've traveled to get to where we're going.

The more we connect to the divine and tap into our higher self with intentional listening, the easier our path becomes because we avoid unnecessary detours.

RITUAL: Have your journal and pen ready for this ritual. You may also want to light a candle and incense to delve into this meditative practice.

Take a few deep, spacious breaths to bring your attention inward. For this ritual, you'll be channeling the divine. As you breathe, bring in love and light. With each exhale, release any places of resistance. Continue breathing until you feel ready to begin. Then, write:

Dear Universe/God/Goddess/Highest vibration of light/ Source/or higher power you feel most aligned with,

"I trust that everything is happening for my highest good. Tell me what I need to know so I may come into alignment with the divine plan."

Now, write as fast as possible and let words pour onto the page while your question is answered. Don't stop to think about spelling, grammar, or how you are scribing. Just write. When you're complete, take a deep breath and express your thanks, then read the wisdom that flowed through you.

The Ecstatic Living Podcast will support your spiritual journey, jumpstart transformation, and enhance the Wealth Codes.
Visit: www.jenpiceno.com/podcast to tune in.

To work privately or to accelerate your Wealth Codes journey, schedule a Wealth Codes Discovery Call here: www.jenpiceno.com/book_now

CHAPTER 21

INVISIBLE ALLIES

HOW TO NEVER FEEL ALONE EVER AGAIN

Atlantis Wolf

"The Possible's slow fuse is lit by the Imagination."

~Emily Dickinson

It always starts with death. It may be an experience of physical death—the loss of your mother, companion, soul friend—or shamanic death—the end of your marriage, a sudden job loss, or first admittance of an addiction—when you feel alone. You feel singular in your despair and isolated in your tomb of pain. It's the bottom-of-the-well feeling, the hushed silence of the ocean depths, the cold white hexagonal bathroom floor tiles pressed into your face as your tear ducts run dry. That's the moment. You make a choice—die or ask for help.

With a final exhale, you reach for God's grace in prayer, surrendering your personal ruin to the venerable divine design, accepting you can't complete your challenges alone. You weren't meant to. That's not the way. Your benediction is answered by a gathering of healers, helpers, and guides stretching to the horizon who are ready to assist you, to transform your pain into a portal of freedom and spiritual evolution. They exist behind the invisible veil in the world of Spirit.

Imagination is the key to entering the Spirit world, the Great Mystery. To imagine moves us to a place where we cognitively accept anything is possible. Oh, not tangible, arcane, or esoteric enough for you? Play with me for a moment. Imagine a time—anytime in your life—when you had a new love, a crush, a fresh lover. Pull into the present their dazzling, shining face, glistening eyes upon your naked skin, arms waiting to seize you, and the deathless, quiet room you shared maybe just once or only in your mind. Use the memories of how you mapped each other's bodies to rekindle a warmth starting at your pelvis and rising to your throat. (Remember the unstoppable scream?) Relive the leisurely steps they took to bring you pleasure, where they kissed you, and how hard. As you recall the sweat and smell of them, fire blazes in the golden bowl that lives between your hip bones. You feel the tips of your nipples tighten. The echo of an orgasm that erupted from your abdomen long ago ripples over your skin even though the soft lips and hungry hands are hundreds of miles away. Or years in the past. Now, does it feel more real? And you didn't need a dusty book of spells to get there.

MY STORY

I see spirits. I hear disembodied voices. I feel the scales of dragon bellies as they fly over my head when I open portals for them to come to the Earth plane. I wasn't born with this awareness, but I live here now. I'm in perpetual conversation with spiritual beings. My experience of what it feels to be me is acknowledging what I receive through my physical senses and feeling into my extrasensory senses to understand the totality, the whole of what is happening to me and around me. Each set of senses—the ones in the physical world and the non-physical world—are two halves of my whole.

Archangel Gabriel was the first spiritual being I saw. I was 38 with no inkling or interest in spiritual matters. I was too busy getting divorced, raising two kids, and hustling for contract work as a project manager at an empty desk in a beige cube. He appeared in a blink, hovering in the corner of my mother's bedroom when she was dying of breast cancer. The ceiling dissolved, and he was looking down from a celestial sky. His hair was a tousle of golden curls, and his long garment was mint green.

My first thoughts: *Gabriel! I haven't seen him in ages. His wings are bigger than I remember. Wow!*

I believe one reason I see so much on the Spirit side is that I naturally greet them all with awe and wonder. I recommend you try this as well. In my last 12 years as a medical massage therapist with over 3,000 clients, I have seen many beings. I see relatives of the client who died, pets that have crossed the rainbow bridge, galactic family (if my client's first incarnation was not Earth), and power animals (like the Kodiak bear that sits on my client's chest and picks off flecks of radiation from bladder cancer treatments). Once I saw a creature made of floating white triangles who made a tinkling sound like a wind chime made of thin shells.

When I asked the triangle being where he came from, he said, *The Edge.*

Me: *That sounds far away. Thank you for coming here today. What can I do for you?*

Triangles: *Nothing. I just wanted to visit here. You opened a loving portal.*

I didn't tell anyone (except my therapist, who was duty-bound to accept what I said and nod) about my Gabriel experience or Triangles. I didn't know how to talk about it because I didn't know what it was. It just happened. After my mom died, I quit my desk job and became a medical massage therapist. The visions came without me doing anything. The spiritual beings appeared more often and with more clarity and details over several years. I was grateful to see them, asked if they wanted my clients to know about them (sometimes yes, sometimes no), and felt comfortable seeing what I saw.

The first time I heard a voice, I almost fell down a stairwell. I was rushing to get to work, came in through the back door with my bags and gear, and bounded up the steps to the second floor, two at a time. At the last step, the booming voice of Cate Blanchett spoke to me, *Manifest your destiny!* I caught myself from falling with my right hand as all my bags fell forward. I paused and thought, *Well, that didn't happen.*

I got to work, settled my things, and greeted my first client, forgetting about the stairwell. As I began the massage, I heard her voice again, the spoken magic of a matriarch, mature and confident, conjured within the sultry notes of bourbon and butterscotch.

Cate: *You won't be doing this for long.*

This caused all the hallmarks of a panic attack.

Me: *I'm working here! You can't say that to a single mother. Give me another message, or I'll turn you off.*

She whispered into my ear: *This will not be your primary source of income.*

Spirit knew how to get my attention. Within a year, I was a #1 bestselling author in six collaborative books (this is book seven), moved my business partner and I into a new suite, and began my career as a shamanic life coach. Thank you, Cate. Come whisper anytime.

Like the triangle creature, my black guardian dragon arrived in my spirit vision while I worked. He's always been with me, but as I practiced seeing into the spiritual world, I began to see him. He stands behind me, has blue-green kyanite eyes, a gold belly, hundreds of sharp, shiny teeth, and often smiles down on me. I feel his belly against my back. He is a shapeshifter, able to morph from scales to feathers. His size varies depending on where we travel together in meditations. Through breathwork, I know he is part of the Galactic Dragon Clan and connected to Archangel Metatron. He is my oldest and best friend.

After working with my dragon for years, I took a dragon activation class offered by the College of Psychic Studies in London. The teacher invited me to be part of a mystical society of women who all work with dragons, anchoring dragon energy for planetary service. These dragon ladies meditate every two weeks from five time zones and share what they see, hear, or feel with each other. These meditations are my supreme joy! Being with the ladies and their dragons in the space of unconditional and egoless service has amplified my ability to pierce the veil into the spirit world. My intuitions are more accurate, my visions are sharper, and at the last meeting, I came to understand where I am in my spiritual evolution.

The dragon ladies each take turns hosting the group over Zoom. It was my turn. After we assembled and chatted, I asked them all to mute their mics and close their eyes. I used my voice and rhythmic beats of my buffalo skin drum to create an energetic bond, stirring our energies together as we imagined sitting around a fire circle in The Blood Temple, a circular, one-room stone sanctuary close to the Earth's core. The fire vortex in the circle of stones had a lick of violet flame in the center, bringing Source (love) energy into our ceremony. I drummed and expanded the fire around the circle, engulfing us in it. I saw all of us in our spirit forms dancing and laughing in the flames.

After I felt a strong connection between us, I guided them to go where they wanted to go and muted my mic. I continued to drum for myself after I checked the timer. We always meditate for 20 minutes. There were 14 minutes left.

As I closed my eyes and relaxed into my journey, I saw the platinum ray dragon, Shimmer, next to me and smiled. When he arrived two weeks ago, he showed me what vibration he had brought. In meditation, we were standing together on Megan's Bay beach in the Caribbean. He pointed to the sparkle on the water, then the sun. I anchor the golden ray helix with the dragons—light codes that activate DNA to remember our past lives when we were all masters of spiritual practices.

Shimmer: *I am the transparent sheath around the golden helix, the quantum, iridescent sleeve around the DNA.*

Me: *The shimmer from the shore?* He smiled.

As I drummed, I felt a hand on my shoulder. I looked right to see Odin. He arrived after I asked the question: *Where am I in my life span, all my lifetimes?* He swept his left hand, and the landscape changed to a hill in the Sedona desert, a favorite meditation spot. He showed me a typical day in the life of a Native American tribe—the men tanning skins, the women making clothes, and the children gathering wood. Then he showed me the chief, sitting alone in his tipi wearing his headdress of eagle feathers and looking forward.

Odin: *Doing versus being.*

Me: *Ah! The tribe needs many people to do multiple tasks, but the chief needs to be the chief, holding "chief space."* Odin nodded.

The desert scene dissolved, and my body began to feel more and more weightless. What felt like the boundary of my skin expanded to a periphery beyond what my mind could hold. I saw only a slice of it. I saw a cosmic, starry background and a faint trace of an outline, whisper-white, a perimeter marker line floating in space, thin and vaporous like a cloud. It was the border of "me" in a state of expanded consciousness, holding everything inside the line as sacred space. The galactic version of me is a field of loving-kindness. On the map of the universe, I said to God, *I got this part!*

Instead of just feeling my body sensations, I felt all beings. It was like being an invisible net cast over a vast expanse of star systems and feeling all their sensations, planetary to cellular. The gentle vibrations of it all lifted and fell like energy traveling through an ocean wave. I was the living connection between everything in my field. I existed inside and outside, like molecules of golden light breathed in and out. Giggling joy. Giddy delight.

I came back to the Blood Temple and peeked at the time. Two minutes left. Odin pointed to the single throne chair up a few marble steps against the wall.

Like chief in the tipi?

He nodded. I'm the High Priestess of the Blood Temple. And the Dragon Medicine Woman. Being in the world is my path. I don't need to do anything to fulfill my soul's purpose. That's my lesson. Be sacred space. Feel the field of conscious awareness. And rest. Your doing days are done.

I unmuted my mic and drummed the group back into the present. Each agreed in the sharing circle that this meditation felt like it stretched for hours, not minutes. The platinum ray dragon, Shimmer, keeper of the quantum field where time and space are not the same as what we see when we look at the clock on the wall, smiled and winked at me.

I opened a portal for you. Take all the time you need. It's infinite.

I love hanging out with dragons.

THE STRATEGY

You can follow the instructions here, or let me guide you with my voice and my drum in this YouTube video: https://youtu.be/NEshVgfF9Qw

Spirits are alive. They communicate with you every moment of your life. Can you hear them, feel them, or see them? You have the tools inside you. Every human being can connect to spirits. You arrived in this lifetime with ways to communicate with beings in the spiritual realms. You are wired to sense them.

Set your scene: You'll need a quiet, comfortable place inside or outside and a source of percussion—a drum, rattle, or creative substitute. You can use a bottle of Advil, a spice jar full of beans or popcorn kernels, or even a toilet paper roll half-filled with M&Ms and taped at each end.

Close your eyes. Breathe until you feel relaxed. Begin your percussive sound. Drum, shake or swirl in a rhythm that matches what you feel is your heartbeat. It might sound like *BOOM-bada-boom-boom* or *boom-boom-boom-BOOM*. Focus your love and attention on your heart and follow its beat. Keep going until the sound replaces all other thoughts in your mind. Continue until the very end of this exercise.

Imagine you and I are in the desert at dusk, sitting on a circle of stones around a fire. The tiny twinkling lights of lightning bugs and fairies dance in the air. You pull the warm smoke into your nose and pop-snap of embers into your ears. Your eyes watch the blue flame up around the curve of the central log in the hottest part of the fire. The fire warms your face while the dark desert air chills your back. A gray wolf howls at the stars, activating your cellular DNA. You check the supply of firewood. Is it enough for the whole night? You reach for the tin cup next to you and drink what's inside, feeling it quench your thirst. You sense invisible beings coming to sit with you in the circle. Greet them with gratitude, awe, and wonder. They love you.

As you and I sit together, our vibration coming into alignment with the element of fire, the veil between the physical world and non-physical world becomes so thin, we can move between the worlds. Reach out to the other side with all your senses, including your internal knowing, intuition, and heart. Greet every being with awe and wonder. You may sense ancestors (even ones you never met in real life), ascended masters (Buddha, Jesus, Mary Magdalene), ancient gods (Anubis, Odin, Athena), animals (pets, familiar creatures, or archetypes of animals), or Star Beings (extraterrestrials who live in other solar systems).

Keep creating your percussion. It will be slow or fast, whatever you need. If you experience a sensation, vision, or hear a message, keep going. You'll remember what you need. If you begin to lose the connection, make the percussion louder and a bit faster. Breathe three times in through your nose and out through your mouth without pausing. Everything you are doing is practice. Let it be what it needs to be this time.

When you feel complete in your journey to the spiritual world, slow your percussion and rest in your breath. Open your eyes and relax your body, lying down if that is comfortable for you. Collect the best pieces of your meditation back to you as if you were putting seashells into a basket. You can't take them all! And you aren't meant to. Just bring back what you need. More details may come when you dream tonight or daydream the next day.

Write about your experience in a journal. Or draw a picture of what you experienced. Pick your favorite creative outlet to express the sensory details that you noticed. That's important. Look for the details that were easy for you - sights, sounds, tastes, or feelings. That is your "clair." That is the extrasensory sense that is strong for you in the spirit world—for example, clairaudience (hearing spirits) or claircognizant (gnosis or knowing from spirits). Pay attention to that one and notice if you receive messages through that sense in your daily life. Practice using that sense when you meditate. Focus your love and attention on that sense and allow it to carry you through the veil again and again.

The personal calamity you endured brought you to the door of a spiritual journey. What feels like isolation is a shamanic initiation into a richer, fully-embodied physical experience. You are never alone and have never been alone. Feeling alone is being disconnected from God. You are a spirit in a physical body supported by other spirits and other celestial bodies. Imagination is the key. Free yourself from the limits of three dimensions and five senses. You have the ability to sense many dimensions with senses designed to guide your life's journey toward your highest and best purpose. The journey within is inevitable. Start now.

I'm Atlantis Wolf, and I believe in you.

Atlantis Wolf is a Shamanic Life Coach who helps people heal from chronic pain using licensed medical massage techniques, emotional release therapy, and spiritual guidance. Her joy is connecting people to the world of Spirit with drumming, guided meditations, and fire circles.

She was spiritually asleep until events around her mother's death awakened her gifts to see and communicate with spiritual beings, power animals, and galactic dragons. She remembers her past lives as an Egyptian healer, Toltec curandera, and Ayurvedic traveling shaman.

Atlantis grew up on a single-lane dirt road in rural Ohio, sure her mother was an angel in human form, whistling to birds and asking herself one question: What am I supposed to be doing here on Earth? She continues to walk into the forest at sunrise in all weather to answer that question almost every day.

She holds dual degrees in Civil Engineering and English with a minor in Environmental Engineering. She has worked as a civil engineer, technical writer, franchise store owner, business analyst, project manager, licensed massage therapist, certified Emotion Code practitioner, marketing consultant, COO, and entrepreneur.

She is a Shamanic Breathwork facilitator and Ordained Shamanic Minister certified by Linda Star Wolf, founder of Venus Rising Association for Transformation and Seneca Wolf Clan lineage keeper. She is also a certified Reiki Master by William Lee Rand, founder of the International Center for Reiki Training.

Atlantis is an Aquarian single mom to three kids and three cats, hot cocoa connoisseur, and six-time Amazon #1 bestselling author. She's available for podcast interviews, retreats, and Shamanic Breathwork events.

Connect with Atlantis:
Website: AtlantisWolf.com
Email: DragonMedicineWoman@gmail.com
Instagram: @DragonMedicineWoman
YouTube: Atlantis Wolf

CHAPTER 22

ANCESTRAL MAPPING OF WEALTH CONSCIOUSNESS

CRAFT YOUR UNIQUE WEALTH IDENTITY USING POTENT DATA FROM YOUR LINEAGE

Laura Mazzotta, LCSW-R, Spiritual Empowerment Coach

MY STORY

"I will never spoil my children."

"There are starving people in Africa."

"Make sure to always have cash on you in case there's an emergency."

Did you hear any of these statements, or something similar, when you were growing up? The first quote was my dad's story because he knew so many whose children were spoiled and entitled. He vowed never to repeat that pattern. The second quote was from several adults in my family, whenever

I wouldn't eat the food on my plate. Their hearts were extending across the globe to show compassion for those in need. The final one was a common theme when I was younger, especially before things were automated and digitized. It was an attempt to keep us safe and sound.

Unfortunately, hearing and repeating these things left me feeling 1) pre-emptively ashamed and afraid that I might become spoiled, always on the edge of my seat to keep tabs on entitlement, 2) guilty that I'm living in a state of privilege and *should* be considering others' hardships *before* listening to my own body, and 3) anxious and mistrusting, always waiting for something bad to happen. All these, combined with other experiences and beliefs I adopted, left me with chronic, persistent anxiety.

I thought it was me, but the problem was the stories underlying each of these beliefs. It wasn't about me at all. Vowing not to spoil your children can be a trauma response to behavior that's made you uncomfortable. You don't want to feel that discomfort or receive the same judgment onto you. However, the message gets encoded in the child's nervous system as money = spoiled. This is not intentional from the person sharing the message, but it's an undesirable byproduct of hearing it repeatedly.

"There are starving people in Africa" gets encoded as, "Don't listen to your body's needs. Instead, honor the collective struggle, first and foremost." This type of statement often turns into people-pleasing or neglecting the signals of your own body. When we do this, our emotional and physical health is sacrificed, little by little, over the course of time.

"Make sure to always have cash on you in case there's an emergency" gets encoded as hypervigilance—always looking over your shoulder for the other shoe to drop. With repetition, this sinks even deeper into a lack of self-trust and lack of trust in the collective, resulting in a persistent state of fear. This is how people end up stuck, seemingly with no way out.

There are always exceptions to these outcomes, of course. Not everyone will interpret these statements the same way. However, I guarantee the impact will be significant if you're an empath. Empaths easily pick up the energy of others and, especially as children, internalize them as truths.

Not knowing I was an empath left me unable to recognize how easily my energy and state of being were persuaded. This left me feeling something was inherently wrong with me, that I was naturally flawed and needed this redirection to be good enough, rather than realizing I was carrying the energy of others.

Later in life, we gain conscious awareness of these belief systems and discover the dissonance between our conditioning and the values on which we desire to structure our lives. We are then left with a decision: Align with our conditioning or align with the future version of ourselves.

It's brave to choose your future self, especially when you're not feeling good enough—what most people don't realize is you get to honor your history while choosing the next-level version of yourself. This isn't a black-and-white situation where you need to choose one or the other.

It can feel that way when we begin to do things differently, and there are reactions from those around us. However, you don't have to internalize this as judgment or pressure. Internalizing leads to performance anxiety and people-pleasing. Instead, you get to share the new version of yourself and communicate the choices you've made to better your life. In fact, you can invite them with you! It's their decision whether they accept that invitation.

Invite and detach from the outcome. The journey of your loved ones differs from your own. You are meant to complement each other's path rather than dictate it.

This is the part where people shrink back: They want to choose themselves, but the guilt and anxiety of setting boundaries with loved ones are too daunting. Do it anyway, gently and lovingly, simply by communicating how new things feel more aligned for your optimal vitality.

One of the best ways to do this is by appreciating others' feedback and assuming the best of intentions. For instance, you could respond with, "Thank you for sharing. I'm so grateful for our connection and always take your thoughts into consideration." By listening to them, you're considering what they've said but ultimately making a sovereign choice from the options on the table.

The other way to communicate new values is using "I" statements. Instead of telling someone what you don't like about their response, share how you feel and what you are and are not available for. For example, you could say, "I am making some changes I know will make me feel better. I'll let you know how it goes." This response indicates you are prioritizing your own state, you're confident about the path you're taking, and you will inform them if you desire to share rather than them intruding on you when they want an update.

Lastly, you aren't required to keep people posted on what you're doing and where you're going in life. That's no one's business but your own. When you shift your values, live your life as you desire and respond as above when others chime in.

It's normal to feel guilt and fear as you share this new version of yourself, but these emotions are not a reason to avoid change. The only way to not fall prey to the guilt and fear long-term is to consistently choose what makes you feel best. Trust that these feelings will gradually dissipate over time. Otherwise, you end up at the beck and call of your emotions.

Trusting is easier said than done, especially if there's been trauma in the family line: I have yet to meet someone whose wealth consciousness isn't firmly rooted in their lineage. This is true for every human being incarnated on this planet, me included. Numerous scientific studies have shown that trauma is passed down through at least three generations.

However, it's very important not to blame the humans who shared conditioned messages with us or passed down their fears. Our ancestors weren't intentionally harming us. They were doing their best to optimize their relationships, mental health, physical health, and day-to-day tasks.

They were sharing wisdom extracted from their lived experience, educating us so we don't make the same mistakes. Their intentions were meant to support our growth, but as society evolves, so do our interpretations of these mistakes.

You're not required to adopt these statements or belief systems as gospel. Ask yourself how these words, and the values underlying them, resonate within your body. Do they feel comfortable? Expansive? Do they get you excited to take on the world?

If not, release them. Know they are no longer yours to carry, even if you don't have all the details of your ancestors' stories. Your ego wants all the nitty-gritty details to create a concrete plan forward. However, you can gather a general understanding of the context from which these stories came without having all the answers, so you can send compassion and love to that layer of your ancestry.

While you consider the lineage that came before you, you get to create your own roadmap from your unique perspective, inner guidance, and the legacy you want to leave behind. This is the exact practice I will be taking you through in just a moment.

I want you to feel empowered and sovereign. I want you to know how deeply you naturally embody wealth consciousness, that your only disconnection from it is conditioning and stories that may or may not have been told by you. I want you to know how powerful you are and your ability to amplify and express this through your wealth identity.

Yes, wealth is an identity. It's a consciousness, a state of being. To embody this involves full appreciation and acceptance of who you are and the distinct magic you bring to the world. Self-love is the surest precursor to and ultimate sustainer of wealth. How can you deeply devote yourself to building momentum toward wealth? How can you nourish yourself at every layer: physical, mental, emotional, energetic, and spiritual?

Money amplifies the best and worst of you (not that anything is technically bad— that's just our own judgment). Raising your vibration, getting clear on where you're going, and sustaining this direction is what will keep you in your wealth identity.

Through the following exercise, I guide you into deeper self-understanding, particularly around wealth consciousness within your lineage, to enhance self-love and appreciation of the journey before and beyond you.

THE STRATEGY

Our ancestors were doing the best they could. They were focused on their relationships, wellness, and daily tasks, not just how they spent or interacted with money and wealth.

They had thoughts about money, of course, but they often came from scarcity. There was a story about the sacrifice that their commitment to more money meant less time with themselves, their families, and freedom. They were stifled by a deep, persistent obligation to provide or else.

This mentality created a tension-filled relationship with money that wasn't initially intended. The energy around this, and the stories told, traveled through the generations to land within our hearts and belief systems.

Now we are confused about what is ours and what is not for us to carry forward. Let's resolve that.

Step 1: Grab a piece of paper and a pen (a colorful one you adore.)

Step 2: Hold the paper in landscape orientation and draw a horizontal line across the page.

Step 3: Close your eyes and take a deep breath, all the way to the base of your spine. Allow a wave of soothing energy to ripple down from your head to your toes. Smile. Drop your shoulders back and down and loosen your jaw. Allow any tension from the day to wash over and through you, dissolving into Mother Earth. Stay here as long as needed to sink into a state of relaxation. You may want to adjust how you are holding your body so you can really settle in and allow your body to be held by the space in which you're sitting. To make this easier and deeper, you can listen as I guide you through this relaxation practice here: https://www.theakashictherapist.com/resources.

Step 4: Think about money. What is the first thought, word, or feeling that pops into your awareness?

Step 5: Jot this down at the end of the line furthest to the right. This is an automatic, subconscious belief about money that is closest to the surface for resolution. The thoughts, feelings, and beliefs that pop up first are ready to be released. They no longer want to be trapped within you. You're giving them a space to land and transform.

Step 6: Now, gaze at this belief on the right end of the line. Trace the line with your finger a couple of inches to the left. Place a dot or heart right at that spot.

Step 7: Close your eyes again, taking another deep breath in, feeling into the first memory you have of this feeling, thought, or belief. Write it down just under this heart or dot you drew.

Step 8: Add as much context as you'd like underneath this memory. Here are a few questions you can tap into to assist with this process:

- Who was there?
- What's the scene look like in your memory?
- Where were you?
- What were you doing?
- Were you engaged or observing?
- How did you feel?
- How did the others in the memory feel?
- What were they thinking?
- What were you thinking?
- What was the lens you were seeing this memory through (meaning, take note of your perspective and mindset you were in at the time?)
- Who was the central player in this memory? In other words, who impacted and imprinted this belief most deeply?

Step 9: Now trace the line with your fingers again, a couple more inches to the left. Place a dot or heart right at that spot.

Step 10: Close your eyes again. Take another deep breath in, feeling into the closest memory/association of the primary player you identified in Step 8. This could involve identifying with the primary player and tuning into what came before this on their behalf. It could also be a memory you were a part of that you know or remember. Whichever it is, write down what first comes to mind under the second heart or dot you drew. Don't get caught up in knowing whether this is fully true. Trust that whatever comes into your mind is what you need to complete this exercise.

Step 11: Add as much context as you'd like underneath this memory. Here are a few questions you can tap into to assist with this process:

- Who was there?
- What's the scene look like?
- Where were you/the primary player?
- What were you/they doing?
- Were you/they engaged or observing?
- How did you/they feel?
- How did the others in the memory feel?
- What were they/you thinking?
- What were the others in the memory thinking?
- What was the lens you/they were seeing this memory through (meaning take note of your/their perspective and the mindset you/they were in at the time?)
- Who was the central player in this memory? In other words, who impacted and imprinted this belief most deeply?

Important note: Be conscious of the current state you're in as you're processing this belief. For instance, if you're angry at your father and this memory brings up your father, recite the Ho'oponopono prayer of forgiveness (Thank you, I love you, Please forgive me, I'm sorry) until you feel the energy start to dissipate, or write a letter to this person, that you don't send, to release whatever is necessary for lightening the space between you. When you are in the space of resentment or conflict, the information coming forward will be distorted by your own lens.

Step 12: Continue tracing the line backward a couple of inches to add another heart or dot. Close your eyes and breathe, activating the relaxation response again, and call forward the next memory, repeating steps 9 - 11 until you feel complete. You will know you're complete when you don't have any information coming forward, or you feel a block in the energy. I usually have about four-to-six hearts on my timeline.

This doesn't mean you're fully complete. It may mean you're complete for now and need the energy to settle for a bit before returning to expand this exercise. There is always room to go deeper, but you get to decide when you feel resolution.

When we refine our wealth consciousness, it's a process of unfoldment. As you integrate this new information into your energy field, new layers of your wealth identity will be revealed. You can always return to this practice to peel back more layers.

Step 13: Once you're complete, glance at your timeline from a bird's eye view. Take in the energy of how this belief progressed and formed into what it is today. Feel into which point holds the greatest potency for transformation. Usually, this is the final heart or dot on the left side of your line, but not always. There may be a point of potency in between.

Trust that where you're drawn is what you're ready to integrate and shift at this time. You may find a point of deeper potency during a subsequent phase of this process.

Step 14: Write a letter to empathize with the primary person's state of being at the time of the memory you've written down. Call in the highest healing light to wash over them, you, and the most potent scene from your timeline. Recite the Ho'oponopono prayer until the energy dissipates. Now place your hands on your heart space and take a deep breath in, honoring yourself for offering to heal yourself, those who came before you, and those who come after you.

Step 15: Call in the energy of the primary person you just wrote to and prayed for. Connect to your most burning desire for this lifetime. Check-in with how your pursuit of this will impact this person. Listen for their response. They may communicate with you through a sensation coming forward in your body, an emotion, a repeating thought, an image, or just a clear knowing. The more relaxed you are, the more data you will collect.

Step 16: With your energy combined, decide what serves you both in your movement forward. How can you collectively lighten your story around and experience of money? What is the legacy you'd both like to leave behind for future generations?

Craft these answers into a mantra to use each time the first belief, on the far right of your timeline, or the energy of it, enters your awareness. The more you practice this, especially in a state of deep relaxation, the more it becomes programmed into your subconscious and energy field.

You have just completed an immersive and profoundly transformative practice for shifting your wealth consciousness. Your thoughts and belief systems shape how you feel and show up in the world. Transforming their content into energy that serves your deepest desire, combined with the legacy of your lineage, will infinitely serve you and generations after you.

You are an alchemist, a powerful being of light meant to transmute the heavy energies we have embodied on this planet. Thank you for your service and for offering yourself the space, time, and compassion to actualize the highest version of yourself. Collective healing begins with us. Celebrate that each step you take in this process enhances the palpable love accessible to this world.

Offer thanks to the person that came forward to experience this exercise with you. Place your hands in a prayer pose and take a deep breath in, allowing a smile to form across your face, knowing how closely connected you are to the lineage with which you are powerfully crafting a new and liberating story of prosperity and wealth.

Wealth gets to mean whatever you desire it to mean. For me, wealth means richness of wisdom, intimacy, connection, and freedom. What does it now mean to you?

Laura Mazzotta, LCSW-R, is a spiritual empowerment coach and therapist with over 18 years of experience. Her mission is to guide multi-passionate women into ditching indecision and confidently owning their multifaceted gifts, so they can thrive with intimacy, abundance, and freedom. Laura knows the most successful formula for optimal vitality, and limitless business expansion is potent, core-level healing combined with uniquely soul-aligned empowerment strategies. With extensive knowledge and skills in modalities such as EFT (tapping), Regression Therapy, Trauma, Inner Child Work, and intuitive development, Laura knows how to guide your healing journey in a unique, compassionate, and highly efficient way.

During her recovery from a serious illness in 2016, Laura exhausted western medicine approaches and realized her deep passion for holistic methods, becoming an even greater advocate for personal development and transformation. Laura knows true healing occurs much more powerfully when all components (physical, mental, energetic, and spiritual) of a person's issue are addressed. She's here to guide her clients in all steps on that journey and empower them to share their natural gifts with the world!

Laura lives in New York with her husband of 20 years, three fabulous children, and one adorable golden retriever.

You can find Laura at www.theakashictherapist.com and join her free Facebook group: The Expansion Portal.

CHAPTER 23

EMBODIMENT OF THE HEALER WITHIN

BALANCING THE REALMS

Hollie Renea

MY STORY

What does it mean to fully embody the healer? I banged my head against the desk, trying to figure out what I was doing with this chapter. I wondered, knowing it was something I always claimed but felt so eager to understand on another level and layer.

For the last eight years, I've lived in direct connection to the higher realms. As I contemplate the story of what it means to understand embodying the healer within, I find myself looking outside of me.

As a professional psychic medium and someone who teaches others how to advance their gifts while owning their mission here on Earth, it's not uncommon for me to call upon my spiritual team and the forces around me who desire to have an influence on what I'm about to talk about. This has been the main source of credit I've given to the evolution of my spiritual journey.

As I sit poolside, feet in the warm water, pondering a deeper explanation for what's going through my mind as I move through a pivotal time in consciousness. I looked down to see a green grasshopper floating in the water. I understand now in my journey that when something is brought to your attention, there is no such thing as coincidence. I dipped my posh cheetah sunglasses into the pool's surface and watched as the grasshopper embraced the life raft in front of him. He took temporary residency on the sunglasses until he could dry off and move forward. I reflected on a time when I had no balance between the physical and spiritual realms.

One evening after a long day of psychic readings, teaching, and mentoring, I found myself in tears, staring into the mirror in complete confusion. At this time in my life, I was doing 20-30 readings a week from my bedside table. I was in a constant state of mental and spiritual exhaustion. I was balancing a business that didn't have a proper energy exchange. I was a mother to a toddler and a wife. And a human who truly felt a call upon her soul to serve the masses.

It was so frustrating to me because this was where I always wished I would be—the place I dreamt of for so long. I felt I had finally stepped into the mission I signed up for in this lifetime. I found myself embodying the channel for the higher realms, embracing myself as the conduit of healing for those who crossed my path.

Prior to this time, the journey was not for the faint of heart. Embodying the healer comes with knowing and understanding what a healer really is.

There was a time in my life when enough was enough. I was shattered with doubt and crippled with anxiety. There was not much more I knew that I could do. In my life up until this point, I had no idea of the true ability I held within. I was constantly in fear, entangled with the beliefs of everyone else around me. I knew no difference between others' energies from my own. I felt different than everyone else.

The room was dim, and the candles lit my swollen eyes as I begged for an understanding of the Divine. "How am I supposed to continue this way? All I ever desire is to serve, I've followed my intuitive promptings, and I feel it's left me with nothing. I cannot keep going on this way."

At the time, my bedside table was crammed with candles, crystals, and symbolic novelties, with a mirror leaning against the wall reflecting the depletion in my face. Anytime I do a session, and I'm drawn to look into my own eyes, I always know there's a specific message coming for me. I felt my eyes rise to the mirror, knowing full well that my higher self desired to have a conversation with me.

Remember the human and allow her to speak. I was immediately taken aback. *What does that mean? She never stops speaking. Haha!*

I sat, a bit confused but did what my higher self suggested. I allowed this version of me to finally be seen. She was abandoned, alone, exhausted, drained, overworked, and confused about what to do next.

You have worked yourself so hard that you've forgotten the part of you so desperately needing your own healing. My higher self chimed in. *There is nothing wrong with owning yourself as the healer. Where you miss the mark is forgetting the one who brings the healing. You're looking at her now.*

I couldn't break eye contact with myself. I was in awe of the remembrance of this vessel I chose to incarnate into.

I began channeling with deep reflection. There is a beauty in tapping into the higher realms and understanding the consciousness we all seek to know. I remembered the embodiment of owning the mission I came here with, to heal the collective. I had quickly forgotten the importance of me— my own healing journey.

Just as I now sit, I realize that in every moment, I've felt as though I must find some way to define what it means to own the title of a healer we humans created. I felt I must be something more than what I already am to embody the healer within. But in reality, it's innately who I already am.

Poolside, I quickly came back to my surroundings with this perspective: I didn't question whether I should have saved the grasshopper. I didn't panic, thinking, *what if he doesn't get on the sunglasses?* Because at that moment, I acted. I took the only tools I had available to assist in the journey of another soul. I didn't do it because someone told me to. I did it because as I fill up my cup, I may also assist those who do so themselves.

As healers, one soul offers another soul, big or small, a helping hand. We use the tools we know to assist in the journey beyond. We are part of one collective mind, desiring to be something that is right within our hearts. Follow the intuitive nudge. Utilize the sources available to you now and release the need to be anything different than who you are.

THE STRATEGY

As healers, we will find ourselves working in higher realms and timelines. This Earth, the reality you're perceiving in front of you right now, is within the 3D realm. We are in human form, experiencing life through our physical eyes. However, beyond that are other higher states of consciousness and awareness. The way it has been shown to me before in meditation is the idea of multiple third eyes. Although we don't have this, we can understand that there are levels and layers to the state of consciousness we see.

The higher the consciousness or realm allows for a shift in perspective that then allows you to see beyond the 3D while still experiencing it. If your focus is only on the higher realms, you'll find yourself becoming disconnected from the reality in front of you. That is not truly living.

The journey of embodying the healer is much simpler than what you may perceive. Embodiment is the essence of fully becoming a version of something. When you identify and know you are the healer, there is nothing more that needs to be done.

The difficulty of this process is when we forget the human. It's when we're so driven to assist the collective that we forget the importance of remembering us as souls experiencing human life. There is nothing wrong with living within the higher realms or higher states of consciousness until it's depleting the human within. The strategy of balancing the realms will be to learn how to remember the human while still existing in a multidimensional frequency that inevitably occurs on the journey as a healer.

As someone who developed and utilized techniques through this process, use some of these to see which fits best for you. As you grow in your state of consciousness and explore the higher realms, these techniques may change or shift.

Let's start with grounding techniques used for the human.

1. Connect to the breath and release. You may be thinking this is so easy. However, when we're tapped into the realms of other states of consciousness, it's very difficult to remember the importance of the body. Our breath takes our awareness back into the body to remind us of our safety here. A big part of healing others means

we can hold a lot of others' energies we may or may not work with. So try this exercise with me. Put your hand on your heart, close your eyes, and take two deep breaths. Ask yourself how much percentage of others people's energy you are holding onto. Once you have received the number from your higher self, take a deep breath of the most beautiful pink color and breathe out any energy that's not yours. Repeat this process until you have made it back to 0%.

2. Utilize the mirror as a portal to come back to the body. How often do you find yourself looking in the mirror and not even acknowledging the human housing your spirit at this time? They're desiring to know you and speak to you, to be honored as you heal those around you. Take a moment throughout your day to make contact with you, the avatar who beats your heart without question, who keeps going even when it needs a break. Remember the human.

3. Feel joy. Yep, you heard me! Stop letting the little stuff steal from your energy. You're just as worthy of enjoying the pleasures of life as any other soul on this planet. You're here to experience you. The rest always will follow. When you're filled with joy, peace, and happiness, it attracts the most abundant version of you available. Now, don't get me wrong. I'm not suggesting you bypass your heavy, dense feelings. That is a part of the journey of being a healer, after all.

While incorporating the higher realms, I've come to find out that nothing in this world is a coincidence. Every single thing caught in your awareness is for some sort of purpose. How can you bring this into human reality?

1. Call upon your spiritual team as much as possible. Each and every one of us has a team of spiritual beings, all existing in higher states of consciousness. Some have experienced this. Some have signed up for a journey to support through the eyes of the healer as they incarnate here on Earth. No matter what their journey, each of you has one. Ask them for a sign throughout the day. Be very specific. A few examples are: 111, a black bird, and a blue giraffe. Get silly with it, and then be open! This is a beautiful technique

that allows the ego to get on board with the understanding that there is much more out there desiring to assist us. The sign can show up anywhere. Remember, as healers, you know exactly what to do.

2. Sit in silence. Simple right? Well, maybe not for some. Our mind is hard-wired to chat, to go a million miles an hour. It's our job to master the mind. I mean, this is Earth, after all. It's a part of the game we're here to play. When we allow the thoughts we've been avoiding to finally be heard, they take away their power over us. Hear them out, honor them, and then let them float away like clouds in the sky. Once the mind is quiet, this is when the higher aspects of you have an opportunity to speak. This is where the ancient knowledge you seek is now able to drop in.

3. Be open to the messages from the beings who enter your reality, big or small. Just like the grasshopper in my story above, there was a message. As healers, we have to begin shifting our perspective to the things we hear and know and the other ways the higher realms may be revealing messages to us. Have no expectations of what will come. Open your heart, open the channel and remember, you are a spiritual being having a human experience. And this experience is meant to be filled with the balance of duality—100% human and 100% Divine.

So to the healer, I say this to you now, thank you for your courage to stand in this human form, to continue to understand the balance of the shadow and the light and the balance of the lower and higher realms. This journey is not easy, but it's rewarding. When you understand the balance of the realms, you understand the balance of what it means to embody exactly who you are, the healer. I see you. I love you. I am you.

Hollie Renea is a professional psychic medium specializing in working closely with higher dimensional beings to assist healers in remembering their mission here on Earth. She teaches the healer how to embody their power, activate their ancient knowledge, and advance their skills to the next level—remembering their deep connection to the higher realms while still honoring the human experience.

As a galactic intuitive, most of the information channeled and shared has been knowledge and techniques that create the happiest human experience available to the soul. The mastery of the matrix while doing the work of a healer.

Hollie loves to enjoy warm baths, color, and paint with her kids! You can catch her outside with a glass of green tea, listening to the birds in the springtime!

Connect with Hollie Renea
Website: Hollierenea.com
Facebook Group: https://www.facebook.com/groups/homeforthehealer
Instagram: https://www.instagram.com/holliereneaxo/
Linktree: https://linktr.ee/Hollierenea

CHAPTER 24

MAGICAL CIRCLE

CHOOSE THE TOOLS TO CREATE YOUR OWN MAGIC

Thais Conte

MY STORY

Who would believe that someone who doesn't like to move would live in so many places? Yes, that's me! I started moving when I was eight and have not stopped until now. I hope it will be in my last place, Georgia, for many years to come.

Good or bad, the things I lived through brought me here today, and this shy girl has become a woman that likes to communicate and connect with people.

We all have our battles, some greater than others. However, we shouldn't try to compare because we all feel them differently. Our perspectives are individual and usually depend on how mature we are and on our life experiences. It's never about winning the battle is about winning the war, and it's not about the struggle itself is what we make from it that will make a difference in our lives. Embrace this knowledge, it usually happens to us for a reason, and we can choose to learn or sink with it.

My personal battle started at the young age of two when I was a perfectly healthy child; suddenly, I stopped eating, talking, and walking and lost control of my tiny little body. This scary situation lasted less than a month, which to my young parents seemed like years. Little did they know at the time that I had a disease similar to Guillain-Barre Syndrome. I miraculously recovered within a month. I never knew what caused it, but certainly, I know that the most significant part of my cure was feeling loved.

LOVE is an essential ingredient for anything in anyone's life, a powerful medicine. I learned over the years that we deserve to be loved and appreciated, though this feeling must start with us. We need to love ourselves to love others truly and to let ourselves be loved.

I have so much to tell you. What I must share today began in early March 2021 when I found a hard and painful mass on my left breast. At first, I thought: *it's probably a cyst and will disappear once I get my period.* My period came, almost a month passed, and it was still there, bigger and beating like a heart. *Hum, I better get this checked; that isn't good, but it's probably nothing serious. As they say, cancer doesn't hurt.*

At the doctor's appointment, I noticed worry on her face. Soon she said, "Thais, this mass is hard and is quite big, I will ask for a mammogram, and they will probably also do an ultrasound, and depending on the results, you will have to do a biopsy."

"No, problem. We do what we got to do to get over with it," I said.

She added, "I will also give you the name of this breast surgeon because even if it is nothing serious, from now on, you will have to follow up with her."

Leaving there, even though I remained calm, I wanted to resolve this problem as fast as I could; I kind of knew I had something and that I'd probably need minor surgery, yet it never crossed my mind how serious it could be.

The mammogram results were no good. Neither was the ultrasound results. So, there I was, scheduling my biopsy.

The doctor was excellent; she explained everything. I liked her. I believe we must trust our doctors and that we need to feel secure when listening to them; otherwise, look for a second opinion.

During the biopsy, she said, "I will give you anesthesia around the tumor, but I cannot give it on the tumor, so I cannot be certain if it's going to hurt or not."

Indeed, I was afraid of it hurting; it hurt all the time. *Let's wait for the worst and hope for the best.* And the best possible scenario happened: I didn't feel a thing, and all went smoothly. I had a huge bruise, though the incision was minimal.

Now, waiting and waiting for results is not an easy task for me. Still, that's what I had for the day.

Before my next appointment, I had the results and was doing my research. I tried to avoid the internet since we know there is a lot of good information and a lot of information that can make us worry more than we should. I remember calling a friend and asking her about her experience and learning about her case. I felt relieved and believed I would have a lumpectomy and radiation, just like her, which didn't seem as scary as the word *chemotherapy*. Even though I understood it was cancer, I remained calm and peaceful. I couldn't understand that feeling. *How could someone be so calm? Maybe I'm in denial and feel guilty for feeling okay when so many suffer and fall into despair.*

I always believe in God for a more significant meaning for things. My life was never perfect or how I planned it, but I was always grateful for what I had—my family, friends, a roof over my head, nature, the beautiful things I saw, and the places and people I was able to meet.

I always knew I would have two beautiful kids. I almost lost my baby girl during birth. When she was about 18 months old, I had my first miscarriage; I tried to get pregnant again after a while. We decided to try artificial insemination and fertilization. That was not a problem since I had the health and means to do it, so I was thankful for at least trying to fulfill my sweetest dream. I knew there was a risk of not fulfilling it, but it was worth trying. At least at the end of the journey, I would know I tried and have no regrets. I had faith; *I know someone is watching over me.* My patience and faithfulness were worth it when my sweet boy was born. Maybe now you understand when I say God prepares us for every moment. So, when I heard the horrific C-word, I knew he had a bigger purpose in my life.

GRATITUDE is being thankful, showing appreciation, and returning kindness. I was always grateful for what I had become, and that is a sum of good and bad moments.

Indeed, having met a few cancer survivors and learning about their stories and victories helped me through the process of accepting my new situation. Tati Lucas, a breast cancer survivor, had a double mastectomy and suffered so much during her treatment. Silu Scheffer and Karina Graham were two more names among so many brave warriors. In trying to understand how calm I was, I realized I felt part of something, that I could feel connected with these brave women.

EMPATHY was a quality I developed along the way. It's the ability to put yourself in other people's shoes!

It was time to tell the family about cancer—first, my husband. I tried to walk him through the situation before telling him about my appointments and exams, but he seemed in another world, focused on his job and daily routine, and never asked about it. Finally, after I talked to the breast surgeon and she sent me to the oncologist, I had to tell him, but first, he told me something else.

"I learned today that I will be without a job in a month."

"Sorry to hear that. Unfortunately, I also have some bad news. I have cancer." Then I told him about my oncologist appointment.

At the oncologist appointment:

"This kind of breast cancer, we usually start with chemo to see how it works on the tumor so when we do the biopsy after the surgery, we will be more certain how effective the treatment went. It will probably shrink your tumor or stop it from growing since this has a greater than 90% proliferation rate."

It was an invasive ductal carcinoma, rare and aggressive, Stage II-A, grade 3, triple negative, size 3.5 cm. "If you choose a mastectomy, you probably won't have to do radiation. If you choose lumpectomy, even if the chemotherapy is extremely successful, you must do the radiation to prevent a recurrence."

I couldn't lose more time. I started my preoperative chemotherapy with dose-dense doxorubicin and cyclophosphamide, followed by paclitaxel the following week. It would be a total of eight chemotherapies every two weeks.

Along with all this, I had to tell my family and friends. I chose to tell only my family in Brazil and my oldest friends since I was afraid of them finding out through someone else and worrying more than they should. After that, I created an Instagram page to keep them updated and to help and inform other Brazilian ladies living abroad. I told my closest friends living in Atlanta, one by one, as they reached me, and most of them only knew after my first or second chemotherapy.

I can't forget to mention that then, like today, I had a full-time job, and I told them as soon as I confirmed the cancer diagnosis. They supported me, and I did my best to work every day of the treatment. Of course, that wasn't possible. In the beginning, I tried, but my body and mind didn't let me perform the way I should've, and that was the first and only time I cried. Due to the chemo, I couldn't process information like an average person, and I wasn't able to finish what I was doing. I finally understood what people said about chemo brain, and I started working from home two days after the chemo, returning to the office on the following Mondays.

ACCEPTANCE is accepting the disease and the means offered to cure it. It was an important step. We must fight for things, for a better life, for our beliefs, earn respect, and not accept less than is fair. The sense of justice is deep in my soul, but when we have problems in our lives beyond our control, we should accept and learn from them to become stronger. A better version of us is under construction!

With all this happing, my husband had to move to another city to start his new job; moving was not an option. We knew that in the beginning he would be here only on the weekends. And as soon as things were under control, he would manage to live part of the month here and avoid the six-hour commute each way. Because of that, my mom came to rescue us.

Keeping an active mind and thinking about other things besides my treatment made everything easier. It certainly saved me from depression and helped me keep a positive attitude.

DO SOMETHING THAT MAKES YOU HAPPY. It's known to be true that hormones of happiness help in the healing process.

236 | WEALTH CODES

Am I getting bald? Not a problem. I can choose the kind of hair to wear and have fun picking wigs. At least that was the idea, but I had a hard time picking a wig and adapting to them. Though I personally never had a problem being bald, losing your hair is challenging. Nevertheless, I loved myself even after losing all the hair on my body. At first, I felt weird with my big white head, and I told myself: *I am a good-looking alien!*

SENSE OF HUMOR in this situation is the ability to choose to laugh and make fun of oneself instead of feeling sorry for yourself.

Although not suffering most side effects of chemo, the journey was a hard and long one that I still feel in my body and soul. After my fifth chemo, my kids and I tested positive for Covid, my son with no symptoms, my daughter with mild symptoms, and I with every single hair of my body. Actually, forget the hair, I had no hair at this point. I felt it with every single part of my body. I was feeling so bad that Wednesday morning, I had to go to the Urgent Care so someone could see me and tell me if I would be okay. Besides the aching, my left arm numbed, and I had pain in my chest since the night before. Never go to Urgent Care complaining of chest pain. They will send you straight to the ER. And that was my first ride in an ambulance. No worries, it was a long day, but everything was fine, though I couldn't tell at the time if it was Covid or the side effects of chemo. As I suspected, I found out it was both.

Confident that I'm no Pollyanna, I believe that being positive during turbulent times will help you move out of the distress zone. I genuinely believed something better would happen, and the bad things that happened were only a chapter of my life. And I, as the writer of my own story, always choose a happy end.

POSITIVENESS is being full of hope and feeling confident that better days will come.

A year has passed since I found out I had cancer. My lumpectomy was a great success with no residual carcinoma. Lymph nodes were negative for metastatic disease. I finished my radiation therapy on December 30th, 2021, and started the new year, leaving all of this behind. Well, almost!

As the new year began, I felt more tired and depressed. No, I'm not Wonder Woman. I was about to burn out. Some say it was PTSD. I counted the days to have my next surgery so I could finally take days off work to rest.

I, someone always afraid of surgeries, looking forward to having another one? Desperate times, desperate thinking!

After my genetic test confirmed that I didn't have the BRAC gene but a genetic predisposition for ovarian cancer, I scheduled a total hysterectomy. As my friend Silvia Osorio knows, ovarian cancer is silent and dangerous, so I did not doubt it was in my best interest to have this surgery. When I found out about the possibility of having ovarian cancer, I understood it as a sign from God telling me to slow down and live more happy moments and that I should seek the means to avoid a more dangerous and deadly cancer. After all the reasons I told you about how calm I was and how well I dealt with this situation, I have to say one last and powerful word: *Faith.*

FAITH is a strong belief in God based on spiritual apprehension rather than proof.

Nowadays, I'm still struggling with my neuropathy. My knees hurt, both feet feel numb, and when I go downstairs, it seems like I have an elephant's leg; when I walk on flat ground, I think I'm walking on the clouds, like magic. Recently my right arm started hurting; it's been over a month, and it doesn't get better. I have made new appointments to investigate if there is something I can do about it. I know that I can manage to live this way and still be happy and full of life, as long as it doesn't get worse than it is. I trust everything will be okay, and meanwhile, I'm trying to have more time for myself and my family and rethinking my life and my choices. Even though I love my job and I need my paycheck, I know that working fewer hours is no longer an option but a reality. I don't have control over everything because I am an adult with kids and have my responsibilities, though I trust my intuition that everything will be all right, that, as always, God will show me the way to a more balanced life.

As a gorgeous warrior once told me:

"I shall walk by faith not by sight." 2 Corinthians 5:7

That was my magical circle, and those were the tools I used. What about yours?

THE STRATEGY

The tool I chose to share is what I just started using on myself. I believe that consciously I have done everything in my power to release all bad energy or feelings. Yet, I realize I cannot control my subconscious. I'm sure that this will allow me to improve the quality of my thoughts and subconscious beliefs to avoid further psychopathic stress, which is the biggest problem in the origin of diseases.

HO'OPONOPONO (pronounced HO-oh-Po-no-Po-no) is an ancient healing practice for forgiveness from Hawaii. Chanting this prayer repeatedly is a way of cleansing your mind and releasing bad feelings and negative thoughts. I'm optimistic that it will work as a mantra of self-love.

"I'm sorry. Please forgive me. Thank you. I love you!"

It works like a meditation, and you can use a Japamala* to guide you with the number of repetitions needed to start working positively on your mind.

There are many tools available for you but remember, nothing is more important than loving yourself and your faith. I'm sure that love, empathy, acceptance, doing something that makes you happy, positiveness, a sense of humor, and faith will make your journey easier.

*A garland, usually with 108 beads, commonly used to aid with meditation and for prayers in other religions, or as I'd rather say, as a spiritual exercise.

Thais Conte, a writer, speaker, ordained minister, and cancer survivor, learned to adapt to new cultures and learned different languages from a young age. Relocating with her family to other countries brought her vast knowledge and diversity into her life. Nowadays, she lives in Atlanta, is currently the president of Rotary Club Atlanta Brazil, is a mother and wife, and works a full-time job.

Instagram:iamthaisconte
Instagram:this_pink_lady
Linktree: https://linktr.ee/thaisconte

CHAPTER 25

VISION CASTING
YOU HAD THE POWER
ALL ALONG

CHANNEL WRITE YOUR WAY TO LIMITLESSNESS

Stephanie Zito, Intuitive Soul Purpose Alchemist

MY STORY

> *"Wealth is the freedom to live a sovereign,*
> *abundant life living your soul's fullest expression."*

You can turn back. You don't have to go. The voice in my head was clear.

The space around me is dead silent.

Everything is still, except for this voice. Seconds before, my red Ford Explorer, packed to the brim with all my belongings for a cross-country move, spins around not once, not twice, but three times and comes to a metal-bending, screeching stop. My heart is pounding. I glance out my side window to see only a guardrail standing between me and a long drop into a weathered ravine.

That was a near miss. I think my guardian angels had my back.

I hit black ice while arguing on my cell phone with my boyfriend, Dave.

This is the same boyfriend I'm driving from Utah to Kentucky for—to start my life with.

I literally just left my job, apartment, and life in Utah. What will I do if I don't continue to Kentucky?

It's not lost on me that my car is literally turned the wrong way on the road, back in the direction from which I came.

After surveying the damage, highway patrol eventually shows up and deems it okay for me to carry on. I throw my SUV bumper in the trunk, pull a u-turn off the breakdown lane, and drive east to Dave.

This isn't how a relationship is supposed to feel.

Six months into my relationship with Dave, I'm so distraught that I'm not sleeping well. In fact, Dave hands me a bottle of melatonin one night to help me. I laugh to myself, knowing it's a Band-Aid for the real issue. Our relationship is breaking down as fast as my Explorer did after the crash. Something has to shift.

You need to leave. The voice in my head urges.

But, I'm afraid.

I hire a wise and patient somatic coach, Madeline Wade.

"Get quiet," Madeline says to me over a phone session, "Listen to your inner voice."

She asks me to scan my body. I come to my heart space, and I feel the pain. My upper back feels like dry driftwood. My heart flushes with sadness, and the tears flow. Madeline invites me to make the following dedication to myself, "I am a commitment to *loving* myself." It feels unexpectedly foreign to me, and I break down sobbing. I land on a version that speaks to me: "I am a commitment to *seeing* myself."

At that moment, I picture myself as a young child. I see her and can feel empathy for her.

That is my first step towards radically loving myself. In doing so, I feel safe trusting my inner voice, just like the one that spoke to me in the car crash months before.

After that session with Madeline, I continue to do the work. Within the next three months, I get crystal clear on what I really want.

"Come to California. You can move in with me," my friend Kelley offers over a phone call. "I even have some work for you when you get here." I release a giant exhale I didn't even know I was holding. Fear begins to shift into the excitement of possibilities.

Is this what it means when they say the Universe has your back?

This is the gateway to my dream location and a coveted job at the therapeutic high school Kelley owns.

I make the radically scary choice to leave what I know, despite not knowing how things will turn out. Now that I'm crystal clear on what I really want, and I say yes to leaping into the unknown, it's as if the Universe lines my dream life up for me.

I pack my new gray Chrysler Sebring convertible (that replaced my totaled Explorer) and leave Dave and Kentucky for California. I get hired full-time at my dream job, getting paid to be me. I start my long-awaited yoga teacher training and meet my now husband, Mark. This all happens within three months of moving and standing for myself.

Is this all really happening? I just fell into my dream life.

Is this what they call a quantum leap?

It's now 2013, and Mark and I live in Encinitas, California, with our firstborn, Bella. I'm feeling this inner nudge to launch my career as a life coach. The whisper "to coach" has nudged me for some time, but I don't know what to call myself or how to describe what I do. I'm afraid people won't get me, as I work with energy, chakras, and intuition. I've had this inkling to launch my coaching practice before but ignored it because of my fears.

How are people going to understand what you do?

Sometimes, our spirit guides give us people and synchronicities to show us the way. We just have to pay attention and say yes. I could have easily missed a crucial message my spirit guide sent me if I had not said yes.

One day, I opened my inbox to find an email from a lady who wanted to buy a hula hoop from me. Let me explain. Before meeting my husband, I had a hoop dance business. I sold adult-sized hula hoops and taught hoop dance all over beaches and yoga studios around Orange County. While Mark and I dated, he accompanied me to farmers' markets and patiently sat with me while I sold hoops. I still had a bunch of hoops in our garage but hadn't been actively teaching for a while. I didn't even realize my hoop dance website, *Hoopify*, was still active.

I saw the email from a lady named Sandra requesting a hula hoop. The only caveat is that Sandra cannot drive. She asks if I can bring the hoop to her. I say yes.

I load up my sweet two-year-old daughter, Bella, and a shiny, pink, and purple striped hula hoop and make the short drive to Sandra. I pull up to Sandra's bungalow, surrounded by lush, tropical plants. Sandra, an older, heavy-set woman in a long flowy dress and kind eyes, greets us at her door, and we enter her small, darkish living room.

Bella's eyes widen, immediately fascinated by trays of sparkling crystals adorning desks and end tables in the room.

As Bella gently explores, Sandra tells me she is a sought-after psychic medium.

"Our meeting isn't about the hoop," Sandra tells me with a knowing look.

"You're meant to read this," she says, pulling a book she wrote off a shelf. (This was so long ago I don't recall the title, as I gave the novel to a friend once I felt complete with its message.) Something felt so right about this meeting; I couldn't wait to begin.

While I could've just left the book on my nightstand to collect dust or made an excuse not to read it, I began that night by devouring the text quickly from cover to cover.

What if something greater than ourselves really guides us? What if something or someone sent Sandra to me?

Within the story, Sandra weaves in a process to manifest what you desire.

Grabbing a notebook and paper, I allow the words to flow as I follow her process. I sign and date the page and put it aside.

So much has unfolded for me since that meeting. I look back at my notebooks and am astonished by all the beautiful events that manifested in my life.

When I say yes to my intuition, my life expands exponentially.

Looking back, I recognize the time I feared my intuition. I feared the unknown on the other side of that big decision to leave Dave.

In a similar vein, I was stuck in inaction, not launching a coaching practice that is my absolute soul's calling. The work I do comes through me from something greater than me. You can call it Source, God, the Universe. I recognize I'm a channel for that work to express itself through me.

My guides lined up that meeting with the psychic so she could give me one of the exact tools I now use to help clients connect with their soul's truth and design their dream life.

Since then, I've downloaded a process called Vision Casting that helps clients manifest their dream jobs, soulmate relationships, start soul-led businesses, and more.

The difference is that before using my intuition, I was just trying to go it alone. I made life a lot harder on myself. After surrendering to my intuition, much greater powers collaborate with me to support my soul's highest calling.

You can make all the money in the world and be miserable, but actual wealth is the freedom to live guided by your truth.

For instance, I could have all the money in the world but stay miserable, locked in that relationship with Dave. Alternately, my husband's career could make us financially set, but I wouldn't have the soul fulfillment that comes from doing my soul's work in the world.

Since I began working with intuition, my knowledge and ability only increased through practice. I went from reading the energy centers of clients to using energy to release their blocks and stuck energy. Through working with intuition, I cracked open the channel to communicate with all the intuitive realms, including the highest self, spirit guides, past loved ones, the Akashic Records, and Source. When I go into the intuitive space, I'm connecting with what is called the channel. This channel connects with the whole quantum field of consciousness itself.

I say this because teaching about intuition is one of the most important things to me. Intuition is our freedom. When you deepen your intuition, you connect with this channel. You receive divine messages to help guide your life for your highest good. You can get messages to help you heal physically, emotionally, and energetically. You can connect with your past loved ones. It's all available to you. It just takes practice.

When you connect with this channel, you gain crystal clear clarity. Decisions come effortlessly in your best interest. You receive messages to help guide you. You become open to receiving the support for your soul's expression. When you're not following the desires of others, and when you're not chained to society's norms and traditions, you are your own sovereign being. You're open to freedom and all the abundance that is the nature of the Universe. You become free.

The strategy I offer is a simple process I call Vision Casting, to call in your soul's desires—not those of society, but your true soul spark.

If freedom is what you yearn for, receive my Vision Casting tool below to connect with your higher guidance and design your dream life. In doing this, you send the coding to the Universe and your own brain to run the programs for what you really desire.

Private coaching, group programs, and energy clearings are available at Stephaniezito.com.

THE STRATEGY

This is the Vision Casting process. In this process, you will connect directly with the channel to have a direct line of connection with the higher realms of spirit guides and Source. Two keys are noteworthy about this process.

The first key is that you're connecting with the high vibe emotions of how it feels to be living your dream life. Higher vibration emotions like love and gratitude strengthen our connection with the supportive spirit realm. The spirit realm can sense your excitement and deliver that which serves you. On the flip side, if you're in a place of fearing what you say you want, you may actually get what will protect you from getting it. For instance, if you wish for career success, but you're afraid you'll be stressed out when you're successful, the Universe will give you what will protect you and keep you safe. You'll find yourself sabotaging that career success. So, get excited about what you envision!

The second key is to write in the present tense as if your desires are happening now. We live life in the present. The Universe also responds to what we desire in the present. If I say what I want in the future tense, then the Universe will always see this in the future for me. How can I ever reach it if I always see it in the future? When I see my desire and am excited about it, the Universe will respond to that and more easily orchestrate the circumstances to support me.

Think of when you're connecting with your soul's desires and writing the vision for what you want; it's as simple as making an order at a drive-through. Let's say you are at a drive-through coffee shop. You don't just ask for any sort of coffee when you place your order. You order exactly what you want. "I'll have a venti, caramel, mocha latte with two pumps of vanilla, please." The barista is clear on what you want and delivers that specifically.

In the same vein, declaring what you desire to yourself and the Universe isn't so different. Do not hold back on what you really want. Get clear. And write it down to the thrilling details.

Let's begin.

Grab paper and a pen. I recommend having a journal dedicated to Vision Casting, but any notebook will do. Then, find a quiet space without distraction.

1. Connect in with the Channel

   a. Find a comfortable place to sit. Close your eyes. Take a few deep breaths. Envision a grounding cord that connects from the base of your spine and travels deep into the earth's center, hooking in and grounding you.

   b. In your mind's eye, see a light beam above the crown of your head. Follow this beam of light up through the sky and space to connect with the spirit realm. This light beam connects with your highest self, your past loved ones who support you, your angels, ascended masters, and Source/God/the Universe.

c. "Om" is the sound of the Universe itself. You clear a channel of connection to this highest realm when you chant "Om." Raise your frequency to connect with this channel by chanting three Oms.

2. Connect with Your Future Self

a. Envision yourself some time in the future. You can choose if this is one year, five years, or even ten years into the future.

b. In the dark space behind your eyelids, envision you're traveling into this future time as you count back from ten to one.

c. You're in your future timeline. Take your time to explore using all your senses. Stay in this space for about three to five minutes.

   • Ask yourself the following questions:
     – Where are you?
     – What are you doing?
     – Who, if anyone, is with you?
     – How do you feel?
     – What is most important to you?
     – What do you smell, taste, or touch?

3. Return to the Present

Envision you travel through the dark space right back to where you now sit. With a few deep breaths, bring your visit to the future to completion.

4. Vision Cast Your Future

a. Divide your journal page into four parts. Write a major category of your life at the top of each section. For instance, I would write the words: career, family, self-care, and personal growth. You can have other categories as well, but we're going to start with the most important ones.

    b. In the present tense, write sentences with the desired emotions of how you feel, for all that you truly want in that category of your life. For instance, when I first did this process, I wrote for the category Career: "I happily get paid to be me." "My soulmate clients find me with ease."

    c. As you write, if you second guess yourself or feel what you're writing is too big or too much, notice that thought. The channel from higher guidance can flow through your pen. See it and just keep going with your big vision.

5. Complete the Process

Sign and date your page. Place this in a safe spot to come back to reflect on at some point. Right now, you have done it! There is nothing more you need to do! You have placed your vision out into the world such that your guides can get to work, in tandem with you, to help bring the people, opportunities, and synchronicities to support your big vision. You just have to say yes when those come your way.

Follow a recorded version of this Vision Casting process at
https://bit.ly/wealthcodeswithsteph

A highly regarded intuitive soul purpose alchemist, **Stephanie Zito,** helps people across the globe discover and realize their best lives with both purpose and passion. She has worked with personal clients and numerous corporations, including AT&T, Park Hyatt Hotels, US Peace Corps, and Sesame Street Research, leading team-building, conflict resolution, and wellness programs.

Stephanie is a visionary, psychic medium, and intuitive channel. She is gifted with a channeled method to identify and release clients' blocks from past generations, past lives, or childhood. Clients frequently say that they do more in an hour's session with Stephanie than they have accomplished in years of therapy.

She is the secret sauce for helping entrepreneurs and CEOs make bold decisions in favor of freedom and abundance.

Stephanie teaches online group classes on intuition and connecting with spirit, including the Akashic Records, soul guides, past loved ones, animal spirit guides, and past lives. You can also find her for in-person soul-purpose sessions, intuitive readings, and sound bath healings at the award-winning boutique wellness retreat, Vera Via, in La Costa, California.

Stephanie is the creator of the card deck "Activate Your Chakras" and the book *Manifesting Magic: 102 Quotes to Manifest Your Best Life,* available at https://linktr.ee/stephaniezito

She is the founder and host of the podcast *This Passionate Life,* sharing her knowledge and insights on finding freedom in living your life's purpose.

Stephanie holds a master's degree in Conflict Analysis and Resolution from George Mason University and certifications in yoga, meditation, and holistic life coaching. She lives in San Marcos, California, where she paddleboards, practices yoga and enjoys exploring the coast and nearby mountains with her husband and two growing children.

Receive Stephanie's bonus resources at https://bit.ly/wealthcodeswithsteph

Connect with Stephanie at:
Website: Stephaniezito.com
Website: https://insighttimer.com/stephaniezito
Email: stephzitocoach@gmail.com
Instagram: https://www.instagram.com/_stephanie_zito/

THANK YOU NOTE
TO OUR READERS

Thank you for reading *Wealth Codes, Sacred Strategies for Abundance,* and embracing the wisdom shared by our talented cast of authors.

I trust that we have served you well and inspired wealth consciousness. May you finish this book with more clarity and become aligned to living an ecstatic lifestyle blessed with wealth in all forms.

No matter what led you to pick up a copy, you now have 25 teachings to escort you further into self-discovery, healing, amplified prosperity, and purpose. Revisit these teachings as needed. Trust that you get to live life on your terms and know that wealth is available to everyone.

I encourage you to reach out to our team of authors and share your experiences. They offer whole-hearted services and are dedicated to impacting the lives of others.

They'd love to hear from you, and so would I. Reach out, drop a message, and connect with us on social media or visit our websites.

If you enjoyed reading this book, please leave a review on Amazon. Reviews help shoppers find the right book and it helps authors share their wisdom with the people who need it most.

Walk your path fiercely,

ABOUT THE AUTHOR

JEN PICENO

GET READY TO ALIGN WITH EVERYTHING YOU'RE MEANT
TO BE IN WAYS YOU'VE NEVER EXPERIENCED

Live your legacy now. Jen Piceno's mission is to ignite worldwide wealth and happiness in homes, lives, and businesses.

As a Wealth Consciousness Coach, bestselling author of *Sacred Medicine, Mystical Practices for Ecstatic Living,* and the host of The Ecstatic Living Podcast, she's empowering women to attain their highest potential without sacrificing joy for success.

Working with Jen leads you into an epic adventure of magic and mystery. She does things differently, and the results save people time, money, and resources. She's a shamanic priestess, ordained and initiated in a powerful lineage. Jen offers diverse practices and strategies to help you achieve bigger visions and better than expected outcomes.

Jen prevailed within corporate America, graced the stage as a professional salsa dancer, and trained as an amateur boxer, martial artist, and figure competitor. She approaches life as a student of higher human potential and mystical practices.

She's a motivational speaker, ghostwriter, and sassy mompreneur savoring life while teaching others to do the same.

With over three decades of experience as a modern mystic, channel, and energy medicine practitioner, Jen does ordinary things in extraordinary ways. You'll learn to love life at a high frequency in her presence. Jen celebrates the human experience in everyday rituals and ceremonies, making the mundane magical for all she serves.

She'll help you bust through limitations so you can solidify your purpose and kickstart the transformation you've been craving.

Jen leads women through life's toughest challenges with heart-centered sacred purpose. You'll transform challenging and traumatic life experiences into soul-aligned purpose and step into what you came to this earth to conquer.

Give self-doubt the middle finger so you can tap into limitless possibilities by honoring your soul purpose and heart's deepest desires.

Manifesting desires unified with our highest potential makes a massive difference in how we show up in life, love, and business.

Unfortunately, most people are unintentionally creating what they don't want. No worries, she'll teach you how to troubleshoot that!

Jen's programs offer one-of-a-kind, personalized sacred experiences that shatter old beliefs and empower limitless abundance in all areas of life.

She activates, aligns, and attunes women with their highest potential. You'll be seen, heard, loved, and appreciated like never before.

Are you ready for this?

When you say "yes," she'll take you on a magical adventure—it's the best part!

She's committed to making a radical difference in the lives of others and is happy to guide you through practices that easily integrate with busy lives.

She lives life fully and doesn't sacrifice family time, pleasure, or success while going after what she wants. Jen's clients are women moving into new life phases, high-achievers, athletes, and celebrities.

As an advocate of ecstatic living, she weaves tantric practices, food, dance, culture, and energetics into sacred experiences that awaken the senses and enhance passion, pleasure, and purpose.

Jen is a double Reiki Master trained in energy balancing, karmic release, and generational healing. She's also a gifted ceremonialist, cacao practitioner, body awareness coach, and culinary enthusiast.

Her ten-year fertility battle taught her the power of womb work and ceremonial healings. Jen's journey to motherhood included a decade of yearly traveling to different areas of Mexico and living in Guadalajara for two months. Ignited and trained by elders along the way, she honors the knowledge learned from expert curanderas, sobadoras, and shamans.

She was initiated all over Mexico in private homes and sacred sites. Then, studied Mayan abdominal massage, Toltec wisdom, and shamanism with spiritual leaders and elders in the US.

She's a mysterious magical being that'll ignite your power and invite it to stay so you can discover the divine essence of who you are while living ecstatically.

HER COMMUNITY

Jen is building a community where women can finally exit survival mode and step into the beauty of ecstatic living: prosperity, passion, pleasure, purpose, and freedom.

When women wake up, remember who they are, and start living on their own terms, they're vibrant, more alive, and energetic. With up-leveled confidence, women become comfortable in their skin and stop looking for outside approval—they glow with magnificence and start getting the love and attention they deserve.

Join Jen so you can be a part of this powerful sacred space and sisterhood. She's celebrating women as they courageously step into authenticity, prosperity, and purpose. That's much different than who you were conditioned or told to be.

Join her online space. She'll lift you up, teach you how to be an unstoppable force of nature, and make sure you have tons of fun living the life of your dreams.

To work with Jen privately, schedule a Discovery Call:

www.jenpiceno.com/book_now

WEBSITE: www.jenpiceno.com

ACADEMY: www.jenpiceno.com/academy

FACEBOOK GROUP: www.facebook.com/groups/jenpiceno

PODCAST: www.jenpiceno.com/podcast

QUICK LINKS: www.jenpiceno.com/links

MY APPRECIATION

Living life ecstatically, consciously, and abundantly is found easily in a state of deep appreciation and gratitude. Within the frequency of gratitude, we become magnetic forces for attracting desires into our life experiences with ease and grace.

This powerful truth anchors us more deeply into prosperity consciousness and invites wealth to flow into all areas of life. It welcomes in a decadent, rich life without us chasing after it.

Within this frequency, I send you all love and appreciation.

Thank you to our cast of authors who shared their stories, expertise, and sacred strategies to encourage abundance in the life of others. Thank you for making beautiful magic together for this wealth-expanding collaboration. Thank you for trusting me to lead this project and for coming together on this writing adventure. We did it! We're already changing lives and creating a flow of wealth throughout the world.

To my husband and son, thank you for the gift of love and laughter that fills our home day and night. I learn, stretch, and grow through all the experiences we share.

To our readers, thank you for trusting this journey and being here with an open heart, ready to savor life. We send you love and blessings as you attract overflowing abundance in love, health, happiness, and wealth into your life.

To Honoree Corder and the 2022 Empire Builders, thank you for your big hearts, powerful words, and incredible wisdom.

To our book designer, Dino Marino, thank you for all you do and for making this book extra magical.

To our cover artists, Guy Graves and Dayna Fellows at Ink Black Designs, thank you for gracing our cover with your gorgeous art.

To all our family, friends, colleagues, and book launch team members, thank you for your support throughout this project. We couldn't have done it without you.

Big love and gratitude to Laura Di Franco and The Breave Healer Productions team. Thank you for your friendship, incredible support, and for encouraging us all to share our brave words with the world one book at a time.

MY ACADEMY

My growing empire includes a space for corporate mystics, holistic and spiritual entrepreneurs, magical households, and seekers looking to activate wealth in all areas of life.

This sacred space is a magical virtual vortex with live and prerecorded offerings.

Taking a step into this academy is like entering a temple that transforms the ordinary into extraordinary and turns the mundane into magical.

Enhance all areas of life with practices that lead to savoring an ecstatic life, growing your business, living a life of pleasure, and simplifying everything so there's more time for joy.

My academy is home to eclectic programs and practitioners with courses charmed for accelerating life's challenges, developing spiritual/psychic gifts, and living life on your own terms. It's filled with soul-aligned sacred strategies, spiritual and business practices, magic, and mystery.

Here's a little taste of what you'll find inside.

<u>Wealth Codes</u>

The Wealth Codes Course: Activate wealth in all areas of life through ceremony and practical action steps with magical innovation. Expand on the ideas of this book and join Jen Piceno for a deeper experience into this holistic wealth series into five pillars of wealth: money, relationships, freedom, vitality, and spirituality.

The Wealth Codes Mastermind: A one-of-a-kind experience with passion and purpose. This is a mission to ignite Wealth Codes into homes, businesses, and incomes. This is a small group container with 1:1 private coaching and bonuses. Auditions for this experience is happening now.

Priestess Initiation Certification

You're meant to have it all. An ecstatic life of impact, purpose, and energetic mastery. Join this intimate container for priestess principles and practices that ignite passion, pleasure, and prosperity.

Intensive program to cultivate big intentions, unify the embodiment of the divine feminine and masculine, and consciously create an ecstatic life.

The Wheel of the Year Tour

Take a tour of the world into eight different cultures to discover how people across the globe celebrate throughout the seasons and sabbaths. Grab your virtual passport so you can come along with Jen Piceno and Kelli Murbach for an online adventure. Learn about festivals, cultural wisdom, and spiritual practices without ever leaving your home.

Initiation (seasonal)

Awaken your most magical self by being initiated into earth-based spiritual practices with Jen Piceno and Cindy Olah. Develop intuition, build confidence, and banish self-doubt.

Muse

A soul aligned writing adventure. Get ahead and feel the flow! MUSE offers authentic expression, healing words, and delicious content creation without the stress. Write for yourself or your audience.

Visit the Academy here:
https:www.jenpiceno.com/academy

PRIVATE COACHING

Private coaching with Jen will catapult you to the next level of living your best life much faster than you can imagine. Her blend of holistic modalities far surpasses traditional coaching and will move you through any blocks or obstacles with better results than you've ever experienced with other coaching methods.

For details, pricing, and information contact her by setting up a support call here: https://www.JenPiceno.com/book_now

WHAT PEOPLE ARE SAYING

"I have had the honor of being a part of what Jen Piceno is doing for the last several months. Jen has a way of getting to the truth in a matter of minutes. She has an innate ability to see what's going on and be available for the solution. She doesn't play small and doesn't allow you to either. I have grown more in the last few months of working with her than I have in almost a decade of personal growth work. I cannot recommend her enough."

~Erin Jones, Urban Evolution Salon

"I love Jen Piceno! Jen is an amazing teacher and ceremonialist. She uses body, mind, Spirit, and creativity to help you move through blocks and embrace your authentic self. Her sessions help heal the past and connect you to your heart again!"

~Sarah Friday

"When I first asked Jen to lead a session with the co-authors of my book Find Your Voice, Save Your Life, my thought was simply about offering a session on celebrating having written our stories for the book. Honestly, I didn't know exactly what to expect. In her most powerful way, Jen took us from a place of acknowledging our work and seeing our words as our own power to help other women heal, to a place of being embraced by our ancestral grandmothers, supporting us to do more. Thanks to Jen, we are off on a challenge to celebrate ourselves, not just today but each day coming. Jen is a spiritual powerhouse who can work with you personally, but also create an incredibly impactful session for your groups or your clients."

~Dianna Leeder, Crave More Life Coaching and author of Find Your Voice, Save Your Life

Jen is full of fire and passion that she pours out to others. She loves what she does, and it shows whether she is healing or teaching. I have experienced Jen in both context, and at all times she is fully present to steer you through your muck. I am always impressed with the questions she asks to enlighten you. I always experience a "lightbulb" moment working with her. No matter how much you're drowning in darkness, Jen will gently guide you to feeling lighter and brighter! But the best part of Jen is her infectious humor. She makes the world a better place.

~Debbie Marshall

THE ECSTATIC LIVING PODCAST

LIVE YOUR LEGACY NOW

Welcome to The Ecstatic Living Podcast hosted by Jen Piceno, bestselling author, mompreneur, celebrated wealth consciousness coach, and Prosperity Priestess! Get ready to align with everything you were meant to be in ways you've never experienced. Are you ready to stop sacrificing joy for success? Become a magnetic force for attracting your desires and welcome in riches without chasing after them. Jen will guide you to increase your passion and live a pleasure-filled life anchored in purpose. Experience overflowing prosperity now!

Girl power; it's a thing. I'm on an epic podcast adventure, but before I share the details with you, I'm giving a shout-out to my friend Kelly Myerson. Her name may sound familiar, she wrote chapter 16 in this book.

We've been cheering for each other, masterminding, and leaning on each other throughout our writing career, mom-life, and business-building process. When I think of girl power, I think of relationships like ours. Friends like this are priceless!

Our virtual conversations are filled with laughter, big smiles, and soul-aligned ideas. I've witnessed her success from concept to the full launch of her show, *The Mystic Nerd Squad Podcast.* I was behind the scenes with Kelly throughout the process, felt the anticipation build, and had the honor of being her first guest. What a wave of emotion!

We celebrated, and then I witnessed magic happen. She aligned more deeply with her passion, and it exploded with clarity as she moved into helping others launch their podcasts.

So, here we are now. *The Ecstatic Living Podcast* is live. Kelly took me through the ins and outs of podcasting with a VIP experience. She can help you with that, too, visit her at https://www.beingwellwithkelly.com/podcast and check out her show while you're there.

Here's the scoop about my show: It's eclectic and magical, just like me! Savoring life, ecstatic living, and living your legacy now makes life delicious. If you want to amplify the wealth codes and integrate them into your lifestyle, this is the show for you. Together we'll embrace magic and energetically align with the vibration of prosperity consciousness.

Stop by to hang out with me. Don't forget to like, share, and subscribe: www.jenpiceno.com/podcast

Topics I'll cover will include (plus whatever mystical musing moves me):

- divine feminine leadership
- spiritual/psychic development
- transformational holistic healing
- the art of ceremony, ritual, and all things magical
- energy-boosting, wealth-creating business energetics
- sacred dance, body love, embodiment, and integration
- money mindset
- running a business and maintaining super mom status
- reconnecting with your partner and up-leveling your relationship
- generational/ancestral healing
- wealth/prosperity consciousness
- tantric practices, all the feels, and orgasmic living
- living a magical life, the goddess path, Priestess-y goodness
- spiritual and holistic businesses building
- entrepreneurship without the grit and grind
- writing to boost your business
- savoring life and living curiously

JEN AS A SPEAKER AND PODCAST GUEST

WHAT PEOPLE ARE SAYING

"Jen brings a fiery, inspirational energy to her guesting game, more than most. Having her as a guest means I can trust we'll have a more-than-engaging conversation; we'll entertain and educate our listeners at another level of badass. Jen isn't afraid to be herself and share that with the world. When she shows up for a podcast, not only is she looking like the shamanic Priestess she is, she's walking the walk during the interview. Jen also clearly understands how to share and promote a show. You won't be sorry you said yes to her. I highly recommend you bring Jen on and create a magical show together."

~Laura Di Franco, Brave Healer Productions

"When I think about Jen, the first thing that comes to mind is "BOSS M.A.M.A.!" Motivated - Ambitious - Mindset - Adventurous. All the traits of a highly effective leader. I highly recommend any boss that needs to be motivated in their ambition with adjusting mindset to embark on this adventure with Jen!"

~SA Grant, Host of the Boss Uncaged Podcast

"Jen was a great guest to work with. She shared some really powerful ideas with our audience, and she kept the conversation going in a fun and free-flowing way. As a host, I never had to prod her to share, rather I was able to just enjoy the flow of good energy and great knowledge. I would definitely have her on again."

~Michael Whitehouse, The Guy Who Knows a Guy

AUTHOR LIFE

JOIN ME ON A WRITING ADVENTURE

I offer book coaching and ghostwriting. Or, if you'd like to ease into author life, you may want to explore joining my next collaborative book project.

Writing a book is more than having your name on the cover. It offers a space to change the world with your words, wisdom, strategies, and practices.

I can't wait to hear your book and story ideas!

Schedule time to chat with me here:

www.jenpiceno.com/book_now

"I learned so much about myself in this process. The journey of excitement to fear of freezing up and back to excitement again. A beautiful journey. Being a writer is a craft; it's a dance with the soul! And the journey has just begun."

~Jessica Wolfe

I had the lovely opportunity to work with Jen in the book Sacred Medicine, Mystical Practices for Ecstatic Living. Jen makes the writing process magical with her sacred practices and intuitive insights. She's an amazing leader who deeply cares about the experience her authors have while working with her. Jen's supportive guidance and cheery attitude makes it easy and enjoyable."

~Amber Dobkins,
Author of *Sacred Legacy, Empowered Generational Healing*

OTHER BOOKS BY AUTHOR JEN PICENO

Sacred Medicine, Mystical Practices for Ecstatic Living by Jen Piceno

Imagine having ancient wisdom. . .

. . .powerful spiritual practices, rituals, and ceremonies that support healing and transformation at its deepest, most foundational level.

In *Sacred Medicine, Mystical Practices for Ecstatic Living,* you'll enjoy the magical, real stories of experts in this field who've made their lives about helping people find the answers to life's greatest questions and the path to their most sought-after desires. This is a book full of master teachers to guide you on this incredible journey.

Because who wouldn't want life-changing clarity about things like peak health, wealth, relationships, or purpose? It's all here, waiting for you to explore!

Grab it now! https://amzn.to/37J1fR4

The Ultimate Guide to Self-Healing, Volume 3

https://amzn.to/3L7YDde
Chapter 16 by Jen Piceno
Energetic Womb Healing:
Reclaiming Your Feminine Power and Fertility Naturally

The Ultimate Guide to Self-Healing, Volume 4

https://amzn.to/3NbYruS
Chapter 3 by Jen Piceno
Balancing Codependence:
Finding Self-Acceptance and Personal Power

The Ancestors Within, Reveal and Heal the Ancient Memories You Carry

https://amzn.to/3w9EyyR
Chapter 23 by Jen Piceno
Ancestral Power:
Claim Your Sacred Wisdom and Magic

Get a signed copies here: www.JenPiceno.com/books

CEREMONIAL GRADE CACAO

**Enhance spiritual and magical experiences with
ceremonial grade cacao**

Jen Piceno is a registered cacao practitioner and teaches the art of ceremony with chocolatey goodness.

This powerful superfood is a delicious plant medicine with many benefits and uses:

- Consciousness & Spirituality
- Workplace Productivity
- Creativity and Art
- Athletics and Physical Training
- Healthy Living
- Heart-Opening Awareness

BUY NOW

Get your Cacao here with my affiliate discount link:

http://www.keithscacao.com/discount/piceno18us62

Jen's Cacao Resource and Ritual:

Basic Ceremonial Cacao Recipe: Aphrodite Ritual with Sacred Cacao:
https://jenpiceno.com/aphrodite-cacao-ritual/

THE END

Goodbyes are never easy for me, so I'm sending you off with the intention that our paths will cross again soon.

If you haven't already picked up a copy of my book *Sacred Medicine, Mystical Practices for Ecstatic Living*, get it here: https://amzn.to/37J1fR4

In the meantime, I'll leave you with this poem.

"I am the ever-flowing outpouring of plenty
the inexhaustible
the never-ending
from the fullness of my being,
I give richly and opulently
generously and copiously
luxuriously and liberally
I am limitless
for I cannot be contained
I am everywhere
and will never cease to be"

~Amy Sophia Marashinsky

Let's stay connected! Here's how to find me:
https://www.jenpiceno.com/links